Mechanics

29
Manuscript and
Letter Form

ms

30
Underlining
for Italics

ital

31
Spelling

sp

32
Hyphenation
and
Syllabication

~

33
The
Apostrophe

'

34
Capital
Letters

cap

35
Abbreviations

ab

36
Numbers

num

Diction and Style

37
Standard
English and
Style

d

38
Wordiness

w

39
Repetition

rep

40
Abstract and
General Words

abst

41
Connotation

con

42
Figurative
Language

fig

43
Flowery
Language

fl

The Process of Composition

44
Clear and
Logical
Thinking

log

45
Writing
Paragraphs

¶

46
Writing
Themes

47
Writing about
Literature

48
Writing the
Research
Paper

Glossaries

49
Glossary
of Usage

gl/us

50
Glossary of
Grammatical
Terms

gl/gr

Practical English Handbook

Practical English Handbook

Sixth Edition

Floyd C. Watkins
Emory University

William B. Dillingham
Emory University

Houghton Mifflin Company Boston

Dallas   Geneva, Ill.   Hopewell, N.J.   Palo Alto

Printed in the U.S.A.

Library of Congress Catalog Card Number: 81-82670

Student's Edition ISBN: 0-395-31734-7

Instructor's Edition ISBN: 0-395-31735-5

Authors of works quoted in the text are identified with the quotations.

Grateful acknowledgement is made to the following publishers and authors for permission to reprint from their works:

William O. Aydelotte. From "The Detective Story as a Historical Source," *The Yale Review* (Vol. ns 39, 1949), copyright Yale University.

James Neal and Suzanne Brown, Reprinted by permission from *Newswriting and Reporting,* by James M. Neal and Suzanne S. Brown. © 1976 by The Iowa State University Press, Ames, Iowa 50010.

James Bush-Brown and Louise Bush-Brown. From James Bush-Brown and Louise Bush-Brown, *America's Garden Book*. Copyright © 1965 by Charles Scribner's Sons. Reprinted with the permission of Charles Scribner's Sons.

Phillip Durham and Everett L. Jones. From *The Frontier in American Literature,* © 1969 by Odyssey Press, The Bobbs-Merrill Co., Inc., Indianapolis, IN 46206.

Theodore Roethke. "My Papa's Waltz," copyright 1942 by Hearst Magazines, Inc., from the book *The Collected Poems of Theodore Roethke* by Theodore Roethke. Reprinted by permission of Doubleday & Company, Inc.

James Thurber. Cartoon "The Seal in the Bedroom." Copyright © 1932, 1950 by James Thurber. *The Seal in the Bedroom,* published by Harper & Row, New York.

Elinor Wylie. From "The Eagle and the Mole." *Collected Poems of Elinor Wylie,* © 1932 by Alfred A. Knopf, Inc., New York.

Stained glass window on cover executed by Susan Heller-Moore and photographed by James Scherer.

Contents

Preface   xiii
Writing and Revising   xv

Grammar   1

The Parts of Speech   2
  Nouns   2
  Pronouns   3
  Verbs   6
  Adjectives   8
  Adverbs   9
  Conjunctions   10
  Prepositions   12
  Interjections   13
The Parts of Sentences   14
  Simple subjects, complete subjects, compound subjects   14
  Simple predicates, complete predicates, compound
    predicates   16

Complements 17
Phrases 20
Clauses 23
The Kinds of Sentences 24

Sentence Errors 27

1 Sentence Fragment 28
2 Comma Splice and Fused Sentence 29
3 Verb Forms 35
4 Tense and Sequence of Tenses 38
5 Voice 44
6 Subjunctive Mood 46
7 Subject and Verb: Agreement 47
  a Compound subject with *and* 47
  b Compound subject with *or, nor,* etc. 48
  c Intervening phrases or clauses 48
  d Collective nouns 49
  e Nouns plural in form but singular in meaning 50
  f Indefinite pronouns 50
  g *None, some, part,* etc. 50
  h *There, here* 51
  i Agreement with subject, not subjective complement 52
  j Relative pronouns 52
  k Titles 52
8 Pronouns: Agreement, Reference, and Usage 56
  a Compound antecedent with *and* 56
  b Compound antecedent with *or, nor,* etc. 57
  c Collective noun as antecedent 57
  d *Each, either,* etc. 57
  e *Which, who, that* 58
  f Vague antecedents 59
  g Ambiguous antecedents 60
  h *-self, -selves* 60

9 **Case** 64
   a Subjects and subjective complements 64
   b Object of a preposition 65
   c Subject of an infinitive 65
   d Appositives 65
   e Pronouns after *than* or *as* 66
   f Words preceding a gerund 66
   g *Of* phrase for possession 67
   h Possessive of personal and indefinite pronouns 67
   i Interrogative and relative pronouns 68
10 **Adjectives and Adverbs** 72
   a Comparative, two things; superlative, more than two 72
   b Forms of the comparative and superlative 72
   c After linking verbs *be, seem, become,* etc. 73
   d After a verb and its object 74

Sentence Structure 77

11 **Choppy Sentences and Excessive Coordination** 78
12 **Subordination** 80
   a Subordination of minor thoughts 80
   b Overlapping subordination 81
13 **Completeness** 84
   a After *so, such, too* 84
   b Omission of verbs and prepositions 84
   c Omission of *that* 85
14 **Comparisons** 85
15 **Consistency** 89
16 **Position of Modifiers** 92
   a Dangling 92
   b Misplaced 94
   c Squinting 94
17 **Separation of Elements** 96
18 **Parallelism** 97
19 **Variety** 101

Punctuation   107

20 The Comma   108
a   Between two independent clauses   108
b   In a series   108
c   Between coordinate adjectives   111
d   After long introductory phrases or clauses   113
e   With nonrestrictive appositives, phrases, and clauses   114
f   With sentence modifiers, conjunctive adverbs, and elements out of order   118
g   With degrees, titles, dates, places, addresses   119
h   For contrast or emphasis   120
i   With mild interjections and *yes* or *no*   120
j   With direct address and salutations   120
k   With expressions like *he said, she remarked*   121
l   With absolute phrases   121
m   To prevent misreading or to mark an omission   121

21 Unnecessary Commas   126
a   Between subject and verb, verb and complement, or adjective and word modified   126
b   Between two compound elements   126
c   Between dependent clauses   126
d   Before *than* or between *as . . . as, so . . . as, so . . . that*   127
e   After *like, such as*   127
f   With period, question mark, exclamation point, dash   127
g   With parentheses   128
h   After coordinating conjunctions and short introductory modifiers   128
i   With restrictive clauses, phrases, and appositives   128
j   Between noncoordinate adjectives   128

22 The Semicolon   130
a   Between independent clauses   130

    b Between long or complex independent clauses   131
    c Between items in a series   131
    d Not between noncoordinate elements   131
23 The Colon   133
    a Before elements introduced formally   134
    b Between two independent clauses   134
    c Before formal appositives   134
    d In times, salutations, and bibliographical entries   135
    e Not after a linking verb or a preposition   135
24 The Dash   135
25 Parentheses   136
26 Brackets   136
27 Quotation Marks   137
    a Direct quotations and dialogue   137
    b Quotation within a quotation   138
    c Titles of short works   138
    d Titles of themes   138
    e For emphasis, slang, irony, and humor   138
    f With other punctuation   139
28 End Punctuation   140
    a Period at the end of a sentence   140
    b Period after abbreviations   140
    c Ellipsis dots for omissions   141
    d Punctuation of titles   141
    e Question mark after a direct question   142
    f Question mark within parentheses   142
    g Exclamation point   142

Mechanics   149

29 Manuscript and Letter Form   150
30 Underlining for Italics   154
    a Titles   154
    b Names of ships and trains   155
    c Foreign words   155

    d   Words, letters, and figures   155

    e   Emphasis   156

    f   Titles of themes   156

31 Spelling   157

32 Hyphenation and Syllabication   162

    a   Compound words   163

    b   Compound adjectives   163

    c   Compound numbers   163

    d   Breaking a word at the end of a line   163

33 The Apostrophe   165

34 Capital Letters   167

35 Abbreviations   170

36 Numbers   171

Diction and Style   175

37 Standard English and Style   176

    a   Slang   177

    b   Illiteracies and dialect   177

    c   Archaic words   178

    d   Improprieties   179

    e   Idioms   180

    f   Specialized vocabulary   182

    g   Triteness   183

    h   Exactness   184

    i   Learning new words   186

38 Wordiness   191

39 Repetition   194

    a   Redundancy   194

    b   Repetition of sounds   195

    c   Repetition for emphasis or clarity   195

40 Abstract and General Words   197

41 Connotation   199

42 Figurative Language   201

43 Flowery Language   203

The Process of Composition 205

44 Clear and Logical Thinking 206
- a Accurate, verified data 207
- b Reliable authorities 207
- c Sweeping generalizations 208
- d Specific evidence 209
- e Sticking to the point 209
- f Conflicting evidence 209
- g Circular reasoning 209
- h Omission of essential steps; unstated assumptions 210
- i Appeal to emotion 210
- j Cause and effect 211
- k Moderation 211
- l Adequate alternatives 212

45 Writing Paragraphs 216
- a Main idea in the topic sentence 216
- b Unity 219
- c Skimpiness 222
- d Excessive length 225
- e Appropriate development 227
- f Transitions 230

46 Writing Themes 232
- a Choosing a subject 237
- b Limiting the topic 238
- c Formulating a thesis 239
- d Appropriate and consistent tone 240
- e Organization 240
- f Examples to illustrate generalizations 243
- g Checklist of essentials 247

47 Writing About Literature 254
- a A subject of personal interest 255
- b Precise title 256
- c Appropriate development 256
- d Excessive summary and paraphrase 258
- e Originality 259

    f   Writing about yourself   259
    g   Sufficient evidence   259
    h   Organization by ideas   260
    i   Moralizing   260
    j   Acknowledgment of sources   261
48 Writing the Research Paper   265
    a   Choosing and limiting a subject   265
    b   Working bibliography   267
    c   Primary and secondary materials   275
    d   Taking notes   275
    e   Outlining   282
    f   Acknowledgment of sources   285
    g   Documentation   287
       Paper: "Hope Through Fantasy in James Thurber's
       Drawings"   295

49 Glossary of Usage   328
50 Glossary of Grammatical Terms   341
Index   349

Preface

This sixth edition of the *Practical English Handbook* comes in the twenty-second year of the book. By this time it is of age and has its own identity. Like a character in a good novel, it remains true to its old self, and certain things cannot be changed. Some of them are the helpful diagrams, the pocket size that fits the hand, exercises based on meaning rather than mere mechanical application of rules, an effectively concise section on writing a literary paper, close adherence (with a few adaptations) to the system of documentation of the *MLA Handbook*, and a practical (as opposed to theoretical) section on logic.

The preservation of traditions in the book is almost matched by the changes in this edition: a new section on grammar, more and better vocabulary tests, a new device to replace the model literary paper, a substantially rewritten composition section, a new model research paper, new varieties of exercises, and some small surprises on many pages. Few things get better and better all the time, but we are confident that each version of the *Practical English Handbook* has been better than the last. Within the given limits, each edition of the book has had special qualities all its own.

This is the first edition of the book without the name of the late Edwin T. Martin as one of the authors. Nevertheless, his teaching and his attitudes toward writing still form the basis of much of the usefulness and practicality of the book.

Directly and indirectly, perhaps nearly all of the more than a million users of this book have had some small hand in making it what it is. Our debts to helpful advisers are enormous and incalculable. A number of individuals offered their assessments of the fifth edition and their suggestions for change. We are grateful to M. Elaine Bell, Harcum Junior College; Peggy F. Broder, Cleveland State University; June Bugg, Gadsden State Junior College; Polly Glover, The University of Tennessee at Martin; Eugene K. Hanson, College of the Desert; Yvonne McLravy, Michigan State University; Lois Poule, Bridgewater State College; Joel D. Rudinger, Bowling Green State University; and Rodelle Weintraub, The Pennsylvania State University. In preparing this edition we have been particularly indebted to John T. Hiers, Marie Morris Nitschke, Eric Nitschke, Peter W. Dowell, Sally Wolff, and Oakley Coburn. We want also to thank the following for their thoughtful reading of the manuscript of the sixth edition and their constructive recommendations: Gregory P. Meyer, The Troy State University System; Steven F. Wozniak, Palomar College; and Shirley Saint-Leon and Joyce Lipkis, Santa Monica College.

We must express our special appreciation to Leon Mandell, Chairman of the Department of Chemistry at Emory University, and to his faculty and staff for their generous hospitality in furnishing two alien English professors with a quiet place in which to contemplate the formulas of grammar and composition. Finally, we believe that our patient wives have been more long-suffering over many years than most spouses who receive the last thoughtful thank you in prefaces.

Floyd C. Watkins
William B. Dillingham

Writing and Revising

Whether the instructor uses this book as a basis for class discussions and exercises or for student self-help, it can be of great use in correcting and revising papers. The model theme on the following pages illustrates how an instructor may mark a paper for revision. The numbers in the margins refer the student to sections in the book which indicate the ways to correct errors. Some instructors prefer to use abbreviations (see a list of them inside the back cover) rather than numbers, and some prefer to use neither but to write brief notes. Often combinations will be used.

Whatever method the instructor uses to mark papers, the student should study the relevant sections with their explanations and make appropriate corrections and revisions as shown on the model theme. These may range from simple to extensive revisions.

It is helpful to keep a chart of the numbers or abbreviations used for errors in order to see how the frequency of errors diminishes and how new kinds of errors occur in later themes.

If the instructor writes overall comments on cover sheets, the student might keep these together and in order; they will provide information about improvement, change, and ways to study and revise. The student or the instructor should keep all themes until the end of the term and study the changes in the writing.

The Trouble With Perfectionists

Of all kinds of people, perfectionists ~~are the kind that~~ bother [38]

[45c] me the most.

They ~~won't~~ *want* to get things right~~,~~ *;* that is ~~great~~ *admirable*. They are certainly [31] [2] [37]

[49] not like ~~alot~~ *a lot* of people who just do not care about their jobs or anything

[39] else. But once you get to know a perfectionist, ~~I guarantee you~~ you

[9e] will feel the same way as ~~me~~ I.

Many people seem to believe that it is ~~complementary~~ *complimentary* to call [31]

someone a perfectionist. They seem to think that the term means a

person who is ~~conscientous~~ *Conscientious*. ~~In my opinion,~~ *a* true perfectionist is not [31] [98]

[31] really ~~conscientous~~ *conscientious* but troubled.

Perfectionists have two problems above all others.
~~Two problems above all other are had by perfectionists.~~ The first [5]

is social; the second is mental. It is hard for a perfectionist to make

friends and keep them because he or she usually is ~~real~~ *really* fussy. The [10]

[0] house of a perfectionist has to *be* kept like a museum ~~or something~~, and if [38]

you sit in a certain place or drop a crumb on the rug, you get the distinct

impression that you will not be welcome in that house again. If a

perfectionist happens to be an executive or an employer, those who work

on a lower level find that no matter how hard they try, they ~~cannot never~~ *can never* [Double Negative 49]

seem to please the perfectionist. So this type of person is likely to

[37a] be ~~more~~ unpopular ~~than a wino~~.

perfectionists have
The second problem that ~~are had by perfectionists~~ is not social but [5]

within the person. Although one might expect a perfectionist to go far

in life, to ~~suceed~~ *succeed* at almost any occupation or ~~prefession~~ *profession*, that is not [31] [31]

[31] the case. Perfectionists are probably less ~~sucessful~~ *successful* than better adjusted

people. Why is this so? ~~In my opinion,~~ it is because they become in a
way paralyzed. ~~What I mean by that is that~~ they will not turn loose of
a piece of work until they feel it is just like they want it; therefore
it is hard for them to finish anything.

~~In the end,~~ Perfectionists tend to quit trying to take on anything
important because they know that what they produce cannot live up to their
own high standard. ~~You can see how~~ they often end up in an unhappy state.

~~Let me just say this.~~ The time to correct this way of thinking is
when it first gets started. It will not become a problem if it is not
allowed to go on for very long. Everyone should recognize that on this
earth there is not such thing as perfection and be content with something
less.

Practical English Handbook

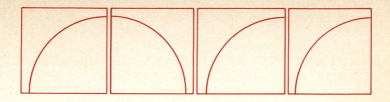

Grammar

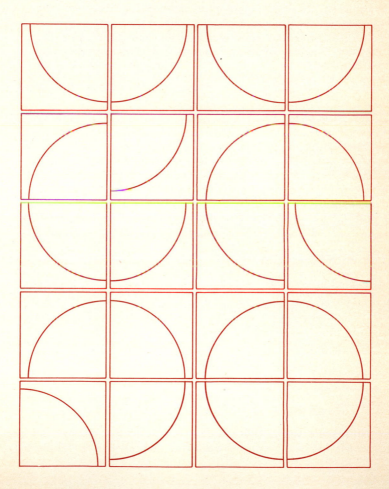

Grammar consists of the basic terms and the descriptions of patterns that are necessary in understanding the workings of a language. You can be a good writer without knowing labels and definitions, but they are often useful. A knowledge of the relatively simple concepts of grammar results in an understanding of language and a self-confidence in speech and writing that are worth the effort. Although many methods have been devised for studying the fundamental elements of English, nothing has worked better and more consistently than the traditional approach. The fundamentals of English grammar are reviewed in this section.

The parts of speech

The eight parts of speech are **nouns, pronouns, verbs, adjectives, adverbs, conjunctions, prepositions,** and **interjections.** Each of these is explained and illustrated below.

NOTE Much of the time, the function of a word within a sentence determines what part of speech that word is. For example, a word may be a **noun** in one sentence but an **adjective** in another.

noun
↓
She teaches in a *college*.

adjective
↓
She teaches several *college* courses.

Nouns

Nouns are words that name. They also have various forms which indicate **gender, number,** and **case** (see **Glossary**

of Grammatical Terms). There are several kinds of nouns.

(a) **Proper nouns** name particular people, places, or things *(Thomas Jefferson, Paris, Superdome)*.

Meet me in *San Francisco* at *Fisherman's Wharf.*

(b) **Common nouns** name one or more of a class or a group *(reader, politician, swimmers)*.

The *women* stared hard and listened intently.

(c) **Collective nouns** name a whole group though they are singular in form *(navy, team, pair)*.

It has been said that an *army* moves on its stomach.

(d) **Abstract nouns** name concepts, beliefs, or qualities *(courage, honor, enthusiasm)*.

Her *love* of *freedom* was no less obvious than her *faithfulness.*

(e) **Concrete nouns** name tangible things perceived through the senses *(rain, bookcase, heat)*.

The *snow* fell in the *forest.*

Pronouns

Most **pronouns** stand for a noun or take the place of a noun. Some pronouns have such general or broad references that they do not directly take the place of a particular noun *(something, none, someone)*.

Pronouns have categories which classify both how they stand for a noun and how they function grammatically in a sentence. (Some of the words listed below have other uses; that is, they sometimes function as a part of speech other than as a pronoun.)

(a) **Demonstrative pronouns** point out (see demonstrative adjectives, page 8). They can be singular *(this, that)* or plural *(these, those)*.

demonstrative pronoun
↓

Many varieties of apples are grown here. *These* are winesaps.

(b) **Indefinite pronouns** do not point out a particular person or thing. They are usually singular, though sometimes plural. (See **8d.**) Some of the most common are *some, any, each, everyone, everybody, anyone, anybody, one,* and *neither*.

indefinite pronoun
↓
Everyone knows that happiness is relative.

(c) **Intensive pronouns** end in *-self* (singular) or *-selves* (plural). An intensive pronoun is used to emphasize a word which precedes it in the sentence.

intensive pronoun
↓

The clown *himself* refused to walk the tight rope.

intensive pronoun
↓
I *myself* will carry the message.

(d) **Interrogative pronouns** are used in asking questions: *who, whom, whose,* and *which. Who* and *whom* combine with *ever: whoever, whomever*.

interrogative pronoun
↓
Who was chosen?

(e) **Personal pronouns** usually refer to a person, sometimes to a thing.

	SINGULAR	PLURAL
First person	I, me, mine	we, us, ours
Second person	you, yours	you, yours
Third person	he, she, it, his, hers, its	they, them, theirs

(f) **Reflexive pronouns** end in *-self* or *-selves* and indicate that the subject acts upon itself.

reflexive pronouns
↓
I hurt *myself*.

Members of an athletic team sometimes defeat *themselves*.

(g) **Relative pronouns** are used to introduce dependent adjective or noun clauses: *who, whoever, whom, whomever, that, what, which, whose.*

relative pronoun
↓
The director could not decide *who* was to act the role of the hero.

▶ Exercise 1

Identify the nouns and pronouns in the following sentences.

1. Everyone knew the adage but the teacher, and she asked a student to recite it.

2. Someone has said that a person who works hard and plays little will be dull.

3. Yosemite National Park is far west of the Mississippi River.

4. The two speakers said that a person who completes college is educated, but they should have said that one who completes college has been exposed to knowledge.

5. It is also possible that those who go to school for only a few years may be intelligent and even learn a great deal by themselves.

Verbs

Verbs express action or a state of being.

action
↓
Twenty-seven mallards *flew* south.

state of being
↓
The twenty-seven birds *were* mallards.

A main verb may have helpers, called **auxiliary verbs,** such as *are, have, will be, did,* and *do.*

auxiliary verb   *main verb*
Twenty-seven mallards *did fly* south.

6   Grammar

auxiliary verbs   main verb

Leif Ericson *may have preceded* Columbus to America.

Linking verbs express condition rather than action: *appear, become, feel, look, seem, smell, sound,* and *taste*. The most common linking verbs, however, are forms of the verb *to be (is, are, was, were,* etc.*).* See page 345.

linking verb

The child *appeared* joyful in the presence of so many toys.

linking verb

The woman with the wax fruit on her hat *is* my mother.

Verbs are either **transitive** or **intransitive** (see pages 44, 348). For **verb tenses,** see pages 38–41. For **verbals,** see pages 20–22 and 348.

▶ Exercise 2

Identify the verbs in each of the following sentences.

1. The long-forgotten recluse wrote a diary.

2. The flight attendant walked among the passengers and looked for the lost purse.

3. The symphony was performed by a renowned orchestra, but the audience was not enthusiastic.

4. Eight of the ten windows and doors were open during the hard rain and strong wind.

5. An appointment with a famous person can be an anxious experience.

Adjectives

Adjectives modify a noun or a pronoun. They limit, qualify, or make more specific the meaning of another word. Generally, they describe. Most adjectives come before the word they modify.

adjective
↓
Sour apples are often used in cooking.

Predicate adjectives follow linking verbs and modify the noun or pronoun which is the subject of the sentence.

subject   *predicate adjective*
↓   ↓
A nap in the afternoon is *restful*.

The three **articles** *(a, an, the)* are classified as adjectives.

Some **possessive adjectives** have forms similar to words which also function as pronouns: *your, her, his, its, our, their*. (Only *her* or *his* may be both pronoun and adjective without changing form.)

Demonstrative adjectives, which have exactly the same forms as demonstrative pronouns, are used before the nouns they modify.

this dog or *that dog; these dogs* or *those dogs*

Indefinite adjectives have the same form as indefinite pronouns: for example, *some, any, each, every*.

(See Section **10** for a discussion of the use of degrees of adjectives.)

Adverbs

Adverbs, like adjectives, describe, qualify, or limit other elements in the sentence. They modify verbs (and verbals), adjectives, and other adverbs.

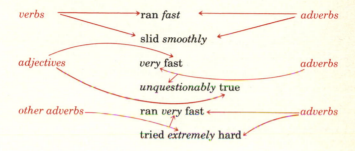

Sometimes adverbs modify an entire clause:

Frankly, *she did not speak the truth.*

Many adverbs end in *-ly (effectively, curiously)*, but not all words that end in *-ly* are adverbs *(lovely, friendly)*.

Adverbs tell how *(slowly, well)*; how much *(extremely, somewhat)*; how often *(frequently, always)*; when *(late, afterward)*; where *(there, here)*. These are the main functions of adverbs, but not the only ones. Words which modify as do adverbs must be determined by what their use is in the sentence; that is, they cannot all be memorized. (For a discussion of the degrees of adverbs, see Section **10**.)

▶ Exercise 3

Identify the adverbs and adjectives in the following sentences. Tell what each one modifies. (Consider a, an, *and* the *as adjectives.)*

1. Slowly and quietly the large automobile glided to a stop.

2. The huge sign was a warning. "Drive carefully and live a long time."

3. Knowing that all things eventually come to an end, one should try to enjoy every moment of life.

4. Two small children ran quickly over the cloth where the food for the afternoon picnic had been spread.

5. Many young couples are carefully restoring the beauties of old homes which have been almost entirely ignored for many years.

Conjunctions

Conjunctions connect words, phrases, or clauses. They are classified as **coordinating, subordinating,** or **correlative.**

Coordinating conjunctions connect elements that are—grammatically speaking—of equal rank. Those most frequently used are *and, but, or, nor, for,* and *yet.*

coordinating conjunction

The orchestra played selections from *Brahms, Beethoven,* and *Wagner.*

coordinating conjunction

The angry candidate left the podium, and *he did not return.*

Subordinating conjunctions introduce a subordinate or

dependent element of a sentence. Examples are *although, because, if, since, though, unless, when, where, while.*

subordinating conjunction
↓
Although many painters sell their work, few become wealthy.

Correlative conjunctions are always used in pairs. Examples are *both . . . and, either . . . or, not only . . . but also, neither . . . nor.* (See Section **18** for discussion of correlative conjunctions and parallelism.)

correlative conjunctions
Not only a well-balanced diet *but also* adequate sleep is needed for good health.

▶ **Exercise 4**
Identify all conjunctions in the following sentences, and tell whether each is coordinating or subordinating or correlative.

1. After a tiring night a sentry leaves his post. As he prepares to rest, he discards from his memory the long hours and the loneliness.

2. When the sun comes up, the world takes on an entirely new appearance, and hope seems to bloom again.

3. The ceilings of the old room were high, but the windows were narrow, and the wind blew hard and whistled through the cracks around the door.

4. After the heat wave had passed, the manager discovered that neither the meats nor the vegetables were spoiled or even discolored.

5. Inquiries and investigations were conducted not only by agencies of the city but also by representatives of the courts.

Prepositions

Prepositions connect a noun or a pronoun (the **object of the preposition**) to another word in the sentence.

Most prepositions are short single words: *above, across, after, against, along, among, at, before, behind, below, beneath, beside, between, by, from, in, into, of, on, over, through, up, upon, with, without.*

A preposition introduces and is a part of a group of words, a phrase, which includes an object. The phrase is used as a unit in the sentence, a single part of speech—usually an adjective or an adverb.

above the clouds   *across the tracks*   *after the game*
by the creek   *through the hallways*   *under the floor*

Groups of words may also serve as prepositions: *along with, according to, in spite of.*

(See **37e** for a discussion of the idiomatic use of prepositions.)

▶ Exercise 5
Identify prepositions, objects of prepositions, and prepositional phrases in the following sentences.

1. For several days Achilles sulked in his tent, and then he joined the battle.

2. According to the rules of the game, the contestant at the front of the line must turn quickly and race toward the rear.

3. There on the table was the book the hostess had given to her friend.

4. Never in the history of the world had such an event occurred so devastatingly.

5. The guest handed the object to the person on his left.

Interjections

Interjections are words that exclaim; they express surprise or strong emotion. They may stand alone or serve as part of a sentence.

Ouch!
Well, that was a shame.

Because of their very nature, interjections are to be found more in speech than in writing, which is generally more planned than spontaneous.

▶ Exercise 6
Name the part of speech of each word underlined and numbered in the following sentences.

1   2   3 4   5   6   7   8 9

<u>Well</u>, <u>questions</u> <u>do</u> <u>not</u> <u>always</u> <u>have</u> <u>answers,</u> <u>but</u> <u>that</u> does not

mean we should stop asking.

10   11   12   13   14   15   16 17 18

<u>In</u> a <u>brown</u> <u>bottle,</u> <u>she</u> <u>discovered</u> a <u>note</u> composed <u>long</u> <u>ago</u> <u>in</u> a

19   20

<u>far</u> <u>country.</u>

The parts of sentences

A sentence, a basic unit of language, has a complete meaning of its own. The essential parts of a sentence are a **subject** and a **predicate.**

    A **subject** does something, has something done to it, or is identified or described.

subject   *subject*   *subject*
  ↓   ↓   ↓
Birds sing.   *Songs* are sung.   *Birds* are beautiful.

A **predicate** expresses something about the subject.

predicate   *predicate*   *predicate*
    ↓   ↓   ↓
Birds *sing.*   Songs *are sung.*   Birds *are beautiful.*

Simple subjects, complete subjects, compound subjects

The essential element of a subject is called the **simple subject.** Usually it consists of a single word.

simple subject
↓
The large *balloon* burst.

The subject may be understood rather than actually stated. A director of a chorale might say "Sing," meaning, "You sing." But her instruction would be a complete sentence.

understood subject predicate
      ↓   ↓
    [You] sing.

All the words which form a group and function together as the subject of a sentence are called the **complete subject.**

complete subject
←——————→
The large balloon burst.

When any similar units of a sentence (subjects, verbs, adjectives) are linked together and function together, they are said to be **compound.**

compound subject
     ↙   ↘
The large *balloons* and the small *bubbles* burst.

Of course pronouns as well as nouns may comprise compound subjects.

compound pronoun subject
↓   ↙
She and *I* sang.

▶ Exercise 7

Identify the subjects and the complete subjects. Tell whether each sentence has a single subject or a compound subject.

1. In the middle of the campus stood the tall, beautiful tower.

2. Swimming against the current, the otter returned to her young.

3. The workers, distracted from their tasks, laid down their tools and stared.

4. The George Washington Bridge and the Golden Gate Bridge are both well known.

5. Six slender trees swayed gracefully in the wind.

Simple predicates, complete predicates, compound predicates

The single verb (or the main verb and its auxiliary verbs) is the **simple predicate.**

simple predicate   *simple predicate*
↓   ↓
Balloons *soar*.   Balloons *are soaring*.

The simple predicate, its modifiers, and any complements form a group which is called the **complete predicate.**

complete predicate
←—————————————→
Balloons *soared over the pasture* .

When two verbs function together and independently in the predicate, they are a **compound predicate**—just as two nouns may be a **compound subject.**

compound predicate

Balloons *soar and burst.*

compound predicate

Balloons *soared over the pasture* and *then burst*.

▶ **Exercise 8**

Identify the verbs and the complete predicates. Tell whether each sentence has a single verb or a compound verb.

1. The scientist left the laboratory and walked to the library.

2. All day long the caravan moved through long valleys and over steep hills.

3. Build beautiful and lasting buildings.

4. People of wisdom exercise their bodies and use their minds.

5. A good writer sometimes composes a first draft, revises it, and then revises again.

Complements

Complements, usually a part of the predicate, complete the meaning of the sentence. They are nouns, pronouns, or adjectives. They function as predicate adjectives or predicate nominatives (both sometimes called **subjective complements**) and direct or indirect objects.

Predicate adjectives
A **predicate adjective** follows a linking verb and modifies the subject, not the verb.

linking
subject *verb* *predicate adjective*
↓ ↓ ↓
The *boots* *were* *muddy*.

Predicate nominatives
Predicate nominatives follow linking verbs and rename the subject. (Compare predicate adjectives above and appositives, page 341.)

predicate
nominative
↓
Bears are *omnivores* .

Direct objects
A **direct object** receives the action indicated by a transitive verb. Naturally, it is always in the objective case. See **9**.

verb *direct object*
↓ ↓
Bears *eat honey*.

Indirect objects
An **indirect object** receives the action of the verb indirectly. The subject (through the verb) acts on the direct object, which in turn has an effect on the indirect object (that is, *it is given to,* or *it is done for*).

		indirect	*direct*
	verb	*object*	*object*
	↓	↓	↓

Rangers *fed*   the *bears honey.*

The sentence can be rearranged to read

				indirect
	verb	*object*	*understood*	*object*
	↓	↓	↓	↓

Rangers *fed honey*   [to]   the *bears.*

When the preposition *(to,* as above, or *for)* is understood, the word is an indirect object. When the preposition is expressed, the word is an object of a preposition:

preposition	*object of preposition*
↓	↓

Rangers fed honey *to* the *bears*.

prepositional phrase

(Grammatically the sentence above has no indirect object.)

▶ Exercise 9

Underline and identify the predicate adjectives, predicate nominatives, direct objects, and indirect objects in the following sentences.

1. The librarian suggested a book which was a popular autobiography.

2. The brick wall was high, but my friend threw me an apple straight over the top.

3. Good peaches are sweet and juicy.

4. Give each of the men and the women a book and a candle.

5. Whoever wins the contest will receive a trophy.

Phrases

A **phrase** is a cluster of words that does not have both a subject and a verb. Some important kinds of phrases are **verb phrases, prepositional phrases,** and **verbal phrases.**

Verb phrases
The main verb and its auxiliary verbs are called a **verb phrase:** *were sitting, shall be going, are broken, may be considered. Were, shall be, are, may be,* and verbs like them are often auxiliary verbs (sometimes called "helping" verbs).

verb phrase

The bear *had been eating* the honey.

Prepositional phrases
Prepositional phrases function as adjectives or adverbs.

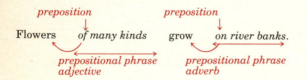

Verbals and verbal phrases
A **verbal** is a grammatical form derived from a verb. No verbal is a complete verb. It may have an object and modifiers. (Adverbs modify verbals as they modify verbs.) A verbal and the words associated with it compose a **verbal phrase.**

There are three kinds of verbals: **gerunds, participles,** and **infinitives.** A gerund is always a noun; a participle is an adjective; an infinitive may be either a noun, an adjective, or an adverb, depending on its use in the sentence.

GERUNDS AND GERUND PHRASES

Gerunds always end in *-ing* and function as nouns.

gerund
↓
Shoeing horses requires care.
←————————→

gerund phrase as noun
(complete subject)

PARTICIPLES AND PARTICIPIAL PHRASES

Participles usually end in *-ing, -ed, -d, -t, -n* (there are many irregular forms also) and always function as adjectives.

participle
↓
Jumping aside, he dodged the ball.
←————————→

participle phrase as adjective
(modifies he*)*

INFINITIVES AND INFINITIVE PHRASES

Infinitives begin with *to,* which may be understood rather than actually stated. They may be used as nouns, adjectives, or adverbs.

USED AS NOUN

infinitive
↓
To rescue the swimmer was easy.
←————————————→

infinitive phrase
used as subject

USED AS ADJECTIVE

infinitive
↓

Charlotte's Web is a good book *to read to a child.*

←————————————→

*infinitive phrase
modifies* book *(noun)*

USED AS ADVERB

infinitive
↓

The novelist was eager *to read a story.*

←————————————→

*infinitive phrase
modifies* eager *(adjective)*

▶ Exercise 10

*Identify phrases in the following sentences and tell what kind
each is: infinitive, gerund, participle, preposition, or verb.*

1. Building the pyramids was an astonishing feat.

2. Working through the night, they completed the musical score

   to be included in the play.

3. Though she had been visiting the resort for many years, she

   still enjoyed its pleasures.

4. Taking the census in modern times is not as simple as it was

   two thousand years ago.

5. Insisting that his vegetables had been grown organically, the

   gardener refused to sell them at a lower price.

Clauses

A **clause** is a group of words with a subject and a predicate. There are two kinds of clauses: **independent** and **dependent** (sometimes called **subordinate**).

Independent clauses

An **independent clause** can stand alone; grammatically it is like a complete sentence. Two or more independent clauses in one sentence may be joined by coordinating conjunctions, conjunctive adverbs, semicolons, and other grammatical devices or punctuation marks.

Hens cackle, and roosters crow.
Hens cackle; roosters crow.

Dependent clauses or subordinate clauses

Like verbals, **dependent clauses** function as three different parts of speech in a sentence: nouns, adjectives, and adverbs. Unlike independent clauses, dependent clauses do not express a complete thought in themselves.

USED AS NOUN (usually subject or object)
That the little child could read rapidly was well known.
    (noun clause used as subject)

The other students knew *that the little child could read rapidly*.
                  (noun clause used as direct object)

USED AS ADJECTIVE

Everyone *who completed the race* won a shirt.
       (modifying pronoun subject)

USED AS ADVERB
When spring comes many flowers bloom.
 (modifying verb)

The kinds of sentences

A **simple sentence** has only one independent clause (but no dependent clause). A simple sentence is not necessarily a short sentence; it may contain several phrases.

Birds sing.
After a long silence, *the bird began to warble a sustained and beautiful song.*
↑
independent clause

A **compound sentence** has two or more independent clauses (but no dependent clause).

independent clause   *independent clause*
Birds sing, and bees hum.

A **complex sentence** has both an independent clause and one or more dependent clauses.

←————————*dependent clauses* ————————→ ←—— *independent clause* ——→

When spring comes and[when] new leaves grow, migratory birds return north.

A **compound-complex** sentence has at least two independent clauses and at least one dependent clause. A dependent clause may be part of an independent clause.

←————————*independent clause* ————————→

When heavy rains come, the streams rise; and farmers know that there will be floods.

dependent adverb clause   *independent clause*   *dependent noun clause used as object*

▶ Exercise 11
Underline each clause. Tell whether it is dependent or independent. Tell the use of each dependent clause in the sentence. Tell

whether each sentence is simple, compound, complex, or compound-complex.

1. People in some towns are awakened in the morning when a factory whistle blows to signal the change in a shift of workers.

2. Moving down the hills and around the curves, the procession of cars was not able to proceed faster than twenty miles an hour.

3. That she had paid the five-dollar debt was proved beyond doubt, so her friend apologized and bought her a red rose.

4. The students who are straggling up the steps seem reluctant, but they are really hoping that they will be allowed to enter the museum.

5. The visitor politely asked to be allowed to speak, and the moderator agreed.

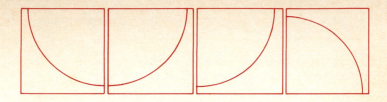

Sentence Errors

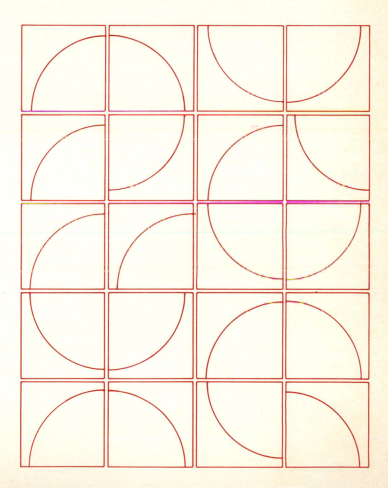

1 Sentence fragment *frag*
Do not write meaningless or ineffective fragments.

A **fragment** is a part of a sentence written and punctuated as a complete sentence. Among a group of several sentences a fragment may seem to make sense at first glance. Standing alone, most fragments are not full and clear. They may be dependent clauses, phrases, or any other word groups which violate the accepted subject-verb sentence pattern. Fragments usually reflect incomplete or confused thinking.

FRAGMENTS

Although grocery prices are still high.
   (dependent clause)
Food being plentiful during this season.
   (noun and phrase)

Food is plentiful.
   (complete sentence)
Prices are declining.
   (complete sentence)

The fragments can be combined with the complete sentences.

COMPLETE SENTENCES

Although grocery prices are still high, food is plentiful.
Food being plentiful during this season, prices are declining.

FRAGMENT

Although some graduates are well schooled in the techniques used by debaters. (dependent clause)

COMPLETE SENTENCE

Some graduates are well schooled in the techniques used by debaters.

FRAGMENT

The green fields humming with sounds of insects. (noun and phrase— no main verb)

COMPLETE SENTENCE

The green fields hummed with sounds of insects.

Fragments are often permissible in dialogue when the meaning is clear.

"See the geese."
"Where?"
"Flying north."

Capable writers sometimes intentionally use fragments for special effects or emphasis.

FRAGMENT FOR SPECIAL EFFECT
The long journey down the river was especially pleasant with just the right amount of rest and just enough action. *And, above all, so much good humor and joy.*

2 Comma splice and fused sentence cs / fus
Use a semicolon or a comma and a coordinating conjunction *(and, but, or, nor, for, yet, so)* to join two independent clauses.

A **comma splice** or **comma fault** occurs when independent clauses have a comma between them but no coordinating conjunction.

SPLICE OR FAULT
Human nature is seldom as simple as it appears, hasty judgments are therefore often wrong.

A **fused sentence** or **run-on sentence** occurs when the independent clauses have neither punctuation nor coordinating conjunctions between them.

FUSED OR RUN-ON
Human nature is seldom as simple as it appears hasty judgments are therefore often wrong.

Comma splices and fused sentences fail to indicate the strong break between independent clauses. They may be corrected in four principal ways:

1. Use a *period* and write two sentences.

   Human nature is seldom as simple as it appears. Hasty judgments are therefore often wrong.

2. Use a *semicolon*. (See also **22**.)

   Human nature is seldom as simple as it appears; hasty judgments are therefore often wrong.

3. Use a *comma* and a *coordinating conjunction*. (See also **20a**.)

   Human nature is seldom as simple as it appears, *and* hasty judgments are therefore often wrong.

4. Subordinate one of the clauses.

   Because human nature is seldom as simple as it appears, hasty judgments are therefore often wrong.
   Human nature is so complex that hasty judgments are often wrong.

   Learn to reduce a fragment or a clause to a phrase or even a single word. The sentence may also be rewritten as follows:

   PHRASE
   Hasty judgments often overlook the complexities of human nature.

   With conjunctive adverbs (*however, moreover, therefore, furthermore,* and so on), use a semicolon to join independent clauses. (See **22a**.)

   The rare book had a torn flyleaf; therefore, it was advertised at a reduced price.

► Exercise 1

Identify each of the following as correct (C), *a comma splice* (CS), *a fused sentence* (FS), *or a fragment* (F).

1. Vitamins are necessary to our health, however, some of them are dangerous if taken in excess.

2. Vitamins are necessary to our health; however, some of them are dangerous if taken in excess.

3. Vitamins are necessary to our health however, some of them are dangerous if taken in excess.

4. Vitamins are necessary to our health. Dangerous, however, if taken in excess.

5. Vitamins are necessary to our health, but some of them are dangerous if taken in excess.

► Exercise 2

Make the following fragments complete sentences by deleting one word, adding one word or a verb phrase, or changing one word.

1. The various colors and designs of academic regalia revealing the wearers' schools, degrees, and fields of learning.

2. That the bald eagle flies high over the mountain tops looking for prey.

3. Rivers with poisonous chemicals from factories, garbage dumped by sportsmen and towns, and various other ugly products of civilization.

4. Because learning may begin when one first understands that there is a problem to be solved.

5. The young artist who won first prize in the autumn exhibit of watercolors.

▶ Exercise 3

Identify (with CS *or* FS*) and correct comma splices and fused sentences. Write* C *by correct sentences.*

1. Television sometimes offers worthwhile programs as well as trivia, it should not be condemned entirely.

2. After twelve years of silence, the great composer finished two brilliant symphonies within six months.

3. Conflicts almost always exist within a family however, it is still the most enduring of social units.

4. One ancient culture practiced the art of carving masks another expressed itself creatively in weaving elaborate tapestries.

5. A famous rose enthusiast wrote that it is necessary to love roses in order to cultivate them successfully the grower must have roses in his heart if he is to have them in his garden.

▶ **Exercise 4**
Identify fragments (F), *comma splices* (CS), *or fused sentences* (FS) *and correct them. Write* C *by correct sentences.*

1. Economy is a virtue up to a point, beyond that it may become a vice.

2. Destroyers uproot trees and move vast quantities of earth but do not replace the soil.

3. The seafood in this cafe probably is fresh; I ate lobster here yesterday.

4. Styles of clothing are not always planned for comfort belts and seams may be designed for looks more than for the natural contours of the body.

5. Difficult puzzles first cause amazement and thought. Then with a change of mood frustration and anger.

6. New York's Washington Square has changed considerably since it was a haven for writers in the 1890's.

7. In a lonely village on the seacoast, where the primitive beauty of nature still survives.

8. New buildings are springing up all over the city the skyline is rapidly changing.

9. For many, swimming is more pleasant than jogging, especially when the weather is hot.

10. An adventurer will sometimes participate in a pastime despite great danger, sky diving, for example, is perilous.

▶ Exercise 5
Follow the instructions for Exercise 4.

1. In some parts of the world marriages are still arranged by parents consequently practical matters take precedence over love.

2. After all, the students argued, any imbecile can punctuate, studying the mechanics of composition is a complete waste of time.

3. Most generous people are naive, they simply do not realize when they are being imposed upon.

4. Some say that nonconformity has become a fad. Nonconformity for its own sake.

5. Science and art are not incompatible, some learned scientists are also philosophers or poets.

6. The art of pleasing is a very necessary one to possess. But a very difficult one to acquire.

7. Kindness can hardly be reduced to rules good will and thoughtfulness will lead to congenial relationships with others.

8. Writing on a blackboard frequently creates a sound which causes an unpleasant sensation.

9. Clothes inappropriate to a place or situation are absurd a mink coat on a beach in July might be comical.

10. If a trout fisherman tires of tangled lines and hooks caught in limbs of trees overhead. He may give up mountain-stream fishing for boats and the open spaces of lakes.

3 Verb forms vb
Use the correct form of the verb.

All verbs have three principal parts: the present infinitive, the past tense, and the past participle. Verbs are regular or irregular.

Regular verbs *(help, talk, nail, open, close)* form the past tense and the past participle by adding *-d* or *-ed* or sometimes *-t* (as in *burnt, dwelt*). Thus the principal parts of *to close* are *close, closed, closed;* those of *to talk* are *talk, talked, talked.*

Irregular verbs usually form the past tense and the past participle by changing an internal vowel: *drink, drank, drunk.* Consult a dictionary when in doubt; if only the infinitive form is given, the verb is regular. For an irregular verb like *think,* the dictionary also gives *thought* (the form of the past tense and the past participle) and *thinking* (the present participle). The principal parts are *think, thought, thought.* For a verb as irregular as *see,* the dictionary lists all three principal parts—*see, saw, seen*—and *seeing.* Know the following troublesome verbs so well that you automatically use them correctly.

INFINITIVE	PAST TENSE	PAST PARTICIPLE
awake	awoke, awaked	awoke, awaked
be	was	been
begin	began	begun
bid (to offer as a price or to make a bid in playing cards)	bid	bid
bid (to command, order)	bade, bid	bidden, bid
blow	blew	blown
bring	brought	brought
build	built	built
burst	burst	burst
choose	chose	chosen
come	came	come
deal	dealt	dealt
dig	dug	dug
dive	dived, dove	dived
do	did	done
drag	dragged	dragged
draw	drew	drawn

INFINITIVE	PAST TENSE	PAST PARTICIPLE
drink	drank	drunk
drive	drove	driven
drown	drowned	drowned
fly	flew	flown
freeze	froze	frozen
give	gave	given
go	went	gone
grow	grew	grown
hang (to execute)	hanged	hanged
hang (to suspend)	hung	hung
know	knew	known
lead	led	led
lend	lent	lent
lose	lost	lost
ring	rang	rung
run	ran	run
see	saw	seen
shine (to give light)	shone	shone
shine (to polish)	shined	shined
sing	sang	sung
sink	sank, sunk	sunk
slay	slew	slain
sting	stung	stung
swim	swam	swum
swing	swung	swung
take	took	taken
teach	taught	taught
throw	threw	thrown
wear	wore	worn
write	wrote	written

In some pairs of verbs, it helps to remember that one is **transitive** (has voice, may take an object) and that the other is **intransitive** (does not take an object):

	PAST TENSE	PAST PARTICIPLE
TRANSITIVE		
lay (to place)	laid	laid
INTRANSITIVE		
lie (to recline)	lay	lain

	PAST TENSE	PAST PARTICIPLE
TRANSITIVE		
set (to place in position)	set	set
INTRANSITIVE		
sit (to be seated)	sat	sat
TRANSITIVE		
raise (to lift)	raised	raised
INTRANSITIVE		
rise (to get up)	rose	risen

NOTE The intransitive verbs *lie, sit,* and *rise* all have the root vowel *i* in the present tense form.

The transitive verb *set* also has intransitive forms (a hen *sets;* concrete *sets;* the sun *sets*).

4 Tense and sequence of tenses *t/seq*
Use verbs to express distinctions in time. Avoid unnecessary shifts in tense.

For each kind of time—present, past, and future—verbs have a different tense form: simple, progressive, and perfect.[1]

	REGULAR	IRREGULAR
SIMPLE		
Present	I walk	I go
Past	I walked	I went
Future	I shall (will) walk	I shall (will) go
PROGRESSIVE		
Present	I am walking	I am going
Past	I was walking	I was going
Future	I shall (will) be walking	I shall (will) be going

---

[1] There are in addition the emphatic forms with the auxiliary *do* or *did* (I *do go* there regularly).

	REGULAR	IRREGULAR
PERFECT		
Present	I have walked	I have gone
Past	I had walked	I had gone
Future	I shall (will) have walked	I shall (will) have gone

In general, the **present tense** expresses present time, but there are exceptions. Compare the following:

I *eat* lunch. (simple present tense—with the force of repeated action)
I *am eating* lunch. (present progressive tense—present action)

I *leave* for New York tomorrow. (present tense—future action)
I *am leaving* in fifteen minutes. (present progressive tense—future action)

As the last two examples illustrate, the time expressed by the tense form is often determined by the rest of the sentence.

In statements about the contents of literature and other works of art, generally use the present tense (historical present).

In Henry James's *The Turn of the Screw,* a governess *believes* that she sees ghosts.

In statements of natural truth or scientific law, use the present tense regardless of the controlling verb.

In 1851, Foucault proved that the earth *rotates* on its axis.
BUT
Ancient Greeks *believed* that the earth *was* motionless.

The three **perfect tenses** indicate one time or action completed before another.

PRESENT PERFECT WITH PRESENT
I *have bought* my ticket, and I **am waiting** for the bus.

The controlling time word may not be a verb.

I *have bought* my ticket **already.**

I *had bought* my ticket, and I **was waiting** for the bus.
I *had bought* my ticket before the bus **came.**

I *shall have eaten* by the time we **go.** (The controlling word, *go,* is
    present tense in form but future in meaning.)
I *shall have eaten by* **one o'clock.**

The future perfect is rare. Usually the simple future tense is
used with an adverb phrase or clause.

I shall have eaten before you go.

I shall eat before you go.

In dialogue, the present tense is often used for the future or
the future perfect.

"When are you leaving?"
"We leave at dawn."

Relationships between verbs should be logical and consistent:

The sailor *stood* on the shore and *threw* shells at the seagulls. (not
    throws)
He *turned* away when he *saw* me watching him.

As the school year *draws* to a close, the students *are swept* into a
    whirl of activities.

An infinitive (see pages 21–22) generally takes the

present tense when it expresses action which occurs at the same time as that of the controlling verb.

NOT
I wanted *to have gone*.
BUT
I wanted *to go*.

NOT
I had expected *to have met* my friends at the game.
BUT
I had expected *to meet* my friends at the game.

NOT
I would have preferred *to have waited* until they came.
BUT
I would have preferred *to wait* until they came.

The perfect participle expresses an action which precedes another action.

Having finished the manuscript, the aged author stored it away in her safe.

▶ Exercise 6
Underline the incorrect verb and write the correction above it. Write C by correct sentences.

1. Before the hen could sit, the eggs disappeared from the nest.

2. The trees stand nearly barren; their leaves lay on the ground.

3. During the play she slowly lies the book on the floor and raises nonchalantly to her feet.

4. The dog had laid on the step without moving for nearly an hour; but he rose quickly when a neighbor set down beside him.

5. Laying on a sofa hour after hour and watching television is not exactly an intellectual activity.

6. Laying in the sun, he dreamed of snowy mountain tops.

7. She just set there, neither excited nor afraid.

8. The artist laid the brush on the stand just after he had painted that portrait, and it has been lying there ever since.

9. The carpenter promised to sit the bucket on the tile, but it has been setting on the carpet for a week.

10. When the door squeaked, the mother slowly raised herself out of the chair, and the boy rose quickly from the floor.

▶ Exercise 7

Underline the incorrect verb and write the correction above it. Write C by correct sentences.

1. In looking back, public officials almost always say they would have preferred to have remained private citizens.

2. After having laid on the bottom of the bay for centuries, the Swedish ship was risen and placed in a museum.

3. Hundreds of dusty arrowheads and spearpoints were laying on the shelves in his study.

4. The actor opened the Bible and begins reading the Song of Solomon.

5. It was Goethe's feeling that genius was simply "consummate industry."

6. After it sets, concrete is a durable material for roads.

7. Joseph Conrad was well into his thirties before he begun to write his novels.

8. After one has already bidden at an auction, it is too late for a change of mind.

9. After the canoe had sank, the explorers continued the journey on foot.

10. The Puritans were in some ways severe, but they lead lives of deep devotion to what they believed.

5 Voice *vo*

Use the active voice except when the context demands the passive.

A transitive verb is either active or passive. (An intransitive verb does not have voice.) When the subject acts, the verb is active. When the subject is acted upon, the verb is passive. In most sentences the actor is more important than the receiver. A weak passive verb may make the doer seem unknown or unimportant.

WEAK PASSIVE
The huge iceberg *was rammed* into by the luxury liner.
STRONG ACTIVE
The luxury liner *rammed* into the huge iceberg.

WEAK PASSIVE
A good race *was run* by the Ferrari.
STRONG ACTIVE
The Ferrari *ran* a good race.

The active voice creates a more concise and vigorous style. The passive voice is sometimes useful, however, when the performer of an action is irrelevant or unimportant:

The book about motorcycles was *misplaced* among books about cosmetics.

The passive voice can also be effective when the emphasis is on the receiver, the verb, or even a modifier:

The police *were* totally *misled*.

▶ Exercise 8
Rewrite the following sentences. Change the voice from passive to active.

1. The insects which were destroying the leaves of the plants were eaten by birds.

2. The trucks were finally loaded by men who used forklifts.

3. Some objects of art were discovered by the amateur archaeologist.

4. The road had been traveled many times by the salesman, but the old house had never before been noticed by him.

5. A safe trip was had by the tourists because the dangers were carefully explained by the guide.

▶ Exercise 9

Change the voice of the verb when it is ineffective. Rewrite the sentence if necessary. Write **E** *by sentences in which the verb is effective.*

1. The nest was flown into directly by the mother bird, which brought a worm to feed its young.

2. Some young people are learning the almost lost art of blacksmithing and shoeing horses.

3. The horse lost the race because the shoe had been improperly nailed to the hoof.

4. Sharp curves are not well negotiated by many people just

   learning to drive.

5. The rare plants were not properly cared for by the gardener.

6 Subjunctive mood *mo*
Use the subjunctive mood to express wishes, orders, and conditions contrary to fact. (See **Mood,** pages 345—346.)

WISHES
I wish I **were** a little child.

ORDERS
The instructions were that ten sentences **be** revised.

CONDITIONS CONTRARY TO FACT
If I **were** a little child, I would have no responsibilities.
If I **were** you, I would not go.
Had the weather **been** good, we would have gone to the top of the
mountain.

Often in modern English other constructions are used instead of the subjunctive, which survives mainly as a custom in some expressions.

SUBJUNCTIVE
The new manager requested that ten apartments **be** remodeled.

SUBJUNCTIVE NOT USED
The new manager decided to have ten apartments remodeled.

▶ Exercise 10
Change the mood of the verbs to subjunctive when appropriate in the following sentences. Put a check by those sentences which already use the correct subjunctive.

1. If this silver dollar was more worn, it would feel entirely smooth.

2. This coin would be worth more money if it were not smooth.

3. The coin dealer wishes that the ancient coin was less worn.

4. The dealer required that the catalog be reprinted.

5. He demanded that his money be refunded because he believed that the coin was a fake.

7 Subject and verb: agreement *agr*

Use singular verbs with singular subjects, plural verbs with plural subjects.

The *-s* or *-es* ending of the present tense of a verb in the third person *(she talks, he wishes)* indicates the singular. (The *-s* or *-es* ending for most *nouns* indicates the plural.)

SINGULAR	PLURAL
The dog barks.	The dogs bark.
The ax cuts.	The axes cut.

7a A compound subject (see page 15) with *and* takes a plural verb.

Work and play **are** not equally rewarding.

Golf and *polo* **are** usually outdoor sports.

EXCEPTION Compound subjects connected by *and* but expressing a singular idea take a singular verb.

A gentleman and a scholar **is** a man of manners and breadth.

When the children are in bed, *the tumult and shouting* **dies.**

7b After a compound subject with *or, nor, either . . . or, neither . . . nor, not . . . but,* the verb agrees in number and person with the nearer part of the subject. (See **8b**.)

NUMBER
Neither the *consumer* nor the *producer* **is** pleased by higher taxes.

Either *fans* or an *air conditioner* **is** necessary.

Either an *air conditioner* or *fans* **are** necessary.

PERSON
Neither *you* nor your *successor* **is** affected by the new regulation.

Colloquially, a plural verb may be used to express a plural idea with *neither . . . nor.*

Neither *television* nor the *press* **are** consistently censored.

7c Intervening phrases or clauses not introduced by coordinating conjunctions do not affect the number of a verb.

Connectives like *as well as* and *along with* are not coordinating conjunctions but prepositions; they do not form compound subjects. Other such words and phrases include *in addition to, together with, with, plus,* and *including.*

The *engine* as well as the wings **was** destroyed in the crash.

The *pilot* along with all his passengers **was** rescued.

7d A collective noun takes a singular verb when referring to a group as a unit, a plural verb when the members of a group are thought of individually.

A collective noun names a class or group: *family, flock, jury, congregation*. When the group is regarded as a unit, use the singular.

The class **holds** its banquet in the auditorium.

When the group is regarded as separate individuals, use the plural.

The class **disagree** among themselves about the best place for a banquet.

7e Most nouns plural in form but singular in meaning take a singular verb.

When in doubt, consult a dictionary.

Economics and *news* are considered singular.

Economics **is** often thought of as a science.

The *news* of the defeat **is** disappointing.

Trousers and *scissors* are treated as plural except when used after *pair*.

The *trousers* **are** unpressed and frayed about the cuffs.

An old *pair* of *trousers* **is** essential for the Bohemian.

The *scissors* **are** dull.

That *pair* of *scissors* **is** dull.

7f Indefinite pronouns *(each, either, neither, one, no one, everyone, someone, anyone, nobody, everybody, somebody, anybody)* usually take singular verbs.

Neither of his themes **was** acceptable.

Everybody **has** trouble choosing a subject for an essay.

Each student **has** chosen a subject for the report.

7g Some words, such as *none, some, part, all, half* (and other fractions), take a singular or a plural verb, depending on the meaning of the noun or pronoun which follows.

            singular
Some of the sugar **was** spilled on the floor.

            plural
Some of the apples **were** spilled on the floor.

            singular
Half of the money **is** yours.

plural

Half of the students **are** looking out the window.

When *none* can be regarded as either singular or plural, a singular or plural verb may be used.

None of the roads **are** (or **is**) closed.

The number is usually singular:

The number of people in the audience **was** never determined.

A number when used to mean *some* is always plural.

A number of the *guests* **were** whispering.

7h In sentences beginning with *there* or *here* followed by verb and subject, the verb is singular or plural depending on the subject.

There and *Here* are devices (**expletives**) sometimes used when the subject follows the verb.

There **was** a long *interval* between the two discoveries.

There **were** thirteen *blackbirds* perched on the fence.

Here **is** a *thing* to remember.

Here **are** two *things* to remember.

The singular *There is* may introduce a compound subject when the first noun is singular.

There is a *swing* and a *footbridge* in the garden.

In sentences beginning with *It*, the verb is singular.

It **was** many years ago.

7i A verb agrees with its subject, not with a subjective complement.

His horse and *his dog* **are** his main source of pleasure.

His main *source* of pleasure **is** his horse and his dog.

7j After a relative pronoun *(who, which, that)* the verb has the same person and number as the antecedent.

antecedent——————→*relative pronoun* ——————→*verb of relative pronoun*

We who **are** about to die salute you.

The *costumes which* **were** worn in the ballet were dazzling.

He was the *candidate who* **was** able to carry out his campaign pledges.

He was one of the *candidates who* **were** able to carry out their campaign pledges.

BUT
He was *the* only *one* of the candidates *who* **was** able to carry out his campaign pledges.

7k A title is singular and requires a singular verb even if it contains plural words and plural ideas.

The Canterbury Tales **is** a masterpiece of comedy.

"Prunes and Prisms" **was** a syndicated newspaper column on grammar
and usage.

▶ Exercise 11

Correct any verb which does not agree with its subject. Write C
by a correct sentence.

1. The sound of hammers mingle with the screech of seagulls
   and the crash of waves on the beach.

2. In O'Neill's *Long Day's Journey into Night,* Mary's smiles
   and laughter is increasingly forced, her resentment is more
   obvious, and her journey into night is more plainly marked.

3. *The Aspern Papers* deal with the subject of the right of
   privacy.

4. A large number of students are now moving away from
   housing provided by universities and colleges.

5. Some of the tailors is unhappy with the scissors that cuts
   poorly.

6. Ethics are the study of moral philosophy and standards of
   conduct.

7. Molasses were used in a great number of early New England recipes.

8. This tribal custom is enforced by strict taboos, the violation of which bring immediate death.

9. Childish sentences or dull writing are not improved by a sprinkling of dashes.

10. Neither money nor power satisfy the deepest human needs of those who seek to fulfill themselves.

▶ Exercise 12
Follow the instructions for Exercise 11.

1. For a certain kind of American, a vacation of at least two weeks have come to be looked upon as a panacea.

2. All year long, the worker who is shackled to his job look forward to the time when he can lounge in endless ease upon the shore of a mountain lake or the white sands by the sea.

3. It is highly improbable that either the white sands or the mountain lake are the answer for this tense city-dweller.

4. Anybody who live a life of quiet desperation for months or even years can hardly expect to forget anxieties at once.

5. Nevertheless, realizing an extreme need to slow down, the American vacationer, along with his entire family, set out.

6. Plan after plan have been made; nothing can go wrong.

7. The trouble is that the family have made too many plans.

8. Father is determined to relax; he somehow fails to see that relaxation and two weeks of feverish activity is not compatible.

9. This man's situation, like that of thousands of others, are the result of his desire on the one hand to slow down and on the other to forget himself, to escape the thoughts that haunts him for fifty weeks of the year.

10. To relax physically and at the same time to escape his frustrations are impossible for him.

11. He thus returns to his job more weary or more worried or both than when he left.

12. The roots of this man's problem goes very deep, and he must search deep within himself for the solution.

13. He must learn to stop frequently and to take account of himself and his values.

14. He must identify himself with values which has proved lasting.

15. Above all, he must learn that there is much worse fates than falling behind the Joneses.

8 Pronouns: agreement, reference, and usage *agr / ref / us*

Use singular pronouns to refer to singular antecedents, plural pronouns to refer to plural antecedents. Make a pronoun refer to a definite antecedent.

The *writer* finished **his** story.

The *writers* finished **their** stories.

8a In general, use a plural pronoun to refer to a compound antecedent with *and*.

The *owner* and the *captain* refused to leave **their** distressed ship.

If two nouns designate the same person, the pronoun is singular.

The *owner and captain* refused to leave **his** distressed ship.

8b After a compound antecedent with *or, nor, either . . . or, neither . . . nor, not only . . . but also,* a pronoun agrees with the nearer part of the antecedent. (See **7b**.)

Neither the *Secretary* nor the *Undersecretary* was in **his** seat.

Neither the *Secretary* nor his *aides* were consistent in **their** policy.

A sentence like this written with *and* is less stilted.

The Secretary and his aides were not consistent in their policy.

8c A singular pronoun follows a collective noun antecedent when the members of the group are considered as a unit; a plural pronoun, when they are thought of individually. (See **7d**.)

A UNIT
The student *committee* presented **its** report.

INDIVIDUALS
The *committee* filed into the room and took **their** seats, some of **them** defiant.

8d Such singular antecedents as *each, either, neither, one, no one, everyone, someone, anyone, nobody, everybody, somebody, anybody* usually call for singular pronouns.

Not *one* of the linemen felt that **he** had had a good day.

Everyone who is a mother sometimes wonders how **she** will survive the day.

Traditionally the pronouns *he* and *his* have been used to refer to both men and women: "Each person has to face **his** own destiny." *He* was considered generic, that is, a common gender. Today this usage is changing because many feel that it ignores the presence and importance of women: there are as many "she's" as "he's" in the world, and one pronoun should not be selected to represent both.

Writers should become sensitive to this issue and strive to avoid offense without at the same time indulging in ridiculous alternatives. Here are three suggestions:

1. Try to make the sentence plural.

    All **persons** have to face **their** own destinies.

2. Use *he or she* (or *his or her*).

    Each person has to face **his or her** own destiny.

NOTE Be sparing in the use of *he or she, his or her*. Monotony results if these double pronouns are used more than once or twice in a paragraph.

3. Use *the* or avoid the singular pronoun altogether.

    Each person must face **the** future.
    Each person must face destiny.

8e *Which* refers to animals and things. *Who* refers to persons and sometimes to animals or things called by name. *That* refers to animals or things and sometimes to persons.

The *boy* **who** was fishing is my son.

The *dog* **which (that)** sat beside him looked happy.

Sometimes *that* and *who* are interchangeable.

A mechanic *that* (*who*) does good work stays busy.
A person *that* (*who*) giggles is often revealing embarrassment.

NOTE *Whose* (the possessive form of *who*) may be less awkward than *of which,* even in referring to animals and things.

The *car* **whose** right front tire blew out came to a stop.

8f Pronouns should not refer vaguely to an entire sentence or clause or to unidentified people.

Some people worry about wakefulness but actually need little sleep.
  This is one reason they have so much trouble sleeping.

This could refer to the worry, to the need for little sleep, or to psychological problems or other traits which have not even been mentioned.

CLEAR
Some people have trouble sleeping because they lie awake and worry about their inability to sleep.

They, them, it, and *you* are sometimes used as vague references to people and conditions which need more precise identification.

VAGUE
They always get **you** in the end.

The problem here is that the pronouns *they* and *you* and the sentence are so vague that the writer may mean almost anything pessimistic. The sentence could refer to teachers, deans, government officials, or even all of life.

NOTE Sometimes experienced writers let *this, which,* or *it* refer to the whole idea of an earlier clause or phrase when no misunderstanding is likely.

The grumbler heard that his boss had called him incompetent. *This* made him resign.

8g Make a pronoun refer clearly to one antecedent, not uncertainly to two.

UNCERTAIN
The agent visited her client before she went to the party.

CLEAR
Before she went to the party, the agent visited her client.

OR
Before the client went to the party, the agent visited her.

8h Use pronouns ending in *-self* or *-selves* only in sentences that contain antecedents for the pronoun.

CORRECT INTENSIVE PRONOUN

The cook **himself** washed the dishes.

FAULTY
The antique dealer sold the chair to my roommate and **myself.**

CORRECT
The antique dealer sold the chair to my roommate and **me.**

▶ Exercise 13
Revise sentences that contain errors in agreement of pronouns.

1. The captain of the freighter let each member of the crew decide whether they wished to remain with the ship.

2. On behalf of my wife and myself, I welcomed the visitors.

3. No matter what the detergent commercials say, no woman is really jubilant at the prospect of mopping their dirty kitchen floor.

4. The drifter, along with his many irresponsible relatives, never paid back a cent they borrowed.

5. Neither the batter nor the fans hesitated to show his ardent disapproval of the umpire's decision.

6. In the early days in the West, almost every man could ride their horse well.

7. The League of Nations failed because they never received full support from the member countries.

8. Did the dignitary hand the certificate to yourself or to your partner?

9. Neither of the two women ever accepted their prize from the advertising agency.

10. The political district have voted against additional taxes.

▶ Exercise 14
Revise sentences that contain vague or faulty references of pronouns.

1. The average factory worker is now well paid, but they have not been able to do much about the boredom.

2. They tell you that you must pay taxes, but most of the time you do not know what they use your money for.

3. In the highly competitive world of advertising, those who do not have it are soon passed over for promotions.

4. They use much less silver now in coins; so the metal in them is worth less.

5. Mail service has not improved over the years though it has gone up.

► Exercise 15

Revise sentences that contain errors in reference of pronouns. Write C by correct sentences.

1. The passerby which saved the two children did not know how to swim.

2. The soles of his shoes were worn, which made him self-conscious.

3. Lawyers generally charge their clients a standard fee unless they are unusually poor.

4. David fought Goliath although he was much smaller in size, and he was an experienced warrior, and he was not.

5. The instructions were brief and clear which was helpful.

6. On the night of July 14, the patriots stormed the doors of the jails, and they were immediately smashed open.

7. Luck is a prerequisite to riches, which is why few people are rich.

8. The poet is widely admired, but it is very difficult indeed to make a living at it.

9. The osprey feeds on fish, which it captures by diving into the water.

10. Typing themes saves a great deal of time in school, but they do not wish to learn to type.

9 Case c

Use correctly the case forms of pronouns and the possessive case of nouns. (See page 342.)

Problems with case arise with the use of the forms of nouns and especially pronouns *(me/I)* in a sentence.

To determine case, find how a word is used in its own clause —for example, whether it is a subject or a subjective complement, a possessive, or an object.

9a Use the subjective case for subjective complements which follow linking verbs and for subjects.

SUBJECTS

This month my sister and *I* **have** not been inside the library. (never *me*)

It looked as if my friend and *I* **were** going to be blamed. (never *me*)

SUBJECTIVE COMPLEMENTS

The guilty ones **were you** and **I.**

In conversation *you and me* is sometimes used. In speech *it's me, it's us, it's him,* and *it's her* are common.

9b Use the objective case for the object of a preposition.

Errors occur especially with compound objects.

FAULTY
The manager had to choose *between* **he and I.**

RIGHT
The manager had to choose *between* **him and me.**

Between you and me presents the same problem.

    Be careful about the case of pronouns in constructions like the following:

FAULTY
A few *of* **we campers** learned to cook.

RIGHT
A few *of* **us campers** learned to cook.

When in doubt, test by dropping the noun (not *of we,* but *of us*).

9c Use the objective case for the subject of an infinitive.

subject of infinitive
The reporter considered **him** *to be* the best swimmer in the pool.

9d Give an appositive and the word it refers to the same case.

The case of pronoun appositives depends on the case of the word they refer to.

SUBJECTIVE

Two *delegates*—**Bill** and **I**—were appointed by the president.

OBJECTIVE

The president appointed two *delegates*—**Bill** and **me.**

9e The case of a pronoun after *than* or *as* in an elliptical (incomplete) clause should be the same as if the clause were completely expressed.

understood
↓
No one else in the play was as versatile as **she** *(was)*.

understood
↓
The director admired no one else as much as *(he did)* **her.**

9f Use the possessive case for most pronouns preceding a gerund. A noun before a gerund (see page 21) may be possessive or objective.

My *driving* does not delight my father.
The **lumberman's** *chopping* could be heard for a mile.

The noun before a gerund is objective when a **phrase** intervenes

Regulations prevented the family **of a sailor** *meeting* him.

the noun is **plural**

There is no rule against **men** *working* overtime.

the noun is **abstract**

I object to **emotion** *overruling* judgment.

the noun denotes an **inanimate object**

The crew did object to the **ship** *staying* in port.

When a verbal is a participle and not a gerund, a noun or pronoun preceding it is in the objective case.

I heard **him** *singing*.
I hear **you** *calling* me.

9g Use an *of* phrase for the possessive of abstractions or inanimate objects.

NOT PREFERRED
The building's construction was delayed.

PREFERRED
The construction of the building was delayed.

There are well-established exceptions: *a stone's throw, for pity's sake, a month's rest, heart's desire, a day's work.*

9h The possessive forms of personal pronouns have no apostrophe; the possessive forms of indefinite pronouns do have an apostrophe.

PERSONAL PRONOUNS
yours its   hers   his   ours   theirs

INDEFINITE PRONOUNS
everyone's other's one's anybody else's

NOTE Contractions such as *it's (it is), he's,* and *she's* require an apostrophe.

9i The case of an interrogative or a relative pronoun is determined by its use in its own clause.

Interrogative pronouns (used in questions) are *who, whose, whom, what, which.* Relative pronouns are *who, whose, whom, what, which, that,* and the forms with *-ever,* such as *whoever* and *whosoever.* Difficulty occurs with *who* and *whoever* (subjective) and *whom* and *whomever* (objective).

    The case of these pronouns is clear in short sentences.

Who *defeated* the **challenger**?

But when words intervene between the pronoun and the main verb, determining the case may be difficult.

Who do the reports say *defeated* the **challenger**?

    Use two simple ways to tell the case of the pronoun in such sentences.

1. Mentally cancel the intervening words:

    Who ~~do the reports say~~ defeated the challenger?

2. Rearrange the sentence in declarative order, subject—verb—complement:

The reports do say who defeated the challenger.

A similar procedure works in determining when *whom* should be used.

NOTE In speech *who* is usually the form used at the beginning of a sentence, especially an interrogative sentence.

Who were you talking to over there?

The case of a relative pronoun is determined by its use in its own clause, not by the case of the antecedent. Three easy steps reveal the correct form:

1. Pick out the relative clause and draw a box around it.

   This is the old man (**who, whom**) the artist said was his model.

2. Cancel intervening expressions (*he says, it is reported,* and so on).

   This is the old man (**who, whom**) ~~the artist said~~ was his model.

3. Find the verb in the relative clause.

   subject   verb
   This is the old man **who** ~~whom~~ was his model.

NOTE Do not confuse the function of the relative pronoun in its clause with the function of the clause as a whole.

   object of verb
   subject
   I know **who**   started the fire.

subject of verb

object

Whom he will appoint is a matter of concern.

Try to avoid writing sentences with elaborate clauses using *who* and *whom*.

▶ Exercise 16

Underline the correct word in each of the following sentences.

1. There was in those days in Paris a singer (who, whom) the secret police knew was a double agent.
2. On the platform stood the man (who, whom) they all believed had practiced witchcraft.
3. On the platform stood the man (who, whom) they all accused of practicing witchcraft.
4. The speaker defended his right to talk critically of (whoever, whomever) he pleased.
5. He (who, whom) would be great of soul must first know poverty and suffering.
6. Wise spending is essential to those (who, whom) have small incomes.
7. On skid row is a little mission which gives (whoever, whomever) comes a hot meal, a dry place to sleep, and a word of encouragement.
8. Will the delegate from the Virgin Islands please indicate (who, whom) she wants to support?
9. (Who, Whom) discovered the human fossils is not known.
10. Truth is there for (whoever, whomever) will seek it.

▶ Exercise 17

Underline the incorrect forms of pronouns and nouns, and write in the correct forms.

1. The director said that the stunt man and myself were the ones most afraid of the white water on the trip down river.

2. After much discussion between the Navajo and she, they agreed that the first chance to buy the turquoise bracelet was her's rather than the man's.

3. No one was able to make more intricate sand designs than him.

4. "You and me," the Chinese man said, "will construct intricate fireworks which will burst into colorful designs."

5. The physician said that he had not objected to the employee returning to work.

6. It was a good days work to repair the house's roof.

7. Deep thinkers have motives and secrets that us ordinary people can never fathom.

8. Who's theory was it that matter can be neither created nor destroyed?

9. Its true that the Potomac got it's name from the Indians.

10. I apologized because I wanted no ill feelings between she and I.

10 Adjectives and adverbs *adj / adv*
Adjectives modify nouns and pronouns. Adverbs modify verbs, adjectives, and other adverbs.

Most adverbs end in *-ly*. Only a few adjectives *(lovely, holy, manly, friendly)* have this ending. Some adverbs have two forms, one with *-ly* and one without: *slow* and *slowly, loud* and *loudly*. Most adverbs are formed by adding *-ly* to adjectives: *warm, warmly; pretty, prettily*.

   Choosing correct adjectives and adverbs in some sentences is simple.

They stood *close*.
The barber gave him a *close* shave.
Study the text *closely*.

   Adjectives do not modify verbs, adverbs, or other adjectives. Distinguish between *sure* and *surely, easy* and *easily, good* and *well, real* and *really, some* and *somewhat*.

NOT
Balloonists *soar* over long distances **easy.**

BUT
Balloonists *soar* over long distances **easily.**

10a Use the comparative to refer to two things; the superlative, to more than two.

Both cars are fast, but the small car is (the) **faster.**
All *three* cars are fast, but the small car is (the) **fastest.**

10b Add *-er* and *-est* to form the comparative and superlative degrees of most short modifiers. Use *more* and *most* (or *less* and *least*) before long modifiers.

	COMPARATIVE	SUPERLATIVE
ADJECTIVES		
	-er/-est	
dear	dearer	dearest
pretty	prettier	prettiest
	more/most	
pitiful	more pitiful	most pitiful
grasping	more grasping	most grasping
ADVERBS		
	-er/-est	
slow	slower	slowest
	more/most	
rapidly	more rapidly	most rapidly

Some adjectives and adverbs have irregular comparative and superlative forms: *good, better, best; well, better, best; little, less, least; bad, worse, worst.*

Some adjectives and adverbs are absolute; that is, they cannot be compared *(dead, perfect, unique)*. A thing cannot be more or less dead, or perfect, or unique (one of a kind). An acceptable form is *more nearly perfect*.

10c Use a predicate adjective, not an adverb, after a linking verb (see page 7) such as *be, seem, become, look, appear, feel, sound, smell, taste.*

He feels **bad.** (He is ill or depressed.)

He *reads* **badly.** (*Reads* is not a linking verb.)

The *tea* tasted **sweet.** (*Sweet* describes the tea.)

She *tasted* the tea **daintily.** (*Daintily* tells how she tasted.)

10d Use an adjective, not an adverb, to follow a verb and its object when the modifier refers to the object, not to the verb.

Verbs like *keep, build, hold, dig, make, think* are followed by an object and an adjective which modifies it. After verbs of this kind, choose the adjective or the adverb form carefully.

ADJECTIVES—MODIFY COMPLEMENTS

Keep your *clothes* **neat.**

Make my *bed* **soft.**

ADVERBS—MODIFY VERBS

Keep your clothes **neatly** in the closet.

Make my bed **carefully.**

▶ **Exercise 18**

Underline unacceptable forms of adjectives and adverbs, and write the correct form. If a sentence is correct, write C.

1. Socrates thought profound about the nature and purpose of

   humanity.

2. The old clockmaker looked sadly when he spoke of the way

   the years whirl by.

3. The young coach was real angry about the controversial decision to fine her.

4. It sure cannot be denied that Tennyson was one of the popularest poets of his time.

5. Hungry birds strip a holly bush of its berries rapid and fly away seeking frantic for other food.

6. The computer, a real complicated mechanical mind, is the most unique instrument of modern civilization.

7. The athlete played awkwardly and badly.

8. Of the two factories, which one makes the most cars?

9. In times of tribulation, you must think logical.

10. The manager, a man of indecision, never knew which of two possibilities was the best.

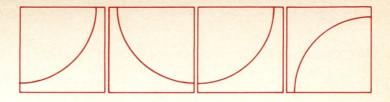

Sentence Structure

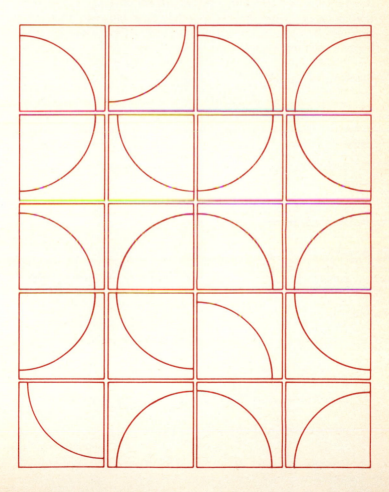

11   **Choppy sentences and excessive coordination**   *chop*
Do not string together short independent clauses or sentences.
(See **19**.)

Wordiness and monotony result from choppy sentences or from brief independent clauses connected by coordinating conjunctions *(and, and so, but, or, nor, for, yet, so)*. Excessive coordination does not show precise relationships between thoughts. English is rich in subordinating connectives, and skillful writers use them often.

STRINGY
Sugarloaf Mountain is four thousand feet high, and it is surrounded by fields and forests, and the air currents are favorable for hang gliding, and many gliding enthusiasts go there in the summer.

CHOPPY
Sugarloaf Mountain is four thousand feet high. It is surrounded by fields and forests. The air currents are favorable for hang gliding. Many gliding enthusiasts go there in the summer.

Make the last clause or sentence the central idea, and improve by using subordinating elements.

IMPROVED
Surrounded by fields and blessed with air currents favorable for hang gliding, four-thousand-foot-high Sugarloaf Mountain attracts many gliding enthusiasts in the summer.

▶ **Exercise 1**
Improve the following sentences by subordinating some of the ideas. Combine choppy sentences into longer sentences.

1. Pagodas are temples or sacred buildings, and they are found in several Eastern countries, and they often have many stories and upward-curving roofs.

2. Sharks are ferocious. And they attack many bathers each year, but they seldom kill; so their reputation as killers is in part undeserved.

3. Some vacationers leave home in search of quiet; so they find a place without a telephone or television, but other people want complete isolation, but they discover that it is difficult to find a state park that is not crowded with trailers and tents.

4. The instructor gave the new student an assignment, and he had to write just one sentence, but he could not think of an interesting subject, and so he did not do the required work.

5. Famous books are not always written by admirable people. Some authors are arrogant. Some are even immoral.

6. The manta ray has a wide, flat body, and it is also called a devilfish, and it is graceful.

7. Headhunters still exist in remote areas of the world, but they are rapidly disappearing, and today we seldom hear of them.

8. Computers calculate rapidly, and they do more work than a human being in the same time, and they threaten many jobs, but we must use them.

9. Women have been discriminated against, and they have been patient, but now they are complaining, and their cause is just.

10. Benjamin Franklin was an American. He was at home wherever he went. He gained wide popularity in France. He was also well known in England.

12   Subordination   *sub*
Use subordinate clauses accurately and effectively to avoid excessive coordination and to achieve variety and emphasis.

Insufficient or excessive subordination may ruin style or create excessively long and stringy sentences. (See also **11**.) Subordinating the lesser thought reveals the relative importance of ideas in a sentence.

12a   Express main ideas in independent clauses, less important ideas in subordinate clauses.

An optimistic sociologist wishing to stress progress despite crime, would write:

Although the crime rate is high, society has progressed in some ways.

A pessimistic sociologist might wish the opposite emphasis:

Although society has progressed in some ways, the crime rate is very high.

Putting the main idea in a subordinate clause is called **upside-down subordination.**

Although the patient recovered fully, the burn had been described as fatal.

12b Avoid excessive overlapping of subordinate clauses.

Monotony and even confusion can result from a series of clauses with each depending on the previous one.

OVERLAPPING
A watch is an intricate mechanism

which measures time,

which many people regard as a gift

that is precious.

IMPROVED
A watch is an intricate mechanism made to measure time, which many people regard as a precious gift.

▶ Exercise 2
The following is an exercise in thinking about relationships, designed to point up differences in meaning that result from subordination. Read the pairs of sentences carefully, and answer the questions.

1. A. After the Roman Empire was considerably weakened, corruption in high places became widespread.
    B. After corruption in high places became widespread, the Roman Empire was considerably weakened.

    Which of these sentences would a historian writing on the causes of Rome's fall be more likely to write?

2. A. Although a lifetime is short, much can be accomplished.
    B. Although much can be accomplished, a lifetime is short.

    Which of these sentences expresses more determination?

3. A. When in doubt, most drivers apply the brakes.
    B. When most drivers apply the brakes, they are in doubt.

    With which drivers would you prefer to ride?

4. A. Despite the fact that he had a speech defect, Cotton Mather became a great preacher.
    B. Despite the fact that he became a great preacher, Cotton Mather had a speech defect.

    In which sentence did he possibly overcome the defect?
    In which sentence did the defect remain noticeable?

5. A. While taking a bath, Archimedes formulated an important principle in physics.
    B. While formulating an important principle in physics, Archimedes took a bath.

    Which sentence indicates accidental discovery?
    In which sentence does Archimedes take a bath for relaxation?

▶ Exercise 3

Rewrite the following sentences to avoid overlapping subordination.

1. *Hamlet* is a play by Shakespeare that tells of a prince who has difficulties making up his mind to avenge the murder of his father.

2. Each musician who plays in the orchestra which performs in the club that is on the side of the lake has at least fifteen years of professional experience.

3. Lobster Newburg is a dish which consists of cooked lobster meat which is heated in a chafing dish which contains a special cream sauce.

4. Few people who smoke realize that the tobacco used in ordinary cigarettes is of the same family as the nightshades which are poisonous.

5. The elevator stuck that had the board member who could have cast a vote that would have changed the future of the corporation.

13 Completeness *compl*
Make your sentences complete in structure and thought.

Sentences should be clear, and every element should be expressed or implied clearly enough to prevent misunderstanding. Do not omit necessary verbs, conjunctions, and prepositions.

13a Make constructions with *so, such,* and *too* complete.

To avoid misunderstanding, be sure that the idea is expressed completely or has adequate context.

NOT CLEAR
The boy was too confused. (Too confused for what?)

CLEAR
The boy was too confused to answer the question.

NOT CLEAR
Her music teacher said she had so much promise. (So much that what?)

CLEAR
Her music teacher said that she had so much promise that she should continue her lessons.

13b Do not omit a verb or a preposition which is necessary to the structure of the sentence.

NOT
The baby was first frightened and then attracted **to** the new kitten.

BUT
The baby was first frightened **by** and then attracted **to** the new kitten.

BETTER

The baby was first frightened **by** the new kitten and then attracted **to** it.

NOT

The *silver* coins **were** scattered and the *paper money* stolen. (Paper money *were* stolen?)

BUT

The *silver coins* **were** scattered, and the *paper money* **was** stolen.

However, when the same form is called for in both elements, it need not be repeated:

To err is human; to forgive, divine.

13c Omission of *that* sometimes obscures meaning.

INCOMPLETE

The labor leader reported a strike was not likely.

COMPLETE

The labor leader reported that a strike was not likely.

14 Comparisons *comp*
Make comparisons logical and clear.

Compare only similar terms.

The *laughter* of a loon is more frightening than an **owl.**

This sentence compares a sound and a bird. A consistent sentence would compare sound and sound or bird and bird.

The *laughter* of a loon is more frightening than the **hoot** of an owl.

A *loon* is more frightening than an **owl**.

The word *other* is often needed in a comparison:

ILLOGICAL
The Sahara is larger than any desert in the world.

RIGHT
The Sahara is larger than any *other* desert in the world.

Avoid awkward and incomplete comparisons.

AWKWARD AND INCOMPLETE
The lily is *as white* if not whiter **than** any other flower. *(As white re-*
quires *as,* not *than.)*

BETTER
The lily is *as* white **as** any other flower, if not whiter. (*Than any other*
is understood.)

AWKWARD AND INCOMPLETE
Canoeing in white water is one of the most dangerous if not the most
dangerous water sport. (After *one of the most dangerous,* the plural
sports is required.)

BETTER
Canoeing in white water is one of the most dangerous water sports if
not the most dangerous one.

OR
Canoeing in white water is one of the most dangerous water sports.

AMBIGUOUS
After many years my teacher remembered me better than my roommate. (Better than he remembered my roommate, or better than
my roommate remembered me?)

CLEAR

After many years my teacher remembered me better than my roommate did.

OR

After many years my teacher remembered me better than he did my
roommate.

NOT COMPLETE

Motion pictures of the 1930s were different.

COMPLETE

Motion pictures of the 1930s were different from those of other decades.
(or, even more exact, *more romantic than* . . .)

▶ Exercise 4

*Correct any errors in completeness and comparisons. Write C by
correct sentences.*

1. Exploring caves is more exciting than any adventure.

2. Visitors to New Lawson discover that the summers there
   are as hot if not hotter than any they have ever experienced.

3. Storms on the open ocean are usually more severe than
   small seas.

4. This sentence is a little different.

5. The baboons ate more of the bananas than the ants.

6. Happy workers always have and still do produce the best
   results.

7. The veterinarian read an article contending that horses like dogs better than cats.

8. For good health, plain water is as good if not better than most other liquids.

9. The lighthouse stood as a symbol and guide to safety.

10. Some laws are so broad that they allow almost unlimited interpretations.

▶ Exercise 5
Follow the instructions for Exercise 4.

1. The river was too shallow.

2. A plant that lives in the air without roots is one of the strangest if not the strangest form of life.

3. The editors say that the headlines have been written and the type set.

4. The children enjoyed singing songs about how we go over the fields and the woods.

5. The attorney saw the witness's composure was lost.

15 Consistency *cons*

Write sentences which maintain grammatical consistency.

Avoid confusing shifts in grammatical forms.

TENSE AND VERB FORMS
Present and past

SHIFT The architect *planned* the new stadium, and the contractor *builds* it. (Use *planned . . . built* or *plans . . . builds*.)

Historical present and past (especially in writing about literature)

SHIFT The heroine *was* an idealist, but her dreams *come* to nothing. (The usual form is *is . . . come*.).

Conditional forms *(should, would, could)*

SHIFT Exhaustion after a vacation *could* be avoided if a family *can* plan better. (Use *could . . . would* or *can . . . can*.)

PERSON

In felling a tree, *a good woodsman* [**3rd person**] first cuts a deep notch near the bottom of the trunk and on the side toward which *he* [**3rd person**] wishes the tree to fall. Then *you* [**2nd person**] saw on the other side, directly opposite the notch.
(The second sentence should read *Then he saws. . . .* Or the first, *you first cut . . . toward which you wish. . . .*)

NUMBER

A *witness* may see an accident one way when it happens, and then *they* remember it an entirely different way when *they* testify. (Use *witness* and a singular pronoun or *witnesses* and *they*.)

MOOD
SHIFTS   *subjunctive*   *indicative*
                                        ↓   ↓
The instructions require that the applicant *fill* in this form and *mails* it. (consistent subjunctive: *fill . . . mail*)

imperative   *indicative*
↓   ↖
First *mail* the application; then the applicant *will go* for an interview. (consistent imperative: *mail . . . go*)

VOICE

SHIFT The chef *cooks* (**active**) the shrimp casserole for thirty minutes and then it *is allowed* (**passive**) to cool. (Use *cooks* and *allows*.)

RELATIVE PRONOUNS AND CONJUNCTIONS
Pronoun

She went to the cupboard *that* leaned perilously forward and *which* always resisted every attempt to open it. (Use *that . . . that* or *which . . . which*.)

Conjunction

The guest came *since* the food was good and *because* the music was soothing. (Use *since . . . since* or *because . . . because*.)

STATEMENTS AND QUESTIONS (EXCEPT IN QUOTATIONS)
Mixed

←———————— *statement*————————→   ←——— *question* ———

The censor says that the book is obscene and why would anyone wish
—————————→
to read it?

Consistent

The censor says that the book is obscene and asks why anyone would wish to read it.

Quotation

The censor says, "The book is obscene. Why would anyone wish to read it?"

▶ Exercise 6

Correct the shifts in grammar in the following sentences.

1. The florist explained that flowers wilt quickly, and why do

    people wait so long to put them in water?

2. A boy who writes an appealing letter to his girl friend will

seem to have personality, but the next time you see her you must be as interesting in person as you are when you write.

3. The failures in the experiments will be avoided this time if the assistants would follow the instructions precisely.

4. The retreating actor backed out of the door, jumped on a horse, and rides off into the sunset.

5. It is wise to start a fire with a wood like pine, and then a heavier wood like oak is used.

6. Use pine first to start a fire since it ignites easily and because it will then make the oak burn.

7. Dedicated joggers run every day; you should not get flabby.

8. Dedicated joggers want to run every day, but occasionally the weather would just be too bad to get outside.

9. For days the engaged couple plans a picnic, but then he decides to go bowling; so she gets angry and called off the wedding.

10. For days the engaged couple planned a picnic which would be by a cool stream and that would give them some precious moments alone.

16 Position of modifiers *po*

Attach modifiers clearly to the right word or element in the sentence.

A misplaced modifier can cause confusion or misunderstanding. Usually a modifying adjective precedes its noun, whereas an adverb may precede or follow the word it modifies. Prepositional phrases (see page 20) usually follow closely, but may precede; adjective clauses follow closely; and adverbial phrases and clauses may be placed in many positions.

16a Avoid dangling modifiers.

A verbal phrase at the beginning of a sentence should modify the subject.

DANGLING PARTICIPLE

Hearing the good news, my *mood* was filled with joy.

CLEAR

Hearing the good news, *I* was filled with joy.

OR

After I heard the good news, my mood was joyful.

DANGLING GERUND

After **searching** around the attic, a *halloween mask* was discovered. (The passive voice in the main clause causes the modifier—a preposition and a gerund—to attach wrongly to the subject.)

CLEAR

After **searching** around the attic, *I* discovered a halloween mask.

DANGLING INFINITIVE

To enter the house, the *lock* on the back door was picked. (*To enter the house* refers to no word in this sentence.)

CLEAR

To enter the house, *he* picked the lock on the back door.

DANGLING PREPOSITIONAL PHRASE

During childhood, *my mother* was a consul in Italy. (In whose childhood?)

CLEAR

During **my** childhood, *my mother* was a consul in Italy.

DANGLING ELLIPTICAL CLAUSE

While still sleepy and tired, the *counsellor* lectured me on breaking rules.

CLEAR

While I was still sleepy and tired, the counsellor lectured me on breaking rules.

Loosely attaching a verbal phrase to the end of a sentence is ineffective:

UNEMPHATIC

Every member of the infield moved closer to the plate, thus preparing for a double play.

Simple coordination is a good way to revise.

BETTER

Every member of the infield moved closer to the plate and prepared for a double play.

NOTE Some verbal phrases need not refer to a single word.

Strictly speaking, does this sentence contain a dangling construction? *To tell the truth,* it does not.

The phrases are sentence modifiers.

16b Avoid misplaced modifiers.

The placement of a modifier in a sentence affects meaning.

He enlisted after he married *again.*
He enlisted *again* after he married.

Almost anything which comes between an adjective clause and the word it modifies can cause confusion.

MISLEADING
Some insecticides are still used on crops that are suspected of being dangerous.

CLEAR
Some insecticides that are suspected of being dangerous are still used on crops.

16c A modifier placed between two words so that it may modify either word is said to squint.

UNCLEAR
The horse which was pawing *violently* kicked its owner.

CLEAR
The horse which was *violently pawing* kicked its owner.

OR
The horse which was pawing *kicked* its owner *violently.*

▶ Exercise 7

Correct the faulty modifiers in the following sentences.

1. Looking through a magnifying glass, the flaw in the diamond appeared to be a dark spot.

2. The courageous patient was able to walk about two weeks after the accident.

3. This computer is seldom used even though it is most effective because of the high cost.

4. To be absolutely certain, the answer must be checked.

5. The restaurant offers meals for children that are inexpensive.

6. Serve one of the melons for dessert at lunch; keep one of them for the picnic in the refrigerator.

7. The carpenter inspected the board before sawing for nails.

8. Although only a freshman, his knowledge of new discoveries in astronomy was impressive.

9. Slowly and relentlessly the historian said that witches attempt to gain control over the minds of others.

10. The woman who was writing hastily rose from the desk and left the room.

▶ **Exercise 8**
Follow the instructions for Exercise 7.

1. The manager gave personal names to every doll, enabling the shop to appeal to the children.

2. Without shoes, the rough stones cut the feet of the hikers.

3. Although hindered by the weather, the bridge was still built by the workers.

4. To taste delicious, the chef should prepare a dressing precisely suitable to the raw spinach salad.

5. The editor only told me that lighthearted columns would be accepted for the children's page.

17 Separation of elements *sep*
Do not needlessly separate closely related elements.

Separation of subject and verb, parts of a verb phrase, or verb and object can be awkward.

AWKWARD
Wild dogs had, *for several sleet-ridden and storm-ravaged winter days when food was scarce,* been seen on the hills.

IMPROVED

For several sleet-ridden and storm-ravaged winter days when food was scarce, wild dogs had been seen on the hills.

PUZZLING

She is the man who owns the service station's wife.

CLEAR

She is the wife of the man who owns the service station.

Do not divide a sentence with a quotation long enough to cause excessive separation.

AVOID

Stephen Crane's view of the place of man in the world,

> A man said to the universe:
> "Sir, I exist!"
> "However," replied the universe,
> "The fact has not created in me
> A sense of obligation,"

is pessimistic.

Split infinitives occur when a modifier comes between *to* and the verb form, as in *to loudly complain*. Some writers avoid them without exception; others accept them occasionally. To avoid objections, do not write this kind of split construction.

18 Parallelism //

Use parallel grammatical forms to express parallel thoughts.

Constructions in a sentence are *parallel* when they are in balance, that is, when a phrase matches up with a phrase, a clause with a clause, a verb with a verb, a noun with a noun, and so forth.

(1) Parallelism in constructions with coordinating conjunctions (*and, or, nor, for,* etc.):

adjective   *verb*

NOT PARALLEL
Sailing ships were *stately* **and** *made* little noise.

adjectives

PARALLEL
Sailing ships were *stately* **and** *quiet*.

nouns   *pronoun*

NOT PARALLEL
Young Lincoln read widely for *understanding, knowledge,* **and** *he* just liked books.

nouns

PARALLEL
Young Lincoln read widely for *understanding, knowledge,* **and** *pleasure*.

NOTE Repeat an article *(the, a, an)*, a preposition *(by, in, on,* etc.), the sign of the infinitive *(to)*, or other key words in order to preserve parallelism and clarity:

UNCLEAR
The artist was **a** painter and sculptor of marble.

CLEAR
The artist was **a** painter and **a** sculptor of marble.

UNCLEAR
They passed the evening **by** eating and observing the crowds.

CLEAR
They passed the evening **by** eating and **by** observing the crowds.

(2) Parallelism in constructions with correlatives (*not only . . . but also, either . . . or,* etc.):

infinitive   *preposition*

NOT PARALLEL
Petroleum is used **not only** *to make* fuels **but also** *in* plastics.

NOT PARALLEL

verb   *preposition*

Not only *is* petroleum used in fuels **but also** *in* plastics.

                            prepositions

PARALLEL

Petroleum is used **not only** *in* fuels **but also** *in* plastics.

                               adverb   *pronoun*

NOT PARALLEL

The lecturer's speeches were **either** *too* long, **or** *they* were not long enough.

NOT PARALLEL

article   *adverb*

Either *the* lecturer's speeches were too long **or** *too* short.

                            adverbs

PARALLEL

The lecturer's speeches were **either** *too* long **or** *too* short.

(3) Parallelism with *and who* and with *and which:*
Avoid *and who* or *and which* unless they are preceded by a matching *who* or *which.*

NOT PARALLEL

The position calls for a person with an open mind *and who* is cool headed.

PARALLEL

The position calls for a person with an open mind and a cool head.

PARALLEL

The position calls for a person *who* is open-minded and *who* is cool-headed.

NOT PARALLEL

A new dam was built to control floods *and which* would furnish rec-reation.

PARALLEL
A new dam was built to control floods and furnish recreation.

PARALLEL
A new dam was built *which* would control floods *and which* would furnish recreation.

▶ Exercise 9
Revise sentences with faulty parallelism. Write C *by correct sentences.*

1. The ideal piecrust is tender, flaky, and tastes good.

2. The new sedan is advertised as attractive, inexpensive, and with a new economical motor.

3. Adjusting to a large college is difficult for a person who has always attended a small school and being used to more individual attention.

4. Roaming through the great north woods, camping by a lake, and getting away from crowds are good ways to forget the cares of civilization.

5. A good listener must have a genuine interest in people, a strong curiosity, and discipline oneself to keep the mind from wandering.

6. A young musician must practice long hours, give up pleasures, and one has to be able to take criticism.

7. A good trial lawyer must be shrewd, alert, and a bold speaker.

8. The delegation found it impossible either to see the governor or any other official.

9. Most slow readers could read much faster if they would not glance back over lines and moving their lips.

10. The jaguar is swift, quiet, and moves with grace.

19 Variety *var*
Vary sentences in structure and order.

An unbroken series of short sentences may become monotonous and fail to indicate such relationships as cause, condition, concession, time sequence, and purpose. (See page 78.)

Structure
Do not overuse one kind of sentence structure. Write simple, compound, and complex patterns. Vary your sentences between loose, periodic, and balanced forms.

A **loose sentence,** the most common kind, makes its main point early and then adds refinements.

LOOSE
Boys are wild animals, rich in the treasures of sense, but the New

England boy had a wider range of emotions than boys of more equable climates.

HENRY ADAMS

Uncle Tom's Cabin is a very bad novel, having, in its self-righteous, virtuous sentimentality, much in common with *Little Women*.

JAMES BALDWIN

A **periodic sentence** withholds an element of the main thought until the end to create suspense and emphasis.

PERIODIC

Under a government which imprisons any unjustly, the true place for a just man is also a prison.

HENRY DAVID THOREAU

PERIODIC

There is one thing above all others that the scientist has a duty to teach to the public and to governments: it is the duty of heresy.

J. BRONOWSKI

A **balanced sentence** has parallel parts which are similar in structure, length, and thoughts. Indeed, balance is simply another word for refined parallelism. (See **18**.) The following sentence has perfect symmetry:

Marriage has many pains, but celibacy has no pleasures.

SAMUEL JOHNSON

A sentence can also be balanced if only parts of it are symmetrical:

Thus the Puritan was made up of two different men, the one all self-
abasement, penitence, gratitude, passion; the other proud, calm,
inflexible, sagacious.

THOMAS BABINGTON MACAULAY

Thus
the Puritan
was made up
of two different men,

the one _____ the other
all self-abasement,____proud,
penitence, _____calm,
gratitude, _____ inflexible,
passion;_____ sagacious.

Order

If several sentences follow the order of subject-verb-complement,
they can be monotonous. Invert the order occasionally; do not
always tack dependent clauses and long phrases on at the end.
Study the variations:

NORMAL ORDER
subject   *verb*   *object*   *modifiers* ———→
  ↓   ↓   ↓
She attributed these *defects* in her son's character to the general weaknesses of mankind.

SENTENCE BEGINNING WITH DIRECT OBJECT
These *defects* in her son's character she attributed to the general weaknesses of mankind.

SENTENCE BEGINNING WITH PREPOSITIONAL PHRASE
To the general weaknesses of mankind she attributed the defects in her
son's character.

SENTENCE BEGINNING WITH ADVERB
Quickly the swordfish broke the surface of the water.

INVERTED SENTENCE BEGINNING WITH CLAUSE USED AS OBJECT
That the engineer tried to stop the train, none would deny.

INVERTED SENTENCE BEGINNING WITH DEPENDENT ADVERBIAL CLAUSE
If you wish to create a college, therefore, and are wise, you will seek to
create a life.

WOODROW WILSON

SENTENCE BEGINNING WITH PARTICIPIAL PHRASE
Flying low over the water, the plane searched for the reef.

▶ Exercise 10
*Rewrite the following sentences and make them periodic. If you
consider a sentence already periodic, put a check mark next to it.*

1. One machine, the typewriter, revolutionized business practices and had a profound influence on the style of many authors.

2. A sense of humor is one quality no great leader can be without.

3. Selfishness, some philosophers maintain, is the reason
   behind every action of any person.

4. The blue whale is the largest known creature on earth.

5. He studied when all other possible methods of passing the
   course proved unworkable.

▶ Exercise 11
*Rewrite the following sentences to give them balanced construc-
tions. Put a check mark by a sentence which is already balanced.*

1. The rewards of youth are obvious, but much more subtle are
   the rewards of age.

2. A successful advertisement surprises and pleases, but not all
   advertisements are successful because some are merely
   boring and irritating.

3. Realists know their limitations; romantics know only what
   they want.

4. A politician is concerned with successful elections whereas
   the future of the people is foremost in the mind of a statesman.

5. A trained ear hears many separate instruments in an orchestra, but the melody is usually all that is heard by the
   untutored.

▶ Exercise 12
*Rewrite the following passage so that it is more varied in sentence
structure.*

The problems of college financing have changed since my

grandfather's day. Like most change, this has been both good and bad. There are good consequences. Families no longer need to make heroic sacrifices to send their children to college. Women are not expected to forsake careers in favor of their male siblings. A college education is accessible to minorities. And the poor. The cost of education has declined steadily, in real terms. The decline has lasted fifty years. At the same time, the system of financial aid that made these improvements possible is increasing college dependency. Colleges depend on the federal government. The dependence is weakening educational institutions. It is making them more expensive and less efficient. Federal subsidy of college expenses is also encouraging irresponsible consumer practices. Subsidy is promoting unethical conduct. Subsidy is promoting a decline in the value we place on education. We are, in short, paying less for education today. We are getting less from it as well.

Adapted from ALSTON CHASE,

Financing a College Education

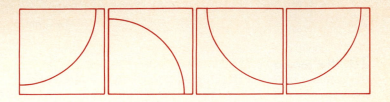

Punctuation

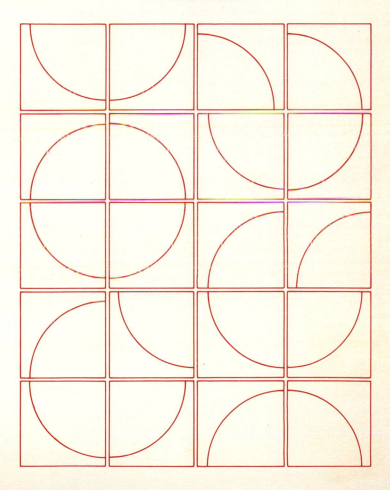

20 The comma   ,
Use commas to reflect structure and to clarify the sense of the sentence.

The **comma** is chiefly used (1) to separate equal elements, such as independent clauses and items in a series, and (2) to set off modifiers or parenthetical words, phrases, and clauses.

Elements which are set off within a sentence take a comma both *before* and *after*.

NOT
This novel, a best seller has no real literary merit.

BUT
This novel, a best seller, has no real literary merit.

20a Use a comma to separate independent clauses joined by a coordinating conjunction.

Nice is a word with many meanings, and some of them are opposite to others.
Sherlock Holmes had to be prepared, for Watson was full of questions.

NOTE The comma is sometimes omitted between the clauses when they are so brief that there is no danger of misreading.

The weather was clear and the pilot landed.

20b Use a comma between words, phrases, or clauses in a series.

The closet contained worn clothes, old shoes, and dusty hats.

The final comma before *and* in a series is sometimes omitted.

The closet contained worn clothes, old shoes and dusty hats.

But the comma must be used when *and* is omitted.

The closet contained worn clothes, old shoes, dusty hats.

And it must be used to avoid misreading.

An old chest in the corner was filled with nails, hammers, a hacksaw and blades, and a brace and bit.

Series of phrases or of dependent or independent clauses are also separated by commas.

PHRASES
We hunted for the letter in the album, in the old trunks, and even under the rug.

DEPENDENT CLAUSES
Finally we concluded that the letter had been burned, that someone had taken it, or that it had never been written.

INDEPENDENT CLAUSES
We left the attic, Father locked the door, and Mother suggested that we never unlock it again.

In a series of independent clauses, the comma is not omitted before the final element.

▶ Exercise 1
Insert commas where necessary in the following sentences.

1. Some prominent women authors took masculine pen names

in the nineteenth century for they felt that the public would not read novels written by women.

2. A good orator should prepare well for a talk speak clearly enough to be understood and practice the art of effective timing.

3. The markings on the wall of the cave were not as ancient as others but none of the experts could interpret them.

4. The hamper was filled with cold cuts mixed pickles bread and butter.

5. Some government documents are classified secret for the safety of the country must be preserved.

6. The sensitive child knew that the earth was round but she thought that she was on the inside of it.

7. The city planner stated that taxes were already high that personal incomes were low and that rapid transit is expensive.

8. For breakfast the menu offered only bacon and eggs toast and jelly and hot coffee.

9. Careless driving includes speeding stopping suddenly turning from the wrong lane going through red lights and so forth.

10. Driving was easy for the highway was completed and traffic was light.

20c Use a comma between coordinate adjectives not joined by *and.* Do not use a comma between cumulative adjectives.

Coordinate adjectives modify the noun independently.

COORDINATE
We entered a forest of tall, slender, straight pines.

Ferocious, alert, loyal dogs were essential to safety in the Middle Ages.

Cumulative adjectives modify the whole cluster of subsequent adjectives and the noun.

CUMULATIVE

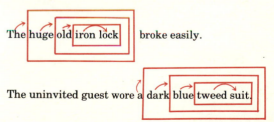

The huge old iron lock broke easily.

The uninvited guest wore a dark blue tweed suit.

Two tests are helpful.

Test one
And is natural only between coordinate adjectives.

tall *and* slender *and* straight
ferocious *and* alert *and* loyal dogs

BUT NOT
dark *and* blue *and* tweed suit
huge *and* old *and* iron

Test two
Coordinate adjectives are easily reversible.

straight, slender, and tall
loyal, alert, ferocious dogs

BUT NOT
tweed blue dark suit
iron old huge

The distinction is not always clear-cut, however, and the sense
of the cluster must be the deciding factor.

She was wearing a full-skirted, low-cut velvet gown.

  (a velvet gown that was full-skirted and low-cut, not a gown that
  was full-skirted and low-cut and velvet)

▶ **Exercise 2**
*Punctuate the following. When in doubt, apply the tests described
above. Write* C *by those which require no comma.*

  1. a   graceful   agile   cat

  2. large   glass   front   doors

3. a little black recipe book

4. gaudy shiny earrings

5. a wrinkled brown paper bag

6. a hot sultry depressing day

7. the gloomy forbidding night scene

8. expensive new electric typewriter

9. a woebegone ghostly look

10. beautiful Persian rugs

20d Use a comma after a long introductory phrase or clause.

LONG PHRASE
With this severe part of the trek behind him, the trapper felt more confident.

LONG CLAUSE
When this severe part of the trek was behind him, the trapper felt more confident.

When the introductory element is short and there is no danger of misreading, the comma is often omitted.

SHORT PHRASE
After this ordeal the trapper felt more confident.

SHORT CLAUSE
When this ordeal was over the trapper felt more confident.

Commas after these introductory elements would be acceptable. Use of the comma here may depend on personal taste.

Introductory verbal phrases, however, are usually set off by commas.

PARTICIPLE
Living for centuries, redwoods often reach great heights.

INFINITIVE
To verify his or her hypothesis, a scientist performs an experiment.

GERUND
After surviving this ordeal, the trapper felt relieved.

A phrase or a clause set off by a comma at the beginning of a sentence may not require a comma if it is moved to the end of the sentence.

BEGINNING
Because of pity for creatures that must live in cages, some people refuse to go to the zoo.

END
Some people refuse to go to the zoo because of pity for creatures that must live in cages.

20e Use commas to set off nonrestrictive appositives, phrases, and clauses.

A **nonrestrictive modifier** describes and adds information but does not point out or identify; omit the modifier, and the sentence loses some meaning but does not change radically or become meaningless.

NONRESTRICTIVE
Shakespeare's last play, *The Tempest*, is optimistic and even sunny in mood.

Taxicabs, *which are always expensive*, cost less in New York than else-
    where.
Abstract words, *which do not convey images*, are necessary in language.

In these three sentences the italicized modifiers add information, but they are not essential to the meaning of the sentence.

NOTE *That* never introduces a nonrestrictive clause.

   A **restrictive modifier** points out or identifies its noun or
pronoun; remove the modifier, and the sentence radically
changes in meaning or becomes nonsense.

RESTRICTIVE
The play *Macbeth* has been studied for over three hundred years.
Taxicabs *that are dirty* are illegal in some cities.
Words *which convey images* are important in poetry.

In all these sentences, the italicized expressions identify the
words they modify; to remove these modifiers would be to
change the meaning or to make the sentences false.
   Some modifiers can be either restrictive or nonrestrictive,
and use or omission of the commas changes the sense.

The coin which gleamed in the sunlight was a Spanish doubloon. (There
    were several coins.)
The coin, which gleamed in the sunlight, was a Spanish doubloon.
    (There was only one coin.)

In speech a nonrestrictive modifier is usually preceded by a
pause, whereas a restrictive modifier is not.

▶ Exercise 3
*The following pairs of sentences illustrate differences in meaning
which result from use or omission of commas with modifiers.
Answer the questions about each pair of sentences.*

1. A. In Allison Long's novel, *Only Once,* the heroine is a physician.
   B. In Allison Long's novel *Only Once,* the heroine is a physician.

   In which sentence has Allison Long written only one novel?

2. A. The posts which are cut from locust trees will last a long time.
   B. The posts, which are cut from locust trees, will last a long time.

   In which sentence is there only one kind of posts?

3. A. The plant, which has an elaborately designed pot, is not as pretty as the container.
   B. The plant which has an elaborately designed pot is not as pretty as the container.

   Which of these sentences would be the one more likely spoken by a florist? Why?

4. A. Young drivers, who are not well trained, cause most of our minor automobile accidents.
   B. Young drivers who are not well trained cause most of our minor automobile accidents.

   Which sentence shows a prejudice against young drivers?

5. A. Anthropologists, who respect native ways, are welcome among most tribes.
   B. Anthropologists who respect native ways are welcome among most tribes.

   Which sentence reflects confidence in anthropologists?

▶ Exercise 4

Insert commas for nonrestrictive modifiers; circle all unnecessary commas. Write C by correct sentences.

1. The name Rover was often associated with dogs which were happy.

2. Barbers, who are bald, often authoritatively discuss baldness with their customers, who are worried about losing their hair.

3. The wealthy who keep their expensive jewelry in bank vaults sometimes hire people to wear their pearls for them so that the gems will not lose their luster.

4. Americans who have grown up on the prairies may feel shut in when they move to forest regions or to cities with buildings which have more than ten stories.

5. Adam's son Abel was a shepherd.

6. Abel Adam's son was a shepherd.

7. The tree, that stood despite the high winds, was planted by my paternal grandfather who was born over a hundred years ago.

8. The most beautiful photograph a shadowy shot of a white bird against a dark sky was made on a small island which is about a mile off the eastern coast.

9. Courses, which are not challenging, usually do not instruct the students who have the best minds.

10. Shaw's play, *Pygmalion,* was the basis for a musical which was entitled *My Fair Lady.*

20f Use commas with sentence modifiers, conjunctive adverbs, and sentence elements out of normal word order.

Modifiers like *on the other hand, for example, in fact, in the first place, I believe, in his opinion, unfortunately,* and *certainly* are set off by commas.

Only a few poets, unfortunately, make a living by writing.
Thomas Hardy's poems, I believe, cause lingering meditation.

Commas are frequently used with conjunctive adverbs: *accordingly, anyhow, besides, consequently, furthermore, hence, indeed, instead, likewise, meanwhile, moreover, nevertheless, otherwise, still, then, therefore, thus.*

optional

BEFORE CLAUSE
The auditor checked the figures again; therefore, the mistake was discovered.

optional

WITHIN CLAUSE
The auditor checked the figures again; the mistake, therefore, was
discovered.

Commas always separate the conjunctive adverb *however* from
the rest of the sentence.

The auditor found the error in the figures; however, the books still did
not balance.
The auditor found the error in the figures; the books, however, still did
not balance.

Commas are not used when *however* is an adverb meaning "no
matter how."

However fast the hare ran, he could not catch the tortoise.

Use commas if necessary for clearness or emphasis when
part of a sentence is out of normal order.

Confident and informed, the young woman invested her own money.

OR
The young woman, confident and informed, invested her own money.

BUT
The confident and informed young woman invested her own money.

20g Use commas with degrees and titles and with elements
in dates, places, and addresses.

DEGREES AND TITLES
Arthur Weiss, M.A., came to the picnic.
Louis Ferranti, Jr., Chief of Police, made the arrest.

DATES

Sunday, May 31, is her birthday.

August 1973 was very warm. (Commas around *1973* are also acceptable.)

July 20, 1969, was the date when a human being first stepped on the moon. (Use commas *before* and *after*.)

She was born 31 December 1970. (Use no commas.)

The year 1980 was a time of change. (Restrictive; use no commas.)

PLACES

Cairo, Illinois, is my home town. (Use commas *before* and *after*.)

ADDRESSES

Write the editor of *The Atlantic*, 8 Arlington Street, Boston, Massachusetts 02116. (Use no comma before the zip code.)

20h Use commas for contrast or emphasis and with short interrogative elements.

The pilot used an auxiliary landing field, not the city airport.

The field was safe enough, wasn't it?

20i Use commas with mild interjections and with words like *yes* and *no*.

Well, no one thought it was possible.

No, it proved to be simple.

20j Use commas with words in direct address and after the salutation of a personal letter.

Mary, have you seen the portrait?

Dear John,
    It has been some time since I've written. . . .

20k Use commas with expressions like *he said, she remarked,* and *she replied* when used with quoted matter.

"I am planning to enroll in Latin," she said, "at the beginning of next term."
He replied, "It's all Greek to me."

20L Set off an absolute phrase with commas.

An **absolute phrase** consists of a noun followed by a modifier. It modifies the sentence as a whole, not any single element in it.

←—— *absolute phrase* ——→
Our day's journey over, we made camp for the night.

←—— *absolute phrase* ——→
The portrait having dried, the artist hung it on the wall.

20m Use commas to prevent misreading or to mark an omission.

After washing and grooming, the pup looked like a different dog.
When violently angry, elephants trumpet.
Beyond, the open fields sloped gently to the sea.

verb omitted
↓
To err is human; to forgive, divine.

▶ Exercise 5

Add necessary commas. If a sentence is correct as it stands, write C *by it.*

1. Inside the convention hall resembled a huge, overcrowded barn.

2. A few hours before he was scheduled to leave the mercenary visited his father who pleaded with him to change his mind and then finally said quietly "Good luck."

3. Seeing a nightingale the American ornithologist recognized its resemblance to other members of the thrush family.

4. Seeing a nightingale for the first time is disappointing; hearing one for the first time unforgettable.

5. History one would think ought to teach people not to make the same mistakes over again.

6. Despite the old saying to the contrary you can sometimes tell a book by its cover.

7. The Vandyke beard according to authorities was named after Sir Anthony Van Dyck a famous Flemish painter.

8. Only after reading a book either very carefully or more than once should a critic write a review.

9. While burning cedar has a distinct and strong odor.

10. The cloverleaf a road arrangement that looks somewhat like a four-leaf clover permits traffic to flow easily between two intersecting expressways.

▶ Exercise 6
Follow the instructions for Exercise 5.

1. The hippopotamus has a stout hairless body very short legs and a large head and muzzle.

2. The tarantula a large hairy spider looks frightening; it is not however highly venomous.

3. Before students can understand the principles of quantum physics they must master simple algebra.

4. The ancient urn labeled 6-01 stood in the corner of the garden and the honeysuckle vines almost hid it from view.

5. While the mystery writer was composing his last novel

The Tiger's Eye he received a note warning him not to write about anyone he knew in the Orient.

6. The barber having finished cutting his hair the youth climbed from the chair and called his friend "Now Jack get your hair cut."

7. The geographer said that he had spent most of his life living in Taos New Mexico.

8. The hungry prospector turned from the window looked into his cabinet and saw that he still had some tomato ketchup dried white beans and beef jerky.

9. Atlanta Georgia is lower in latitude than Rome Italy. Miami furthermore is not as far south as the equatorial zone is it?

10. Towers domes and stadiums provided little contrast with the low overhanging clouds.

▶ **Exercise 7**
Add necessary commas.

1. Attempting to save money as well as transportation costs

some shoppers go to the grocery store only once a month; others however choose to go more often.

2. The menu included beets carrots and radishes for the chef was fond of root foods.

3. However the travelers followed the worn outdated city map they always returned to the same place.

4. The last selection on the program Chopin's Polonaise brought the most applause I believe.

5. The American frigate *Constitution* it is true fought in the War of 1812.

6. She wished the warm sunny day would last forever but she realized that winter was coming.

7. High over the mountain clouds looked dark ominous.

8. Edward Friar Ph.D. was awarded his honorary degree on June 1 1947 in Fulton Missouri.

9. With a renewed sense of the importance of his experiment the chemist continued his work.

10. Yes friends the time has come for pausing not planning.

21   Unnecessary commas *no ,*
Do not use commas excessively.

A comma at every pause within a sentence is not necessary.

21a   Do not use a comma between subject and verb, between verb or verbal and complement, or between an adjective and the word it modifies.

NOT
The guard with the drooping mustache, snapped to attention.
Some students in the class, admitted, that they had not read, "Mending Wall."
The stubborn, mischievous, child refused to respond.

A phrase set off by two commas may be used between subject and verb.

The malamute, an Alaskan work dog, can survive extraordinarily cold weather.

21b   Do not use a comma between two compound elements, such as verbs, subjects, complements, or predicates.

compound verb

He **left** the scene of the accident and **tried** to forget that it had happened.

no comma

21c   Do not use a comma before a coordinating conjunction joining two dependent clauses.

dependent clauses

The contractor testified **that the house was completed** and **that the work had been done properly.**

no comma

21d Do not use a comma before *than* in a comparison or between compound conjunctions like *as . . . as, so . . . as, so . . . that.*

no comma

John Holland was more delighted with life on the Continent than he had thought he could be.

21e Do not use a comma after *like* and *such as.*

commas here   not here

Some languages, such as Latin and Anglo-Saxon, are no longer spoken.

A comma is used **before** *such as* (as above) only when the phrase is nonrestrictive.

21f Do not use a comma with a period, a question mark, an exclamation point, or a dash. These marks stand by themselves.

no comma

"Did you get the job?" her roommate asked.

21g   A comma may be used after a closing parenthesis, but not before an opening parenthesis.

no comma
↓

After reading *The Pilgrim's Progress* (the most popular allegory in the

comma
↓

language), he turned next to *Oliver Twist*.

21h   A comma is not used after coordinating conjunctions. A comma is not required after short introductory adverbial modifiers. (See **20d.**)

NOT
But, some people are excessively tolerant.
Thus, he passed the examination.

OPTIONAL
After he had slept, he felt more confident.

21i   Do not use commas to set off restrictive clauses, phrases, or appositives. (See **20e.**)

NOT
People, who live in glass houses, should not throw stones.

21j   Do not use a comma between adjectives which are not coordinate. (See **20c.**)

FAULTY
The tired, old, work horse stopped.

▶ **Exercise 8**
Circle all unnecessary commas, and be prepared to explain your decisions.

1. Soccer is a popular sport in Great Britain, where it is sometimes called, football.

2. The secretary bird is so named, because, on its crest, it has feathers which resemble quill pens.

3. Restaurants, that serve excellent food at modest prices, are always popular among local people, though tourists seldom know about them.

4. Riding horses, and driving cattle were more strenuous work, than he expected.

5. Riding horses, (new for him), travel on freight trains, and rowing boats were strenuous tasks.

6. That summer he tried many new activities, such as, riding horses, traveling on freight trains, and rowing boats.

7. Communities, near large airports, have become increasingly aware that noise pollution can be just as unpleasant as impurities in the air or in streams.

8. Once, huge movie houses were fashionable, but now these

palaces are like dinosaurs, extinct, giants, curious remind-

ers, of the past.

9. The Olympic runner was disqualified, after he ran out of his

lane, but he would not have won a gold medal, anyway.

10. The gardener vowed that he would never work for the mil-

lionaire again, and that he would go back to his small farm.

22 The semicolon ;

Use a semicolon between independent clauses not joined by coordinating conjunctions *(and, but, or, nor, for, so, yet)* and between coordinate elements with internal commas.

Omitting a semicolon between independent clauses may result in a comma splice or a fused sentence. (See **2.**)

22a Use a semicolon between independent clauses not connected by a coordinating conjunction.

WITH NO CONNECTIVE
For fifteen years the painting stood in the attic; even Kirk forgot it.

WITH A CONJUNCTIVE ADVERB
A specialist from the museum arrived and asked to examine it; **then** all the family became excited.

See **20f** for use of commas with conjunctive adverbs, such as *however, therefore, moreover, then, consequently, nevertheless.*

The painting was valuable; **in fact,** the museum offered ten thousand dollars for it.

See **20f** for use of commas with sentence modifiers, such as *on the other hand, for example, in fact, in the first place.*

22b Use a semicolon to separate independent clauses which are long and complex or which have internal punctuation.

In many compound sentences either a semicolon or a comma may be used.

COMMA OR SEMICOLON
Moby-Dick, by Melville, is an adventure story, *(or ;)* and it is also one of the world's great philosophical novels.

SEMICOLON PREFERRED
Ishmael, the narrator, goes to sea, he says, "whenever it is a damp, drizzly November" in his soul; and Ahab, the captain of the ship, goes to sea because of his obsession to hunt and kill the great albino whale, Moby Dick.

22c Use semicolons in a series between items which have internal punctuation.

The old farmer kept a variety of poultry: chickens, for eggs and Sunday dinners; turkeys, for very special meals; and peacocks, for their beauty.

22d Do not use a semicolon between elements which are not coordinate.

dependent clause   *independent clause*
After the tugboat had signaled to the barge twice; it turned toward
  the wharf.

▶ Exercise 9
*Circle unnecessary semicolons and commas, and insert necessary
ones. Write* C *by sentences which are correct.*

1. The sound of Niagara Falls is deafening it truly demon-
   strates the power of the cascade.

2. The stipulations of the agreement were; that each company
   would keep its own name that profits would be evenly
   divided and that, no employees would lose their jobs; because of the merger.

3. An advanced civilization is guided by enlightened self-
   interest; however, it is also marked by unselfish good will.

4. The sound of the banjo drifted up from the floor below, it
   blended with the chatter of typewriters; and the droning of
   business conferences.

5. After a prolonged and severe economic depression; people
   are hesitant to spend money freely; because they are afraid
   hard times will recur.

6. The hallway was long, and dark; and at the end of it hung a dim, obscure painting representing a beggar; in eighteenth-century London.

7. The mutineers defeated the loyal members of the crew; took command of the ship; and locked the captain and other officers in the brig.

8. Winning is important, and rewarding; but sportsmanship is more essential in building character.

9. Fortunetelling still appeals to many people even when they realize it is superstitious nonsense; they continue to patronize charlatans, like palm readers.

10. The making of pottery, once a necessary craft as well as an art, has again become popular, and hundreds of young people, many of them highly skillful, have discovered the excitement of this art.

23 The colon :
Use a colon as a formal and emphatic mark of introduction.

23a   Use a colon before quotations, statements, and series which are introduced formally.

Some of the buildings on the tour were unusual: antebellum two-storied homes, built mainly in the 1840's; smaller houses, which had long open hallways; and stores, some of which had two stories with porches.

A colon may be used to introduce a quotation formally.

The warden began with a sharp reminder: "Gentlemen, you are now almost free; but some of you will not remain free long."

23b   Use a colon between two independent clauses when the second explains the first.

Music communicates: it is an expression of deep feeling and ethical values.

23c   Use a colon before formal appositives, including those introduced by such expressions as *namely* and *that is.*

One factor is often missing from modern labor: pleasure in the work.
The author made a difficult decision: he would abandon the manuscript.

NOTE The colon comes before *namely* and similar expressions, not after.

The author made a difficult decision: namely, that he would abandon the manuscript.

23d Use a colon between figures used to indicate hours and minutes, after the salutation of a formal letter, and between city and publisher in bibliographical entries.

12:15 P.M.   Dear Dr. Tyndale: Boston: Houghton Mifflin, 1929

23e Do not use a colon after a linking verb or a preposition.

NOT AFTER LINKING VERB
Some chief noisemakers **are**: automobiles and airplanes.

NOT AFTER PREPOSITION
His friend accused him **of**: wiggling in his seat, talking during the lecture, and not remembering what was said.

24 The dash —
Use a dash to introduce summaries and to indicate interruptions, parenthetical remarks, and special emphasis.

In typing, a dash is made by two hyphens (--) with no space before or after it.

FOR SUMMARY
Attic fans, window fans, air conditioners—all were ineffective that summer.

FOR SUDDEN INTERRUPTIONS
She replied, "I will consider the—No, I won't either."

FOR PARENTHETICAL REMARKS
Three horses came from the water—a fourth had disappeared—and struggled up the bank.

FOR SPECIAL EMPHASIS
Great authors quote one book more than any other—the Bible.

25 Parentheses ( )
Use parentheses to enclose a loosely related comment or explanation or to enclose figures which number items in a series.

The frisky colt (it was not a thoroughbred) was given away.
The prospector refused to buy the land because (1) the owner had no clear title, (2) it was too remote, (3) it was too expensive.

A parenthetical sentence within another sentence has no period or capital, as in the first example above. A freestanding parenthetical sentence requires parentheses, a capital, and a period.

capital   period here
↓   ↓

At the moment all flights are late. (The weather is bad.) Listen for further announcements.

26 Brackets [ ]
Use brackets to enclose interpolations within quotations.

In the opinion of Arthur Miller, "There is no more reason for falling down in a faint before his [Aristotle's] *Poetics* than before Euclid's geometry."

Sometimes parentheses within parentheses are replaced by brackets ([ ]). Try to avoid constructions which call for this intricate punctuation.

27   Quotation marks   " "

Use quotation marks to enclose the exact words of a speaker or writer and to set off some titles.

Most American writers and publishers use double quotation marks (". . .") except for internal quotations, which are set off by single quotation marks ('. . .').

27a   Use quotation marks to enclose direct quotations and dialogue.

DIRECT QUOTATION

At a high point in *King Lear,* the Duke of Gloucester says, "As flies to wanton boys, are we to the gods."

NOTE Do not use quotation marks to enclose indirect quotations.

He said that the gods regard us as flies.

In dialogue a new paragraph marks each change of speaker.

DIALOGUE

    "What is fool's gold?" asked the traveler who had never before been prospecting.

    "Really," the geologist told him, "it's pyrites."

    In typing, indent ten spaces and single-space prose quotations which are longer than four lines. Do not use quotation marks to enclose these blocked quotations.

    Poetry of four lines or more is single-spaced and indented ten spaces. Retain the original divisions of the lines.

> If you would keep your soul
> From spotted sight or sound,
> Live like the velvet mole;
> Go burrow underground.

Quotations of three lines of poetry or less may be written like the regular text—not set off: Elinor Wylie satirically advises, "Live like the velvet mole; / Go burrow underground."

27b Use single quotation marks to enclose a quotation within a quotation.

The review explained: "Elinor Wylie is ironic when she advises, 'Go burrow underground.' "

27c Use quotation marks to enclose the titles of essays, articles, short stories, short poems, chapters (and other subdivisions of books or periodicals), dissertations (see page 290), episodes in television programs, and short musical compositions.

D. H. Lawrence's "The Rocking-Horse Winner" is a story about the need for love.
Chapter VII of *Walden* is entitled "The Beanfield." (For titles of books, see **30a.**)
My younger brother likes to watch "Sesame Street."

27d Do not use quotation marks around the title of your own theme.

27e Do not use quotation marks to emphasize or change the usual meanings of words or to justify slang, irony, or attempts at humor.

The beggar considered himself a "rich" man.
Some of the old politician's opponents were hoping that he would "kick the bucket" before the next election.

27f Follow established conventions in placing other marks of punctuation with quotation marks.

Periods and **commas** in American usage are placed *inside* quotation marks.

All the students had read "Lycidas."
"Amazing," the professor said.

Semicolons and **colons** are placed *outside* closing quotation marks.

The customer wrote that she was "not yet ready to buy the first edition"; it was too expensive.

A **question mark** or an **exclamation point** is placed *inside* quotation marks only when the quotation itself is a direct question or an exclamation. Otherwise, these marks are placed *outside*.

He asked, "Who is she?" (Only the quotation is a question.)
"Who is she?" he asked. (Only the quotation is a question.)
Did he ask, "Who is she?" (The quotation and the entire sentence are questions.)
Did he say, "I know her"? (The entire sentence asks a question; the quotation makes a statement.)
She screamed, "Run!" (Only the quotation is an exclamation.)
Curse the man who whispers, "No"! (The entire statement is an exclamation; the quotation is not.)

After quotations, do not use a period or a comma together with an exclamation point or a question mark.

NOT
"When**?**", I asked.

BUT
"When**?**" I asked.

28 End punctuation .?!
Use periods, question marks, or exclamation points to end sentences.

(These marks also have special uses indicated in **28b, c, d, f,** and **g.**)

28a Use a period after a sentence which makes a statement or expresses a command.

Some modern people claim to practice witchcraft**.**
Water the flowers**.**
The gardener asked whether the plant should be taken indoors**.** (This
   sentence is a statement even though it expresses an indirect question.)

28b Use periods after most abbreviations.

Periods follow such abbreviations as Mr**.**, Dr**.**, Pvt**.**, Ave**.**, B.C.,
A.M., Ph.D., e.g., ibid**.**, and many others. In British usage periods
are often omitted after titles (Mr).
   Abbreviations of governmental and international agencies
often are written without periods (FCC, TVA, UNESCO, NATO,
and so forth). Usage varies. Consult your dictionary.

A comma or another mark of punctuation may follow the period after an abbreviation, but at the end of a sentence only one period is used.

After she earned her M.A., she began studying for her Ph.D.

But if the sentence is a question or an exclamation, the end punctuation mark follows the period after the abbreviation.

When does she expect to get her Ph.D.?

28c Use three spaced periods (ellipsis dots) to show an omission in a quotation.

Notice the quotation below and how it may be shortened with ellipsis marks.

> "He [the Indian] had no written record other than pictographs, and his conqueror was not usually interested, at the time, in writing down his thoughts and feelings for him. The stoic calm of his few reported speeches and poems gives only a hint of the rich culture that was so soon forgotten."

ROBERT E. SPILLER

ELLIPSIS

marks not necessary at beginning of quotation   *one period to end sentence and three for ellipsis*

The Indian "had no written record other than pictographs. . . . The stoic calm of his . . . speeches and poems gives only a hint of the rich

three periods for ellipsis in sentences

culture. . . ."

four at end of sentence

28d A title has no period, but some titles include a question mark or an exclamation point.

The Sound and the Fury   "What Are Years**?**"
*Westward Ho***!**   *Ah***!** *Wilderness*

28e Use a question mark after a direct question.

Do teachers file attendance reports**?**
Teachers do file attendance reports**?** (a question in the form of a de-
    clarative sentence)

Question marks may follow separate questions within an
interrogative sentence.

Do you recall the time of the accident**?** the license numbers of the cars
    involved**?** the names of the drivers**?**

28f Do not use a question mark or an exclamation point within a sentence to indicate humor or sarcasm.

NOT
The comedy (**?**) was a miserable failure.

A question mark within parentheses shows that a date or a
figure is historically doubtful.

Pythagoras, who died in 497 B.C. (**?**), was a philosopher.

28g Use an exclamation point after a word, a phrase, or a sentence to signal strong exclamatory feeling.

Wait**!** I forgot my lunch**!**
Stop the bus**!**
What a ridiculous idea**!**

Use exclamation points sparingly. After mild exclamations, use commas or periods.

NOT
Well! I was discouraged!
BUT
Well, I was discouraged.

▶ Exercise 10

Supply quotation marks as needed in the following passage, and insert the sign ¶ where new paragraphs are necessary.

Alex Tilman, young, vigorous, and alert, walked briskly beside the little stream. As he neared a pond, he thought of Thoreau's essay Walking and the calm that pervaded nature. An old man was fishing with a pole on the bank of the pond. Knowing that fishermen dislike noisemakers, Alex strolled quietly up to him and said, How's your luck today? Oh, about like every other day, except a little worse, maybe. Do you mean you haven't caught anything? Well, a couple of bream. But they're small, you know. Before I left home my wife said to me, If you don't catch any sizable fish today, you might as well give it up. And I'm beginning to wonder if she hasn't got something there. Alex watched the water for a little while, now and then stealing a glance at the unshaved fisherman, who wore baggy breeches and a faded old flannel shirt. Then he dreamily said, Well, I guess most people don't really fish just for the sake of catching something. The old gentleman looked up at him a little surprised. His eyes were much brighter and quicker than Alex had expected. That's right, he said, but, you know, that's not the kind of wisdom you hear these days. You new around here, son? Yes. My wife and I just bought the old Edgewright place. Oh! Well, maybe you can come fishing with me sometime. I'm usually here about this time during the day. Alex was not eager to accept the invitation, but he was moved by a sudden sympathy. Yes. Maybe. Say, if you need any work, I might be able to find something for you to do around our place. My wife and I are trying to get things cleaned up. A slight smile came over the man's face, and he said warmly, Much obliged, but I've got more work now than I know what to do with. So I come out here and hum Lazy Bones and fish. On the way back to his house, Alex asked a neighbor who that old tramp was fishing down by the pond. Tramp! his friend repeated. Good heavens, man, that was no tramp. That was

Angus Morgan, one of the wealthiest men in the country.

▶ Exercise 11

*Add quotation marks where needed; circle unnecessary ones.
Also make all necessary changes in punctuation.*

1. "Failure is often necessary for humanity," Professor Xavier

    said. Without failure, he continued, how can we retain our

    humility and know the full sweetness of success? For, as

    Emily Dickinson said, Success is counted sweetest / By

    those who ne'er succeed.

2. Madam, said the talent scout, I know that you think your

    daughter can sing, but, believe me, her voice makes the

    strangest sounds I have ever heard. Mrs. Audubon took her

    daughter "Birdie" by the hand and haughtily left the room

    wondering "how she could ever have been so stupid as to

    expose her daughter to such a 'common' person."

3. Your assignment for tomorrow, said Mrs. Osborn, is to read

    the following (to use Poe's own term) tales of ratiocination:

    The Purloined Letter, The Murders in the Rue Morgue, and

The Mystery of Marie Roget. When you have finished these stories you might read some of the next assignment.

4. The boy and his great-uncle were "real" friends, and the youngster listened intently when the old man spoke. Son, he would say, I remember my father's words: You can't do better than to follow the advice of Ben Franklin, who said, One To-day is worth two To-morrows.

5. The expression population explosion suggests the extreme rapidity with which the world's "population" is increasing.

6. A recent report states the following: The marked increase in common stocks indicated a new sense of national security; however, the report seems to imply "that this is only one of many gauges of the country's economic situation."

7. Chapter IV, The National Mind, develops one of the most optimistic views of the country's future to be found in "modern" studies of economics.

8. One of Mark Twain's most famous letters, addressed to "Andrew Carnegie," reads as follows:

"You seem to be in prosperity. Could you lend an admirer $1.50 to buy a hymn-book with? God will bless you. I feel it; I know it. So will I."

"N.B.—If there should be other applications, this one not to count".

9. In a "postscript," Mark Twain added, Don't send the hymn-book; send the money; I want to make the selection myself. He signed the letter simply Mark.

10. The hermit thought the hiker's question "odd," but he replied, "You ask me, Why do you live here? I ask you why you do not live here?"

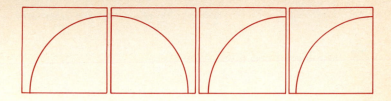

Mechanics

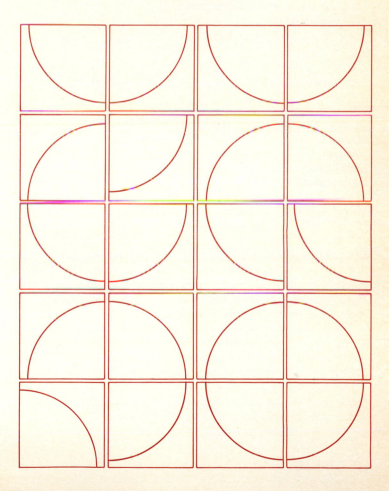

29 **Manuscript and letter form** *ms*
Follow correct manuscript form in your papers and business letters.

Papers
Paper

    typing: white, $8^{1}/_{2}$ by 11 inches

    longhand: ruled

    not: onionskin, spiral, legal size

Lines

    typing: double-space

    longhand: skip every other line (or follow your teacher's instructions)

Title

    center and leave extra space between title and text

Margins

    ample and regular at bottom and top—at least one inch on each side

Page numbers

    Arabic numerals (2, **not** II) in upper right corner except on first page (omit or center at bottom of page)

The business letter
In writing a business letter follow conventional forms. All essential parts are included in the example on page 152. Type if possible; single-space, with double-spacing between paragraphs. Paragraphs may begin at the left margin without indentation in block form, or they may be indented.

    It is best to determine the title and the name of the addressee. Opinions vary widely about the best customs when the name or title of the person is unknown. If the addressee is a man or if the sex is unknown, some write *Dear Sir* or *Gentlemen.* When the sex is unknown, some write *Dear Sir or Madam.* Some omit the salutation entirely. When a woman's marital status is unknown or when she prefers it, use *Ms.*

Example of Correct Manuscript Form

The Trouble With Perfectionists ←——Center

Indent 5 spaces   ←——Triple space

Of all kinds of people, perfectionists bother me the most. ᴧ They 2 spaces

want to get things right; that is admirable. They are certainly not after

periods

like a lot of people who just do not care about their jobs or anything

else. But once you get to know a perfectionist, you will feel the same

as I.

Many people seem to believe that it is complimentary to call someone

a perfectionist. They seem to think that the term means a person who

is conscientious. A true perfectionist is not really conscientious

but troubled.

Perfectionists have two problems above all others. The first is

social; the second is mental. It is hard for a perfectionist to make

friends and keep them because he or she usually is really fussy. The

house of a perfectionist has to be kept like a museum, and if you sit

in a certain place or drop a crumb on the rug, you get the distinct im-

pression that you will not be welcome in that house again. If a per-

fectionist happens to be an executive or an employer, those who work

on a lower level find that no matter how hard they try, they can never

seem to please the perfectionist. So this type of person is likely to

be unpopular.

The second problem that perfectionists have is not social but

within the person. Although one might expect a perfectionist to go

far in life, to succeed at almost any occupation or profession, that is

not the case. Perfectionists are probably less successful than better-

adjusted people. Why is this so? It is because they become in a way

Page number for first page

1 ←——————— on bottom line (optional)

                                        141 Oakhurst Drive, Apt. 2A
                                        Singleton, Ohio 54567
                                        March 1, 1982

Mr. Freeman O. Zachary, Manager
Personnel Department
Keeson National Bank
P. O. Box 2387
Chicago, Illinois 34802

Dear Mr. Zachary:

    I am writing to ask if you will have an opening this coming summer
for someone of my qualifications. I am finishing my sophomore year at
Singleton State College, where I intend to major in economics and finance.
I have been active in several extracurricular activities, including the
Spanish Club and the Singleton Players.

    Although I have no previous experience in banking, I am eager to
learn, and I am willing to take on any duties you feel appropriate.
Chicago is my home town, so I am especially anxious to find summer employment there. I will be in Chicago for spring vacation from March 20
to 26 and available for an interview. In addition, I shall be pleased to
furnish you with letters of recommendation from some of my professors
here at Singleton State and with a transcript of my college record. I
appreciate your consideration, and I look forward to hearing from you.

                                    Sincerely yours,

                                    Audrey DeVeers

                                    Audrey DeVeers

Audrey DeVeers
141 Oakhurst Drive, Apt. 2A
Singleton, OH 54567

                                        Place stamp here

                    Mr. Freeman O. Zachary, Manager
                    Personnel Department
                    Keeson National Bank
                    P. O. Box 2387
                    Chicago, IL 34802

Blocked Form of Letter

Address of writer ——————→ 141 Oakhurst Drive, Apt. 2A
Date —————————→ Singleton, Ohio 54567
————→ March 1, 1982

Mr. Freeman O. Zachary, Manager
Personnel Department ←———— Name and title of addressee
Keeson National Bank
P. O. Box 2387
Chicago, Illinois 34802 ←———— Full address

Dear Mr. Zachary: ←———— Salutation and name. Use a colon.

I am writing to ask if you will have an opening this coming summer for
someone of my qualifications. I am finishing my sophomore year at
Singleton State College, where I intend to major in economics and finance.
I have been active in several extracurricular activities, including the
Spanish Club and the Singleton Players.

Although I have no previous experience in banking, I am eager to learn,
and I am willing to take on any duties you feel appropriate. Chicago
is my home town, so I am especially anxious to find summer employment
there. I will be in Chicago for spring vacation from March 20 to 26 and
available for an interview. In addition, I shall be pleased to furnish you
with letters of recommendation from some of my professors here at Singleton
State and with a transcript of my college record. I appreciate your
consideration, and I look forward to hearing from you.

Sincerely yours, ←———————— Complimentary close

Audrey DeVeers ←————————— Signature, handwritten
Audrey DeVeers ←————————— Name, typed

Folding the letter

1

2

1   2   3

Business letters are usually written on stationery 8½ by 11 inches. Fold horizontally into thirds to fit a standard-sized business envelope. For smaller envelopes fold once horizontally and twice the other way.

30   Underlining for italics   *ital*

Underline titles of independent publications (books, magazines, newspapers) and occasionally for emphasis.

Italic type slants *(like this)*. Underline words individually (<u>like</u> <u>this</u>), or underline words and spaces (<u>like this</u>).

30a   Underline titles of books (except the Bible and its divisions), periodicals, newspapers, motion pictures, paintings, sculpture, musical compositions, plays, and other works published separately.

Be precise: watch initial articles *(A, An, The)* and any punctuation.

BOOKS
<u>Adventures</u> <u>of</u> <u>Huckleberry</u> <u>Finn</u> (*not* <u>The</u> <u>Adventures</u> . . .)
<u>An</u> <u>American</u> <u>Tragedy</u> (*not* <u>The</u> <u>American</u> <u>Tragedy</u>)

PERIODICALS
<u>The</u> <u>Atlantic</u> <u>Monthly</u> and the <u>American</u> <u>Quarterly</u>

NEWSPAPERS
<u>The</u> <u>New</u> <u>York</u> <u>Times</u> or the <u>New York Times</u>

MOTION PICTURES
<u>Citizen</u> <u>Kane</u>

MUSICAL COMPOSITIONS
Bizet's <u>Carmen</u>
Beethoven's <u>Mount of Olives</u> (**but not** Beethoven's Symphony No. 5)

PLAYS
<u>The Cherry Orchard</u>

30b   Underline names of ships and trains.

the <u>Queen Elizabeth</u> II   the U.S.S. <u>Hornet</u>   the <u>Zephyr</u>

30c   Underline foreign words used in an English context, except words which have become part of our language.

Consult a dictionary to determine whether a word is still considered foreign or has become part of the English language.

French
↓

He claimed extravagantly to have been <u>au courant</u> since birth.

But

Some words which may seem foreign have become a part of the English language: *faux pas, amigo, karate.*

30d   Underline words, letters, and figures being named.

The word <u>puppy</u> usually has delightful connotations.
Don't forget to dot your <u>i</u>'s.

NOTE Occasionally quotation marks are used instead of underlining.

30e Avoid excessive underlining for emphasis.

Weak writing is seldom improved by mechanical tricks. Do not sprinkle a page with underlinings, dashes, or exclamation points.

30f Do not underline the title of your own theme.

▶ **Exercise 1**
Underline words as necessary in the following sentences. Put an X *over words unnecessarily underlined.*

1. The customer was <u>irate</u> when he found no one to help him.

2. The Los Angeles <u>Times</u> announced the arrival of the ship Tropical Explorer.

3. The author's last novel, The Green Summer, was reviewed in The Philadelphia <u>Inquirer</u>.

4. The word fabulous is overused.

5. The <u>limousine</u> was used in a motion picture entitled The Years of Hope.

6. Mona Lisa continues to be one of the most popular paintings at the Louvre.

7. Jack London's short story "To Build a Fire" is published in the latest edition of the anthology America's Great Tales.

8. The periodical <u>Harper's</u> has an article on the modern opera <u>Streets of the City.</u>

9. He made his <u>i's</u> with little circles over them instead of <u>dots</u>.

10. While on the train <u>The Northern Star,</u> she saw a large moose.

31 Spelling   *sp*
Spell correctly; use a dictionary to look up words you are un-sure of.

Spelling is troublesome in English because many words are not spelled as they sound *(laughter, slaughter);* because some dis-tinct pairs and triplets sound the same *(capital, capitol; there, they're, their; to, too, two);* and because many words are pro-nounced with the vowel sound "uh," which gives no clue to spell-ing (sens*i*ble, cap*a*ble, defi*a*nt).

Many misspellings are due to the omission of syllables in habitual mispronunciations *(accident-ly* for *acciden-tal-ly);* the addition of syllables *(disas-ter-ous* for *disas-trous);* or the chang-ing of syllables *(prespiration* for *perspiration).*

There are no infallible guides to spelling in English, but the following are helpful.

ie or *ei*?

Use *i* before *e*
Except after *c*
Or when sounded as *a*
As in *nei*ghbor and *wei*gh.

WORDS WITH IE
bel*ie*ve, ch*ie*f, f*ie*ld, gr*ie*f, p*ie*ce

WORDS WITH EI AFTER C
rece**i**ve, rece**i**pt, c**ei**ling, dec**ei**t, conce**i**ve

WORDS WITH EI SOUNDED AS A
fr**ei**ght, v**ei**n, r**ei**gn

EXCEPTIONS TO MEMORIZE
either, n**ei**ther, l**ei**sure, s**ei**ze, w**ei**rd, h**ei**ght

Drop final silent *e*?

DROP When suffix begins with a *vowel*		**KEEP** When suffix begins with a *consonant*	
curse	cursing	live	liv**e**ly
come	coming	nine	nin**e**ty
pursue	pursuing	hope	hop**e**ful
arrange	arranging	love	lov**e**less
dine	dining	arrange	arrang**e**ment

TYPICAL EXCEPTIONS	**TYPICAL EXCEPTIONS**
coura**ge**ous	awful
noti**ce**able	ninth
d**ye**ing (compare *dying*)	truly
sin**ge**ing (compare *singing*)	argument

Change *y* to *i*?

CHANGE When *y* is preceded by a *consonant*		**DO NOT CHANGE** When *y* is preceded by a *vowel*	
gully	gullies	valley	valle**ys**
try	tried	attorney	attorne**ys**
fly	flies	convey	conve**y**ed
apply	applied	pay	pa**ys**
party	parties	deploy	deplo**y**ing

When adding *-ing*

try	tr**y**ing
fly	fl**y**ing
apply	appl**y**ing

Double final consonant?

If the suffix begins with a consonant, do not double the final consonant of the base word *(man, manly)*.

If the suffix begins with a vowel:

DOUBLE
When final consonant is preceded by single vowel

DO NOT DOUBLE
When final consonant is preceded by two vowels

despair	despairing
leer	leering

Monosyllables

pen	penned
blot	blotted
hop	hopper
sit	sitting

Words ending with two or more consonants preceded by single vowel

jump	jumping
work	working

Polysyllables accented on last syllable

defér	deferring
begín	beginning
omít	omitting
occúr	occurring

Polysyllables not accented on last syllable after addition of suffix

defér	déference
prefér	préference
devélop	devéloping
lábor	lábored

Add *s* or *es*?

ADD S
For plurals of most nouns

girl	girls
book	books

ADD ES
When the plural is pronounced as another syllable

church	churches
fox	foxes

For nouns ending in *o* preceded by a vowel

radio	radios
cameo	cameos

Usually for nouns ending in *o* preceded by a consonant (consult your dictionary)

potato	potatoes
Negro	Negroes

BUT
flamingos *or* flamingoes

NOTE The plurals of proper names are generally formed by adding *s* or *es (Darby,* the *Darbys; Jones,* the *Joneses).*

Words frequently misspelled

Following is a list of over two hundred of the most commonly misspelled words in the English language.

absence	benefited	dining
accidentally	boundaries	disappearance
accommodate	Britain	disappoint
accumulate	business	disastrous
acquaintance	calendar	discipline
acquitted	candidate	dissatisfied
advice	category	dormitory
advise	cemetery	eighth
all right	changeable	eligible
altar	changing	eliminate
amateur	choose	embarrass
among	chose	eminent
analysis	coming	encouraging
analyze	commission	environment
annual	committee	equipped
apartment	comparative	especially
apparatus	compelled	exaggerate
apparent	conceivable	excellence
appearance	conferred	exhilarate
arctic	conscience	existence
argument	conscientious	experience
arithmetic	control	explanation
ascend	criticize	familiar
athletic	deferred	fascinate
attendance	definite	February
balance	description	fiery
beginning	desperate	foreign
believe	dictionary	formerly

forty
fourth
frantically
fulfill or fulfil
generally
government
grammar
grandeur
grievous
height
heroes
hindrance
hoping
humorous
hypocrisy
immediately
incidentally
incredible
independence
inevitable
intellectual
intelligence
interesting
irresistible
knowledge
laboratory
laid
led
lightning
loneliness
maintenance
maneuver
manufacture
marriage
mathematics
may

maybe
miniature
mischievous
mysterious
necessary
ninety
noticeable
occasionally
occurred
omitted
opportunity
optimistic
parallel
paralyze
pastime
performance
permissible
perseverance
personnel
perspiration
physical
picnicking
playwright
possibility
practically
precede
precedence
preference
preferred
prejudice
preparation
prevalent
privilege
probably
professor
pronunciation

prophecy
prophesy
quantity
quiet
quite
quizzes
recede
receive
recognize
recommend
reference
referred
repetition
restaurant
rhythm
ridiculous
sacrifice
salary
schedule
secretary
seize
separate
sergeant
severely
shining
siege
similar
sophomore
specifically
specimen
stationary
stationery
statue
studying
subtly
succeed

successful	temperamental	their
supersede	tendency	thorough
surprise		

▶ **Exercise 2**

In each of the following groups of words one, two, or three are misspelled. The others are correct. Put an X over incorrectly spelled words.

1. lizard, blizard, gizard, wizard, sizzler

2. accommodate, acumulate, comming, blooming, ramming

3. percieve, believe, recieve, acheive, conceive

4. mountain, villian, protein, maintainance, certian

5. credence, precedence, balence, existance, independance

6. tallys, valleys, bellys, modifys, fancies

7. defys, relays, conveyes, carries, dirtys

8. obedience, modifyer, complience, applience, guidance

9. incredible, detectable, delectible, dependible, reversible

10. loveable, receivable, likeable, likible, noticeable

32 Hyphenation and syllabication ～
Use a hyphen in certain compound words and in words divided at the end of a line.

Two words *(campaign promise)* not listed in a dictionary are usually written separately.

32a Consult a dictionary to determine whether a compound is hyphenated or written as one or two words.

HYPHENATED	ONE WORD	TWO WORDS
drop-off	droplight	drop leaf (noun)
white-hot	whitewash	white heat
water-cool	watermelon	water system

32b Hyphenate a compound of two or more words used as a single modifier before a noun.

HYPHEN	NO HYPHEN AFTER NOUN
She is a *well-known* executive	The executive is *well known*.

A hyphen is not used when the first word of such a group is an adverb ending in *-ly*.

HYPHEN	NO HYPHEN
a *half-finished* task	a *partly finished* task

32c Hyphenate spelled-out compound numbers from *twenty-one* through *ninety-nine*.

32d Follow conventions in dividing a word at the end of a line.

Monosyllables
Do not divide.

thought   strength   cheese

Single letters
Do not put a one-letter syllable on a separate line:

NOT
a-bout   might-y

Prefixes and suffixes
May be divided.

separ-able   pre-fix

Avoid carrying over a two-letter suffix.

bound-ed   careful-ly

Compounds with hyphen
Avoid dividing and adding another hyphen.

self-satisfied

NOT
self-satis-fied

▶ ## Exercise 3
Underline the correct form for the words indicated. Use a dictionary when needed.

1. The (muchdrilled, much-drilled, much drilled) (rescueteam, rescue-team, rescue team) worked fast.
2. (Snowdrifts, snow-drifts, snow drifts) had not yet blocked the

(heavilytraveled, heavily-traveled, heavily traveled) road-way.

3. The (foxhound, fox-hound, fox hound) was (welltrained, well-trained, well trained) not to chase rabbits.
4. The (twentyone, twenty-one, twenty one) dancers did not know how to (foxtrot, fox-trot, fox trot).
5. Several words in the paper were hyphenated at the end of lines: a-round, almight-y, al-most, self-in-flicted, marb-le.

33 The apostrophe '

Use the apostrophe for the possessive case of many nouns, contractions, omissions, and some plurals.

Use **'s** for the possessive of nouns not ending in *s*.

SINGULAR
child**'s**, man**'s**, deer**'s**, lady**'s**, mother-in-law**'s**

PLURAL
Children**'s**, men**'s**

Use **'s** for the possessive of singular nouns ending in *s*.

Charles**'s**, Watts**'s**, Dickens**'s**, waitress**'s**, actress**'s**

NOTE When a singular noun ending in *s* is followed by a word beginning with *s,* use only the apostrophe, not *'s*.

the actress**'** success, Dickens**'** stories

Use **'** without **s** to form the possessive of plural nouns ending in *s*.

the Joneses**'** car, the Dickenses**'** home, waitresses**'** tips

Use **'s** to form the possessive of indefinite pronouns.

anybody**'s**, everyone**'s**, somebody else**'s**, neither**'s**

NOTE Use no apostrophe with personal pronouns like *his, hers, theirs, ours, its* (meaning "of it"). *It's* means "it is."
Use **'s** with only the last noun for joint possession in a pair or a series.

the architect and the builder**'s** plan (The two jointly have one plan.)
the architect**'s** and the builder**'s** plans (Both have plans.)

Use **'** to show omissions or to form contractions.

the roaring **'**20**'**s, o**'**clock, jack-o**'**-lantern
we**'**ll, don**'**t, can**'**t, it**'**s (meaning "it is")

Use **'s** to form the plural of numerals, letters, and words being named.

three 7**'s** (but *three sevens*), four *a***'s**, six *the***'s**

▶ Exercise 4
Underline the words that contain correctly used apostrophes.

1. the people's favorite, a persons' favorite, everybody's favorite
2. sheeps' wool, deer's horns, cats' eyes, a cat's eyes
3. the Williams' lawn, the Williamses' lawn, all the neighbor's lawns
4. the youths' organization, the women's club, the womens' club
5. it's food, its food, hers, her's
6. wasnt, wasn't, two ms, three n's

7. three *why's,* four *hows*
8. one o'clock, two oclock, three opossums
9. Mary and Martin's store (together they own one store)
   Mary's and Martin's stores (each owns a store)
10. our's, ours', its', it's

34 Capital letters *cap*

Use a capital letter to begin a sentence and to designate a proper noun (the name of a particular person, place, or thing).

Capitalize the first word of a sentence, the pronoun *I,* and the interjection *O.*

How, O ye gods, can I control this joy?

Capitalize first, last, and important words in titles, including the second part of hyphenated words.

Across the River and into the Trees
"The Man Against the Sky"
"After Apple-Picking"

NOTE Articles *(a, an, the),* short prepositions, and conjunctions are not capitalized unless they begin or end a title.

Capitalize first words of direct quotations and words capitalized by the author.

Carlyle said, "Meanwhile, we will hate Anarchy as Death, which it is. . . ."

Capitalize titles preceding a name.

President Truman

Capitalize the title of the head of a nation.

The **P**resident is not expected to arrive today.

Capitalize titles used specifically as substitutes for particular names.

Lieutenant Yo pleaded not guilty; the **L**ieutenant was found innocent.

NOTE A title not followed by a name is usually not capitalized.

The stockholders sat down, and the president called for order.

Titles which are common nouns that name an office are not capitalized.

A college president has more duties than privileges.
A lieutenant deserves a good living allowance.

Capitalize degrees and titles after a name.

Jeffrey E. Tyndale, Sr., **P**h.**D**., **J.D**.
Abraham Lincoln, **A**ttorney at **L**aw

NOTE Do not capitalize names of occupations used as appositives or as descriptions.

Abraham Lincoln, a young lawyer from Springfield, took the case.

Capitalize words of family relationship used as names when not preceded by a possessive pronoun.

USED AS NAMES
After **F**ather died, **M**other carried on the business.
BUT
After my father died, my mother carried on the business.

Capitalize proper nouns but not general terms.

PROPER NOUNS	GENERAL TERMS
Plato, **P**latonic, **P**latonism	pasteurize
Venice, **V**enetian blind	a set of china
the **W**est, a **W**esterner	west of the river
the **R**epublican **P**arty	a republican government
the **S**enior **C**lass of **I**vy **C**ollege	a member of the senior class
Clifton **S**treet	my street
the **M**ississippi **R**iver	the Mississippi and Ohio rivers
the **R**omantic **M**ovement	the twentieth century

Capitalize months, days of the week, and holidays.

April, **F**riday, the **F**ourth of **J**uly, **L**abor **D**ay

NOTE Do not capitalize seasons and numbered days of the month unless they name holidays.

spring, the third of July

Capitalize **B.C.**, **A.D.**, words designating the Deity, religious denominations, and sacred books.

in 273 **B.C.**
the **M**essiah, our **M**aker, the **T**rinity, **Y**ahweh, **A**llah, **B**uddha, **J**esus
"**P**raise **G**od from **W**hom all blessings flow."
Catholic, **P**rotestant, **P**resbyterian
the **B**ible, the **K**oran

NOTE Pronouns referring to the Deity are usually capitalized.

From **H**im all blessings flow.

Capitalize names of specific courses.

I registered for **S**ociology 101 and **C**hemistry 445.

NOTE Do not capitalize studies (other than languages) which do not name specific courses.

I am taking English, sociology, and chemistry.

35 Abbreviations *ab*
Avoid most abbreviations in formal writing.

Spell out names of days, months, units of measurement, and (except in addresses) states and countries.

Friday (*not* Fri.)
February (*not* Feb.)
pounds (*not* lbs.)
Sauk Centre, Minnesota (*not* Minn.)

EXCEPTION Washington, D.C.
      The following abbreviations are **acceptable** in any context.

ABBREVIATIONS BEFORE NAMES
Mr., Mrs., Ms., Messrs., Mmes., Dr., St. *or* Ste. (for *Saint,* not *Street*), Mt., Rev. (but only with a first name: *the Rev. Ernest Jones,* not *Rev. Jones*)

ABBREVIATIONS AFTER NAMES
M.D. (and other degrees), Jr., Sr., Esq.

ABBREVIATIONS IN FOOTNOTES AND BIBLIOGRAPHIES (see 48)

ABBREVIATIONS WITHOUT PERIODS FOR MANY AGENCIES AND ORGANIZATIONS
TVA, NAACP, FBI

ABBREVIATIONS WITH DATES AND TIME
B.C. and A.D. (with dates expressed in numerals, as *500 B.C.*) A.M. and P.M. or a.m. and p.m. (with hours expressed in numerals, as *4:00 A.M.*)

36 Numbers *num*
Spell out numbers that can be written in one or two words.

twenty-three, one thousand

Use figures for other numbers.

123   1¹³/₁₆   \$1,001.00

NOTE Newspapers and government publications generally use figures for numbers above ten.

EXCEPTIONS Never use figures at the beginning of a sentence. Spell out the number or recast the sentence.

Use numerals for figures in sequences.

One polar bear weighed 200 pounds; another, 526; the third, 534.

Use figures for dates, street numbers, page references, percentages, and hours of the day used with A.M. or P.M.

USE FIGURES
July 3, 1776 (*not* 3rd)
1010 State Street
See page 50.
He paid 15 percent interest.
The concert begins at 6 P.M.
 (or 6:00 P.M.)

SPELL OUT
the third of July
Fifth Avenue
The book has fifty pages.

The concert begins at
 six o'clock.

▶ Exercise 5
Supply capitals as needed below. Change capital letters to lower case as necessary.

1. The book was entitled *the long road to wealth and the short*

    road to poverty.

2. The small Country appeared to be headed for a Civil War, but the Factions arrived at a peace settlement.

3. Captain Kaplan, united States army, arrived on wednesday to find that he was late for the tour of buddhist temples.

4. When she registered for Chemistry, martha was told that she would need to take Algebra 101.

5. Alfred Curall, m. d., attended the meeting of the American Medical association and returned home before thanksgiving day.

6. Out west Cowboys were numerous in the Nineteenth Century.

7. In the Winter we sat around the fire, thinking of the Spring thaw and the pleasure of swimming again in the Ohio river.

8. Though the printer lived for a while on Magoni avenue, he moved to detroit last August.

9. The Salk Vaccine has all but eliminated the dangers of Polio, according to an article in a Medical Journal.

10. She wanted to become a Lawyer, she explained, because she saw a direct connection between the Law and Morals.

Place an X by the following which are not acceptable in formal writing, a ✔ by those which are acceptable.

1. May thirteenth
2. Twelve thirteen Jefferson Street
3. Jefferson Ave.
4. Mister and Mrs. Smidt
5. the biography of the ste.
6. Minneapolis, Minn., on 3 June 1940
7. Eng. 199 in the Dept. of English
8. the Cumberland and Tennessee Rivers
9. Page 10 in Chapter 11
10. Geo. Smith
11. William Adams, Junior
12. 300 B.C.
13. etc.
14. five hundred dollars
15. five hundred and ten bushels
16. December 24th, 1981
17. Interstate Seventy-Five
18. five million dollars
19. Friday, June 13
20. 103 lbs.

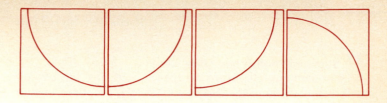

Diction and Style

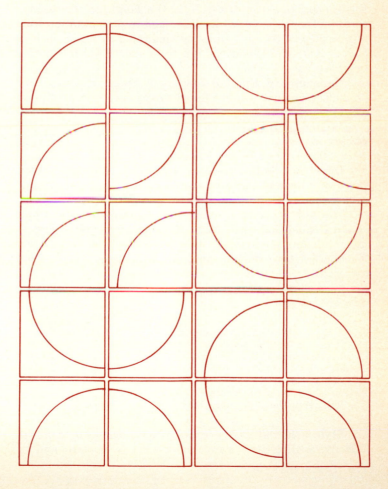

37 **Standard English and style** *d*
Use Standard English except on special occasions, and consult
your dictionary on usage. Make your style appropriate to your
subject.

Standard English is the generally accepted language in
English-speaking countries. It is the language of educated
persons. Though it varies in usage and in pronunciation from
one country or region to another (indicated by labels such as
U.S. or *Brit.* in dictionaries), it is the standard which is taught
in schools and colleges.

Nonstandard English consists of usages, spellings, and
pronunciations not usually found in the speech or writing of
educated persons.

Diction is the choice and use of words. Consult your dictionary for definitions of the labels it employs (for example,
Slang, Dialect, Vulgar, Poetic, Informal, Obsolete).

Informal or **colloquial** language (terms used almost inter-
changeably) is appropriate in certain situations though not in
college themes. **Colloquial** does not mean **dialect.**

The best sources of information are dictionaries, which
record current and past usage. They tell who uses what. In
minor matters dictionaries do not always agree. In current
dictionaries, for example, you will find disagreement about
cooperate, co-operate, and *coöperate.*

Particularly useful at the college level are the following
desk dictionaries:

The American Heritage Dictionary of the English Language. Boston:
Houghton Mifflin Company.
The Random House College Dictionary. New York: Random House.
Webster's New Collegiate Dictionary. Springfield, Mass.: G. & C. Mer-
riam Company.
Webster's New World Dictionary of the American Language. Cleveland:
William Collins Publishers, Inc.

Style is the way writers express their thoughts in language.
Effective writing always involves the choice of words and ex-

pressions, the arrangement of words, and variety in the patterns of sentences. The ways in which similar ideas are expressed may have vastly different effects, and much of the difference is a matter of style. Writing may be whimsical, poetic, terse, flippant, imaginative, literal, and so on. Develop the habit of noticing the style and tone of what you read and what you write. Your style should be appropriate to your subject and to your own personality.

37a   Use slang only when nothing else will serve as well.

Slang is a nonstandard language which according to the *American Heritage Dictionary* consists "typically of arbitrary and often ephemeral coinages and figures of speech characterized by spontaneity and raciness."

Too often slang is a popular rubber stamp which only approximates exact thought. The expression "He's a jerk" would not communicate much. What precisely does this mean—except that he is in some vague way unattractive?

Slang in student papers is usually out of place. Slang expressions are particularly inappropriate in a context that is otherwise dignified.

The violin virtuoso's performance on the cello was a *real bomb*.
When Macbeth recoiled at the thought of murder, Lady Macbeth urged him not to *chicken out*.

Slang which is vivid and useful sometimes becomes standard. "Skyscraper," "bus," and "mob" were once slang; and because no other word was found to convey quite the same social meanings as "date," it is no longer slang.

37b   Avoid illiteracies and dialect.

Illiteracies, which are found in the language of uneducated people, should not be used in speech or writing.

NOT

She *ain't* ready yet. Would you care to *set* awhile?

    Dialect, words and usages peculiar to one section of the country, should be avoided except to give a deliberate flavor of local speech. Similarly, the speech and linguistic patterns of a particular social or ethnic group are often termed dialect.

    There is no reason to erase all dialectal characteristics from your language. They are a cultural heritage and a source of richness and variety. But in general communication avoid expressions which are local or nonstandard.

37c   Avoid archaic words.

Archaisms, out-of-date words, are seldom appropriate in modern speech or writing. *Oft, yon,* and *holp* (past tense of *help*) are examples.

▶ **Exercise 1**

Using your own judgment, point out and label any slang words and expressions, illiteracies, dialectal words, and archaisms in the following sentences.

  1. Overdue books always gross out fussy librarians.

  2. What cleared him was that the police discovered the goods in his friend's pad.

3. She was instructed to lug the bread back to the vault and to follow the boss to his office.

4. The hairdresser was shook up because the shoppe had been sold.

5. We heard on our ears that smokey was only three miles down the blacktop.

6. Pipe smoking just ain't as popular as it used to be, but some devoted pipe freaks are still around.

7. The award went to a little-known actress who played good the part of a raving beauty who married a deformed dwarf.

8. I reckon the plane will arrive betimes, provided of course that the runways are not congested.

9. He couldn't do nothing without the supervisor giving him the eyeball and coming down on him.

10. Before the rain ceased, the group of tourists were besprinkled, but their enthusiasm was not dampened.

37d Avoid improprieties. Use words in their correct functions and meanings.

An **impropriety in function** is the use of a word as the wrong part of speech.

IMPROPRIETIES IN FUNCTION	PROPER FORMS
psychology approach (noun for adjective)	*psychological* approach
suspicioned (noun made into a verb)	*suspected*
good *eats* (verb for noun)	good *eating,* good *food*
stagnate waters (verb for adjective)	*stagnant* waters
surprising large number (adjective for adverb)	*surprisingly* large number

An **impropriety in meaning** is the incorrect use of a word for another vaguely similar word.

IMPROPRIETIES IN MEANING	PROPER WORDS AND MEANINGS
invoke a response	*evoke* a response
congenial infirmity	*congenital* infirmity
make due with a little	*make do* with a little

37e Use correct idioms.

An **idiom** is an accepted expression or construction with its own meaning. Literally the words mean one thing; collectively, they assume a different distinctive meaning. Such expressions as "catch the eye" and "by and large" cannot be understood literally.

A wrong word in an idiomatic expression can cause awkwardness or an error in meaning.

Many common errors in idiom result from use of a preposition and a verb which do not belong together.

UNIDIOMATIC	IDIOMATIC
according with	according to
capable to	capable of

UNIDIOMATIC	IDIOMATIC
conform in	conform to (*or* with)
die from	die of
ever now and then	every now and then
excepting for	except for
identical to	identical with
in accordance to	in accordance with
incapable to do	incapable of doing
in search for	in search of
intend on doing	intend to do
in the year of 1976	in the year 1976
lavish with gifts	lavish gifts on
off of	off
on a whole	on the whole
outlook of life	outlook on life
plan on	plan to
prior than	prior to
similar with	similar to
superior than	superior to
try and see	try to see
type of a	type of

▶ **Exercise 2**

Mark the improprieties or the incorrect idioms in each of the following groups.

1. her advise and consent, her advice and consent

2. accede to, accede with, accede for, accede about

3. preposition phrase, prepositional phrase

4. inferior of, inferior from, inferior about, inferior to

5. the statue on the square, the statute on the square, the stature on the square

6. abide with, abide by, abide for

7. agree to, agree on, agree with, agree for

8. food, the eats, victuals

9. oblivious of, oblivious to, oblivious about

10. society problems, social problems, societal problems.

37f   Avoid specialized vocabulary in writing for the general reader.

All specialists, whether engineers, chefs, or philosophers, have their own vocabularies. Some technical words find their way into general use; most do not. We know the plant *red clover,* but not its botanical name *Trifolium pratense.*

Trouble comes when specialists either cannot or do not see the need to express their ideas in language for the general reader. The following passage, for instance, would not be addressed to a general group or a wide audience.

> The neonate's environment consists in primitively contrasted perceptual fields weak and strong: loud noises, bright lights, smooth surfaces, compared with silence, darkness and roughness. The behavior of the neonate has to be accounted for chiefly by inherited motor connections between receptors and effectors. There is at this stage, in addition to the autonomic nervous system, only the sensorimotor system to call on. And so the ability of the infant to discriminate is exceedingly low. But by receiving and sorting random data through the identification of recurrent regularity, he does begin to improve reception. Hence he can surrender the more easily to single motivations, ego-involvement in satisfactions.
>
> JAMES K. FEIBLEMAN,
> *The Stages of Human Life: A Biography of Entire Man*

Contrast the foregoing passage with the following, which is on the same general subject of the infant but which is written so that the general reader—not just a specialized few—can understand it.

> Research clearly indicates that an infant's senses are functional at birth. He experiences the whack from the doctor. He is sensitive to pressure, to changes in temperature, and to pain, and he responds specifically to these stimuli. . . . How about sight? Research on infants 4–8 weeks of age shows that they can see about as well as adults. . . . The difference is that the infant cannot make sense out of what he sees. Nevertheless, what he sees does register, and he begins to take in visual information at birth. . . . In summary, the neonate (an infant less than a month old) is sensitive not only to internal but also to external stimuli. Although he cannot respond adequately, he does take in and process information.
>
> IRA J. GORDON,
> *Human Development: From Birth through Adolescence*

The only technical term in the passage is *neonate;* and unlike the writer of the first passage, who also uses the word, the second author defines it for the general reader. Special vocabularies may obscure meaning. Moreover, they tempt the writer into the use of inflated words instead of plain ones—a style sometimes known as *gobbledygook* or *governmentese* because it flourishes in bureaucratic writing. Harry S. Truman made a famous statement about the presidency: "The buck stops here." This straightforward assertion might be written by some bureaucrats as follows: "It is incumbent upon the President of the United States of America to uphold the responsibility placed upon him by his constituents to exercise the final decision-making power."

37g Avoid triteness. Strive for fresh and original expressions.

Clichés are worn out phrases and figures of speech. Once the speaker or writer has begun the expression, the reader may know the remainder of what he will say. Trite writing contains few surprises. Avoid extravagance; be original enough so that your words have the freshness of a newly typed page rather than the faint tracings of a carbon copy.

The following twenty phrases are trite. Study them as examples. This list will show you the characteristics of triteness so that you can avoid these expressions and, more important, others like them.

interesting to note	in the final analysis
last but not least	in a very real sense
few and far between	to make a long story short
in this day and age	straight from the shoulder
slowly but surely	method in their madness
better late than never	other side of the coin
easier said than done	tempest in a teapot
all walks of life	as luck would have it
the bottom line	each and every
conspicuous by its absence	no sooner said than done

37h   Be exact. Use words in their precise meanings.

Knowledge of idiom, use of a dictionary, and a good vocabulary —all these are necessary for precise writing. Misuse of a word like *preservation* for *conservation* results in vagueness and confusion. Correct use of words usually requires sensitivity to language. The words in the following sentences express inexact meanings.

She was *overtaken* by the heat. (*Overcome* was intended.)
Foremost, both librarians lost their patience. (Was *immediately* intended? or *first*?)

Misuse of one word for another that is somewhat like it can make a sentence ridiculous. (See **37d.**)

Her dishonesty hurt her conscious. (The word is *conscience.*)

Hamlet wished to get *avenge* for the murder of his father. *(revenge)*
As the sun beams down upon the swamp, no different varieties of color are reflected, only the unreal grayish color of dead *vegetarian.* *(vegetation)*

Other examples are *climatic* for *climactic, statue* for *stature* (or vice versa), *incidences* for *incidents,* and *course* for *coarse.* Nonwords should never be used: for example, *interpretate* for *interpret, predominately* for *predominantly,* and *tutorer* for *tutor*.

▶ Exercise 3

Point out clichés and inexact words and expressions in the following sentences.

1. It goes without saying that the value of a college education cannot be measured in money, but tuition is high as a kite.
2. The meal was fabulous, and the service was fantastic.
3. Although the model claimed she wanted to marry a strong, silent type, she tied the knot with a man who could talk the horns off a billygoat.
4. Holidays always repress some people.
5. On the outskirts of the small town a sign was erected that renounced that this was the home of the one and only Fitz Fritzsimmons.
6. The survivor was weak as a kitten after eight days on the ocean, but his overall condition was unbelievable.
7. The brothers were as different as night and day, but each drank like a fish.
8. The eager young attorney jumped to her feet and cried, "That is irrevelant and immaterial."
9. At the retirement dinner the corporation president toasted the old engineer and told him that his daily presents in the building would be soarly missed.
10. As he looked back, the farmer thought of those mornings as cold as ice when the ground was hard as a rock and when he shook like a leaf as he rose at the crack of dawn.

37i Add new words to your vocabulary.

Good writers know many words, and they can select the precise ones they need to express their meanings. A good vocabulary displays your mentality, your education, and your talents as a writer.

In reading, pay careful attention to words you have not seen before. Look them up in a dictionary. Remember them. Recognize them the next time you see them. Learn to use them.

General exercises

▶ Exercise 4
Underline the letter identifying the best definition.

1. *contingency:* (a) series (b) important point (c) possible condition (d) rapidly
2. *aegis:* (a) sponsorship (b) eagerness (c) foreign (d) overly proper
3. *summit:* (a) highest point (b) total amount (c) heir (d) exhibition
4. *magnanimity:* (a) state of wealth (b) excellent health (c) strong attraction (d) generosity
5. *credibility:* (a) debt (b) kindness (c) knowledge (d) believability
6. *gullible:* (a) capable of flight (b) flexible (c) easily tricked (d) intelligent
7. *patent:* (a) obvious (b) long suffering (c) omen (d) victim
8. *audible:* (a) capable of being heard (b) overly idealistic (c) easily read (d) tasty
9. *adamant:* (a) without measure (b) unyielding (c) fragrant (d) judicial decision
10. *travesty:* (a) long journey (b) congested traffic (c) scaffolding (d) mockery

11. *innate:* (a) void of sense (b) inborn (c) applied (d) digestible
12. *acrimonious:* (a) bitter (b) ritualistic (c) hypocritical (d) massive
13. *insurgents:* (a) deep cuts (b) rebels (c) music makers (d) physicians
14. *duress:* (a) fancy dress (b) with quickness (c) stress (d) penalty
15. *flagrant:* (a) odorous (b) conspicuously bad (c) beaten (d) delicious
16. *substantive:* (a) substantial (b) in place of (c) religious (d) hardheaded
17. *imprudent:* (a) unwise (b) lacking modesty (c) ugly (d) incapable of proof
18. *solicitous:* (a) seeking sales (b) without energy (c) heroic (d) concerned
19. *valid:* (a) butler (b) favorable (c) desirable (d) founded on truth
20. *charlatan:* (a) robe (b) quack (c) high official (d) strong wind

▶ Exercise 5
Underline the letter identifying the best definition.

1. *impetus:* (a) egomaniac (b) incentive (c) ghost (d) perfectionist
2. *dire:* (a) terrible (b) bare (c) final (d) dishonest
3. *subpoena:* (a) below ground (b) in disguise (c) legal summons (d) unspoken
4. *commentary:* (a) explanations (b) military store (c) grouch (d) headland
5. *prodigy:* (a) extraordinary person (b) wasteful person (c) lover of children (d) musician
6. *vacillate:* (a) oil (b) repair (c) waver (d) empty
7. *peer:* (a) an equal (b) an ideal (c) an emotion (d) intense
8. *poignant:* (a) housecoat (b) fruitful (c) hostile (d) piercingly effective

9. _spurious:_ (a) brimming over (b) pricking (c) not genuine (d) affectionate

10. _perennial:_ (a) continuing (b) circus show (c) circular (d) filial

11. _contend:_ (a) incantate (b) appease (c) compete (d) look after

12. _scapegoat:_ (a) one being sought (b) one taking blame for others (c) one who looks stupid (d) one guilty of crime

13. _pomposity:_ (a) heaviness (b) splendor (c) scarcity (d) arrogance

14. _banal:_ (a) commonplace (b) fatal (c) aggressive (d) tropical

15. _parameter:_ (a) restatement (b) expansion (c) limit (d) device for measuring sound

16. _acute:_ (a) appealing (b) critical (c) average (d) unorthodox

17. _vibrant:_ (a) blunted (b) double (c) irritating (d) energetic

18. _presume:_ (a) guess (b) judge (c) know (d) take for granted

19. _gesture:_ (a) demonstration (b) internal disorder (c) joke (d) court clown

20. _veracity:_ (a) boldness (b) speed (c) great anger (d) truthfulness

▶ Exercise 6
Put the matching number on the left by the letter on the right.

1. heady		a.	exaggeration
2. reciprocate		b.	customary
3. dispiriting		c.	repay
4. literally		d.	a ranking
5. consecrate		e.	imitation
6. bolster		f.	basic
7. ideology		g.	in actuality
8. anticipate		h.	unreal
9. incorrigible		i.	opposition
10. fantastic		j.	impetuous
11. antagonism		k.	a showing forth
12. hyperbole		l.	one who comes before

13. conventional
14. manifestation
15. mimicry
16. seminal
17. hierarchy
18. predecessor
19. distort
20. labyrinth

m. twist
n. not reformable
o. disheartening
p. foresee
q. make sacred
r. set of beliefs
s. maze
t. support

▶ Exercise 7
Select the word or phrase that most exactly defines the italicized word in each sentence.

1. An *obdurate* attitude seldom leads to prosperity. (egotistical, hard-hearted, wasteful, false)
2. He felt it his *prerogative* to speak out. (turn, responsibility, right, nature)
3. The speech was marked by *vapid* expressions. (inspiring, dull, vigorous, sad)
4. The *renowned* singer performed in the small town. (famous, unknown, opera, talented)
5. *Gluttony,* explained the slim traveler, was not one of his faults. (hitchhiking, stagnation, overeating, speeding)
6. The banker's *salient* traits were frugality and kindness. (prominent, best, hidden, lacking)
7. Imagining himself a great statesman, he was the prime minister's *lackey.* (assistant, servile follower, hair groomer, moral superior)
8. The *laconic* old woman stood out among the group of excited young men. (untalkative, diseased, depressed, evil)
9. Not all those who took part in the robbery were *depraved.* (needy, evil, prepared, punished)
10. The gem was pronounced an *authentic* emerald. (genuine, artificial, rare, expensive)

▶ Exercise 8

Follow the instructions for Exercise 7.

1. The judge found the defendant's answer _incredible._ (highly impressive, wonderful, not believable, awful)
2. A _transcript_ was made of the tapes. (recording, written copy, mockery, extension)
3. To discuss the matter further would be to _obfuscate_ it. (avoid, obscure, criticize, clarify)
4. I _deplore_ the method used to recover the gems. (praise, understand, regret, follow)
5. The poem was composed by an _anonymous_ author. (dead, foreign, excellent, unknown)
6. Finding the essay _provocative,_ she discussed it with her tutor. (stimulating, disgusting, prolonged, offensive)
7. The child _reluctantly_ joined her brother in the swimming pool. (rapidly, hesitantly, joyfully, playfully)
8. _Platitudes_ can quickly destroy the effectiveness of a lecture. (catcalls, stutterings, stale truisms, bad jokes)
9. A _sorcerer_ was said to be the king's only companion. (healer, valiant warrior, jester, wizard)
10. Make the report as _succinct_ as possible. (colorful, concise, long, accurate)

▶ Exercise 9

Dictionaries disagree about the levels of particular words. Read the preliminary pages in your dictionary, and study the labels which it applies to particular words. Webster's New Collegiate Dictionary _uses fewer and less restrictive labels than other college dictionaries. Without your dictionary, put by each of the following words the label which you believe it should have. Then look the word up and determine the label which it has in your dictionary._

1. yon

2. ain't

3. lift

4. learn

5. blockhead

6. TV

7. bull (nonsense)

8. phony

9. kid (child)

10. a creep

38 Wordiness w
Do not use needless words and irrelevant ideas.

Conciseness increases the force of writing. Do not pad your paper merely to obtain a desired length or number of words.

Use one word for many.

The love letter was written by somebody who did not sign a name. (13 words)
The love letter was anonymous (*or* not signed). (5 or 6 words)

Use the active voice for conciseness. (See **5.**)

The truck was overloaded by the workmen. (7 words)
The workmen overloaded the truck. (5 words)

Revise sentence structure for conciseness.

Another element which adds to the effectiveness of a speech is its emotional appeal. (14 words)
Emotional appeal also makes a speech more effective. (8 words)

Avoid constructions with *It is . . .* and *there are . . . .*

NOT
There are some conditions **that** are satisfactory.
BUT
Some conditions are satisfactory.

NOT
It is truth **which** will prevail.
BUT
Truth will prevail.

Do not use two words with the same meaning (tautology).

basic and fundamental principles (4 words)
basic principles (2 words)

Study your sentences carefully and make them concise by
using all the preceding methods. Do not, however, sacrifice concreteness and vividness for conciseness and brevity.

CONCRETE AND VIVID
At each end of the sunken garden, worn granite steps, flanked by
 large magnolia trees, lead to formal paths.
EXCESSIVELY CONCISE
The garden has steps at both ends.

▶ Exercise 10
*Express the following sentences succinctly. Do not omit important
ideas.*

1. The custom which has always been so popular in the country of waving to strangers as you pass them is gradually fading out.

2. There are several reasons why officers of the law ought to be trained in the law of the land, and two of these are as follows. The first of these reasons is that policemen can enforce the law better if they are familiar with it. And second, they will be less likely to violate the rights of private citizens if they know exactly and accurately what these rights are.

3. Although the Kentucky rifle played an important and significant part in getting food for the frontiersmen who settled the American West, its function as a means of protection was in no degree any less significant in their lives.

4. Some television programs assume a low level of public intelligence and present their shows to the public as if the audience were made up of morons.

5. The distant explosion was audible to the ear.

6. The Japanese beetle is a beetle which was introduced into America from Japan and which thrives on fruits and roots of grass.

7. The judge who will try the case is an honorable woman, and she is highly intelligent.

8. It is not true that he is guilty.

9. It is a pleasure for some to indulge in eating large quantities of food at meals, but medical doctors of medicine tell us that such pleasures can only bring with them unpleasant results in the long run of things.

10. The essay consists of facts which describe vividly many of the events in the life of a typical juggler. In this description the author uses a vocabulary which is easy to understand. This vocabulary is on neither too high a level nor too low a level, but on one which can be understood by any high school graduate.

39   Repetition   *rep*
Avoid redundancy—excessive repetition of words and sounds. Repeat for emphasis rarely and carefully.

Unintentional repetition is seldom effective. Avoid by using synonyms and pronouns and by omitting words.

39a   Do not needlessly repeat words.

The history of human flight is full of histories of failures on the part of
those who have tried flight and were failures.

The history of human flight recounts many failures.

Do not revise by excessively substituting synonyms for repeated words.

The history of human flight is full of stories of failures on the part of
those who have tried to glide through the air and met with no
success.

39b Do not needlessly repeat sounds.

The biologist again *checked* the *charts* to determine the *effect* of the
poison on the *insect*.

The biologist again studied the charts to determine the effect of the
poison on the moth.

39c Repeat only for emphasis or for clarity.

Effective repetition of a word or a phrase may create emphasis,
especially in aphorisms or poetry.

Searching without knowledge is like *searching* in the dark.
"Beauty is truth, truth beauty."

JOHN KEATS

Diction and style   195

▶ **Exercise 11**
Rewrite the following passage. Avoid wordiness and undesirable repetition.

A large number of people enjoy reading murder mysteries regularly. As a rule, these people are not themselves murderers nor would these people really ever enjoy seeing someone commit an actual murder, nor would most of them actually enjoy trying to solve an actual murder. They probably enjoy reading murder mysteries because of this reason: they have found a way to escape from the monotonous, boring routine of dull everyday existence.

To such people the murder mystery is realistic fantasy. It is realistic because the people in the murder mystery are as a general rule believable as people. They are not just made-up pasteboard figures. It is also realistic because the character who is the hero, the character who solves the murder mystery, solves it not usually by trial and error and haphazard methods but by exercising a high degree of logic and reason. It is absolutely and totally essential that people who enjoy murder mysteries have an admiration for the human faculty of logic.

But murder mysteries are also fantasies. The people who read such books of fiction play a game. It is a game in which they suspend certain human emotions. One of these human emotions that they suspend is pity. If the reader stops to feel pity and sympathy for each and every victim that is killed or if the reader stops to feel terrible horror that such a thing could happen in our world of today, that person will never enjoy reading murder mysteries. The devoted reader of murder mysteries keeps uppermost in mind always and at all times the goal of arriving through logic and observation at the final solution to the mystery offered in the book. It is a game with life and death. Whodunits hopefully help the reader to hide from the hideous horrors of actual life and death in the real world.

40 Abstract and general words   *abst*

Do not write abstractly or vaguely. Choose specific and concrete words.

Abstract writing may communicate little information or even cause misunderstanding.

Words which pinpoint the meaning are the basis of the most exact and the best writing. To describe a sofa as **pleasing** is to be less precise than to say it is **comfortable.** Specific words say

Diction and style   197

what you think. They do not leave your reader wondering what you mean.

NOT SPECIFIC
The leader told his followers they were in danger.

SPECIFIC
The head of the troop whispered that a mountain lion was in the branches of the tree overhead.

Concreteness is relevant to all kinds of writing: a college catalogue; a business letter; instructions on how to put together a gas grill; a speech; a theme; art (fiction or poetry).

▶ Exercise 12

The following ten words or phrases are general. For any five of them substitute four specific and concrete words. Do not let your substitutions be synonymous with each other.

EXAMPLE moved with the feet   *jogged, danced, ambled, raced*
Answers will vary greatly.

1. communications

2. entertainments

3. foods

4. organizations

5. living things

6. instruments

7. machines

8. books

9. emotions

10. occupations

▶ **Exercise 13**
Write your personal definition of one of the following abstract terms in a paragraph of about two hundred words. Give concrete examples from your experience.

wisdom   love   progress   peace of mind

41 **Connotation**   *con*
Choose words with connotations appropriate to tone and content.

Many words carry special associations or suggestions — **connotations. Denotations** of words are precise meanings, the exact definitions given in dictionaries. Denotatively, the word *dog* arouses no emotional response of any kind, no hatred, no affection. Dog is a four-legged carnivorous domesticated animal.

Connotations include emotional responses. What *dog* suggests in addition to *four-legged carnivore* is connotation, which can be pleasant or unpleasant. To one person *dog* may suggest friendship; to another once attacked by a dog, the word may connote terror.

A good writer uses connotations to evoke planned emotional reactions. To suggest sophistication, the writer may mention a *lap dog;* to evoke the amusing or the rural, *hound dog.* To connote a social or moral distinction, the writer may call someone a *cur.* Even this word may have different connotations: a social worker may react sympathetically to it; a snob, contemptuously. Consider the associations aroused by *canine, pooch, mutt, mongrel, puppy,* and *watchdog.* Even some breeds arouse different responses: *bloodhound, shepherd, St. Bernard, poodle.*

Words that are denotative synonyms may have very different connotative overtones. Consider the following:

drummer—salesperson—field representative
slender—thin—skinny
resolute—strong-willed—stubborn

The exact writer avoids a word with unwanted connotations and chooses an appropriate synonym. Be sure that your words give the suggestions you wish to convey. A single word with the wrong connotation can easily spoil a passage. Only one word has been changed in the following quotation:

Let us never bargain out of fear. But let us never fear to bargain.

President Kennedy actually wrote:

Let us never negotiate out of fear. But let us never fear to negotiate.

The word *bargain* ruins the tone of the statement even though it is a close synonym for *negotiate*.

▶ **Exercise 14**

The words in each group below have different connotations. Rate each word for favorability of connotation: 1 for most favorable, 2 for second, 3 for least. Be prepared to explain the different shades of connotation.

1. frolic
   clown
   cut up
2. innocent
   naive
   simple
3. garbage
   rubbish
   trash
4. impractical
   quixotic
   romantic

5. economical
   stingy
   thrifty
6. job
   profession
   position
7. decay
   decompose
   rot
8. inexpensive
   cheap
   reasonable
9. remedy
   medicine
   cure-all
10. enthusiast
    extremist
    fanatic
11. fat
    overweight
    stout
12. little
    petite
    small
13. stream
    gutter
    rivulet
14. famous
    notorious
    well known
15. diseased
    ill
    sick

42 Figurative language *fig*

Avoid mixed and inappropriate figures of speech. Use fresh figures.

Figures of speech compare one thing (usually abstract) with another (usually literal or concrete).

Mixed figures associate two things which are not logically consistent.

MIXED

These corporations lashed out with legal loopholes.
(You cannot *strike* with a *hole*.)

Inappropriate figures of speech compare one thing with another in a way that violates the mood or the intention.

INAPPROPRIATE
Then, like a thief in the night, my father passed away.
    (It is unfortunate to compare a dying father to a thief.)

Use figurative comparisons (of things not literally similar) for vivid explanation and for originality. A simile, a metaphor, or a personification gives you a chance to compare or to explain what you are saying in a different way from the sometimes prosaic method of pure statement, argument, or logic.

METAPHORS (IMPLIED COMPARISONS)
Archaeologists constantly stir the **ashes of the past.**
The mind is a **house of many mirrors.**

SIMILES (COMPARISONS STATED WITH LIKE or AS)
Old courthouse records are often *like* **fallen leaves.**
The mind is *like* a **house of many mirrors.**

PERSONIFICATIONS
Father Time
Money talks.

▶ Exercise 15
Explain the flaws in these figures of speech.

1. Like a trenchant sword, the speaker removed the ground

   from his opponent's argument.

2. The language of the politician was as flowery as a giant oak.

3. A novelist carefully ties together the threads of the stream of

   time.

4. The pollster wished to keep his pulse on the movement of the people.

5. Like the sensitive fingers of a safe-breaker, the adviser sought for the student's hidden problems in order to help her.

▶ **Exercise 16**
Compose and bring to class two fresh figures of speech.

43 **Flowery language** *fl*
Avoid ornate or pretentious language.

Flowery language is wordy or artificial. It is often misplaced or inappropriate elegance or grandeur. It calls attention to itself as words without stressing the point. Naturalness and sincerity disappear into affectation.

PLAIN LANGUAGE	FLOWERY LANGUAGE
The year 1981	The year of 1981
Now	At this point in time
Lawn	Verdant sward
Shovel	Simple instrument for delving into Mother Earth
A teacher	My fellow toiler in the arduous labors of pedagogy
Reading a textbook	Following the lamp of knowledge in a textual tome
Eating	Partaking of the dietary sustenance of life
Going overseas	Traversing the ever-palpitating deep

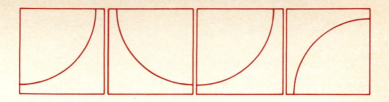

The Process of Composition

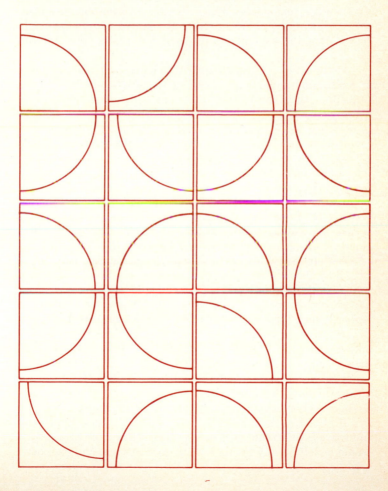

44   **Clear and logical thinking** *log*

The two most common kinds of logic or reasoning are **inductive** thinking and **deductive** thinking.

Inductive reasoning is mainly scientific and factual. It begins with collected data, which is derived from statistics, experiments, examples. When enough information has been collected, one who induces arrives at a statement of a principle taken from the examples, and then he or she notes all the exceptions.

Deductive reasoning begins with a principle and applies it to a situation, a person, an action, or some kind of condition. Deductive thinkers believe that the principle is always or usually true. The position they begin with may derive from any kind of source. They apply moral principles, religious beliefs, scientific statements, psychological or philosophical systems, governmental regulations or laws—any kind of rule or principle —to a new situation.

The conclusions of deductive thinkers may be less certain, more disputable, than the conclusions of inductive thinkers, who arrive at a principle instead of starting from one. Deductive thinkers are accurate only to the extent that their principle is correct and only to the extent that they have applied it truly.

Both inductive and deductive thinking are tested and questioned by those to whom the conclusions are presented. Of an inductive thinker, one asks whether the facts are true, whether the exceptions have been noted, whether the selection of materials is representative, whether the conclusions are truly and accurately drawn from the data, whether the conclusions are stated precisely or exaggerated. Of a deductive thinker, one asks whether the given principle is true, whether purely personal opinion is given credence, whether it is applied to materials relevantly, whether the conclusion is accurate according to the principle, whether exceptions have been noted.

If all conclusions reached by all thinkers deductively and inductively were true, no room for disagreement on any subject would be left for any thinker. With good motives and bad, however, with honesty and with deceit, different thinkers reach different conclusions derived from the same data or from the same principles. You should learn to test the logic, the accuracy of the thinking, of anything you read or hear. Indeed, when you write, you must test your own reasoning severely and carefully. The following sections should enable you to begin reading and writing with some accuracy in your thinking.

44a Use only accurate and verified data.

Facts are demonstrable. They are the basis of judgments. A writer should distinguish carefully between the facts and the judgments derived from them and then explain how one comes from the other.

Errors of fact, ignorance, or dishonesty make the reader suspicious and lead to distrust and doubt. The following statements contain factual errors.

The traveler testified that he had entered the country on June 31, 1976. ("Thirty days hath June.")

Only wealthy people buy original oil paintings. (The facts do not bear out this contention.)

44b Use reliable authorities.

Specialists in the same field may disagree. Therefore, in evaluating an authority you may use some of the following criteria and perhaps additional methods.

1. When was the work published? An old publication may contain superseded information.
2. Who published the work? University presses and well-established publishing houses employ informed consultants.

3. How has the work been evaluated by other authorities in annotated bibliographies and reviews?
4. Is the presumed authority writing about his or her own field? (An atomic scientist may not be an expert on world records in baseball.)
5. Are the language and the tone reasonable, or does the authority attempt to persuade by using ornate rhetoric or slanted words and terms?
6. Is the authority fair-minded enough to admit the existence of facts that seem contradictory?
7. Does the authority distinguish fact from opinion?

44c Avoid sweeping generalizations.

Generalize with great care. If you know that three of your friends oppose capital punishment, you should not assert that "Everyone wishes to have capital punishment abolished" or even that "Most people wish to have capital punishment abolished." These statements are too broad for the evidence on which they are based. Sweeping generalizations like the following may contain an element of truth, but it is lost in exaggeration.

A poor person cannot get a fair trial in America.
Russian athletes are the best in the world.

Sweeping generalizations about nationalities and races are among the most pernicious. If you have not done extensive and conclusive research on your subject, qualify your opinions.

Some poor people feel that they cannot get a fair trial in America.
Many Russian athletes are among the best in the world.

Resist the temptation to claim too much. Remember that a sweeping generalization is often a falsification.

44d   Use enough specific and accurate evidence to support your argument.

Truth and accuracy depend on an adequate number of examples. Statistics and samplings of opinions, polls, and other kinds of data should be not only sufficiently extensive but also fairly and representatively chosen. Sometimes it is not enough that data should be picked at random. A public opinion poll taken from only one social, educational, or occupational group, for example, would probably be misleading.

44e   Stick to the point.

Do not introduce irrelevancies or wander off the subject. First or last paragraphs of papers may be especially irrelevant because they begin or end at a point too far removed from the subject. Digression is a sign of failure to focus attention on the problem at hand.

44f   Do not ignore conflicting facts or evidence.

Be aware of facts and instances which seem to refute or qualify your views and conclusions. Deal with them fully and honestly. You can actually strengthen your case by taking opposing evidence into consideration.

44g   Do not reason in a circle.

A writer who reasons in a circle (or begs the question) assumes that something is true and then reaches a conclusion which merely restates the assumption.

CIRCULAR REASONING
Good raincoats shed water well because they are rainproof.

The writer is reasoning in a circle by simply stating the assumption in two different ways.

44h Do not omit essential steps in thought or draw false conclusions from unstated assumptions.

An error in logic occurs when the omission of a step in reasoning leads to a false conclusion. The argument that "He cannot be elected to Phi Beta Kappa because he is a football player" is based on a false assumption: that no football player ever makes good grades, or that Phi Beta Kappa will refuse to elect someone who plays football. Similar omissions of parts of the argument occur in the following sentences. What are the unstated assumptions, and why are the conclusions false?

Since she made good grades in high school, she will undoubtedly be a good student in college.
She will not make a good judge because she was once fined for speeding.
He has a wonderful personality and will certainly be a successful salesman.

44i Do not substitute an appeal to emotions for an appeal to reason.

Name-calling attempts to appeal to prejudice. Calling an opponent irresponsible beclouds an issue. This is argument against a person rather than against a principle or a point of view.

Loaded words and **labels** attempt to shape an attitude through prejudice instead of reason. In loaded terms a government subsidy plan might be described as a "hand-out scheme that a bunch of radical do-gooders are trying to fasten on the taxpayers."

Flattery attempts to persuade through excessive praise. The political candidate who tells the people that he knows they will vote for him because of their high intelligence is attempting to convince by flattering.

Snob appeal asserts that one should adopt a certain view because all the better people do. The use of athletes, beauty queens, or motion picture stars in advertising is a form of snob appeal.

Mass appeal attempts to persuade by asserting that everyone follows a certain pattern. It suggests that one who does not follow the herd is in error (*everyone ought* to go to college; *everyone ought* to own a home).

44j Do not draw false conclusions about cause and effect.

When two things happen in sequence, the second is not necessarily caused by the first. If a man walks under a ladder and shortly thereafter loses his wallet, he should not assume that he lost his wallet *because* he walked under the ladder. To show a cause-and-effect relationship between two events, it is necessary to produce evidence of real causation.

44k Be moderate.

Be temperate in your judgments and in your choice of words.

Overstatement, overemphasis, and dogmatic assertion not only irritate most readers but arouse doubt or even disbelief. The good writer is not cocksure and brash.

44L Allow for adequate alternatives.

On some questions it is false logic to assume that there are *two and only two* alternatives. Often other possibilities exist. If, for example, a father tells his son that he must go to college or fail in life, he has not recognized that his son may succeed without a college education.

▶ **Exercise 1**
Describe the errors in content and thought in each of the following.

1. The fact that the lexicographer wrote the publisher about his objections to the novel proves that as fiction it was not worth publishing.

2. Boys are good in mathematics and science; girls are good in English and the fine arts.

3. An interjection is a word or a clause used to express a strong emotion.

4. Russian medicine is far behind that in this country because Russia has so many young doctors.

5. The book which you reviewed favorably is trash, the kind of dirty garbage found on the cheapest shelves of pornographic bookstores.

6. Anyone who reaches the age of eighteen is old enough to make decisions without advice from other people.

7. John Quincy Adams, the second President of the United States, was respected for his idealism and great knowledge.

8. Nearly all the great monuments of this world are made of marble.

9. All college graduates are unusually intelligent; otherwise, they could not have passed the courses and completed their education.

10. The fact that you could espouse the cause of those rebels shows me that you are a coward and a degenerate.

11. After only one week at Reduso Spa, Mrs. Wentworth lost sixteen pounds. Enroll now if you really wish to lose weight.

12. My professor must be a good scholar; he is a member of the Modern Language Association.

13. All students should go to trade school before going to college because it is extremely difficult for college graduates to get good jobs unless they can do something with their hands.

14. Order our new device for restoring hair in your bald spots, and new hair will begin to grow within two weeks.

15. The only good kinds of narratives are fiction and auto-biography.

16. Her parents deserted her when she was an infant. No wonder she has spent much of her life in prison.

17. The welfare system in this country makes the people who have earned their money give it away to lazy good-for-nothings who are not willing to work for themselves.

18. Joseph Conrad was the greatest novelist who ever lived.

19. Our commune has a definite philosophy; those who follow it will have no serious problems in life.

20. Freedom is a necessary ingredient in the life of every woman, and every woman should make her decisions without advice because of her need for liberation.

21. According to the high school chemistry text, the article in *Chemical Research Journal* cannot be correct.

22. Subscribe to *Now,* the intellectual's magazine, and join the most enlightened readers of the day.

23. Shakespeare did not write the plays attributed to him. This fact has been proved by a famous surgeon who recently retired from a medical career to which he had devoted almost all his energy.

24. Fortunetellers are not fakes. The palmist said that I was going to Alaska within three months, and I did.

25. A good theme must be written in chronological order.

45 Writing paragraphs ¶

A **paragraph** develops one idea. In itself it is an independent unit, but it also functions as part of a larger work—a theme or a chapter. When the purpose of the paragraph is not clear, the direction of the paper is lost for the moment.

A paragraph may appear to be a simple construction, but underlying it is a definite structure of parts and connections.

45a State the main idea of a paragraph in a topic sentence.

The **topic sentence** is the crucial part which attaches the paragraph to the whole and also defines the function of the sentences it controls and manages. Topic sentences supply the direction. Other sentences add evidence, make refinements, develop the main idea; but as a rule they do not control the purpose of the paragraph. Consequently, taken together, the topic sentences of a paper are a sort of skeleton of the whole. Reading only the topic sentences may show a writer whether the lines of thought are clear. The topic sentences also may enable a reader to scan a piece of writing and to see generally its major points.

Test your own papers by examining the topic sentences. If they move logically and clearly through the main outlines of your work, that is a good sign. If not, you may have omitted ideas, arranged thoughts in the wrong sequence, or neglected to state purpose and direction. Then you may need to replan your paper, to rewrite topic sentences, or to formulate ideas which you have previously just assumed.

Topic sentences do not have to come at the beginning of a paragraph. They may appear almost anywhere. Most of them, however, come at the beginning or the end.

A topic sentence at the beginning of a paragraph usually states a general thought, and then the following sentences exemplify, modify, qualify, add, or develop it in a variety of ways.

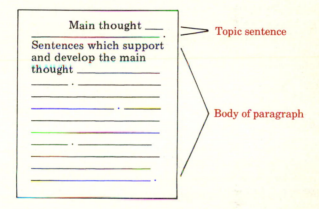

A topic sentence may come at the end of a paragraph. Here the writer collects a series of facts or examples or pieces of information. The paragraph then concludes with a topic sentence which not only sums up and brings together all the previous sentences but also shows their connection to the central thought and the rest of the paper. This kind of paragraph is usually based on inductive thinking (see pages 206–207).

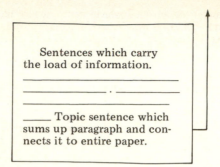

In a well-structured paper, every part looks back to what has gone before and forward to what will come later. Leaving out any necessary part of a theme is a failure as serious as the omission of an essential structural element of a building. Omit the floors or the beams, and the thought collapses.

The following selection about gardening illustrates a skillful method of writing good paragraphs.

Gardening is one of the oldest of the arts. The ancient Egyptians, the Assyrians and the Persians developed gardens of majestic grandeur and opulence. The Chinese, with their deep sensitiveness to beauty, laid the foundations for a form of garden art which was later to have great influence upon other lands.

The Greeks gave to the world a new concept of gardening. Their homes were adorned with flowers, but it was in their civic design that they most skillfully applied their garden art. Their temples were surrounded by groves of trees, and trees lined the important streets and market places in their principal cities.

Much of the knowledge and skill in garden craft which the Romans possessed was acquired from the Greeks. In the second century A.D. the Romans began to build gardens of tremendous scale, inspired by the precedent of the vast palace gardens of Mesopotamia which they had conquered. They studied hydraulics and brought water from great distances by conduit to supply the ornamental fountains which adorned their villa gardens. These great villas were later to inspire the Italian garden architects to follow the Roman precedent.

Through the Dark Ages, those centuries of almost complete barbarism and ignorance, the art and practices of gardening were kept alive by the monks in the monasteries. They were scholarly men of faith who made their work the interpretation of goodness and their study the means of gaining a deeper knowledge of life.

The gradual emergence of Europe into an era of revived culture and intellectual enlightenment; the spread of the study of the classics, brought about by the founding of the universities; the rise of an independent class of citizen craftsmen, unattached to the feudal system; the growing importance of the great free cities of Europe—all combined to usher in an age of greater prosperity and greater accomplishment in the arts. It was a remarkable era, destined to become known as "The Renaissance," the time of rebirth of Western Civilization.

JAMES BUSH-BROWN AND LOUISE BUSH-BROWN,
America's Garden Book

Notice the strong topic sentence in each paragraph and the varying lengths of topic sentences. Each lends a sense of direction to the passage. Each paragraph deals clearly with a single period in the development of gardening: the first to its historical origins, the second to the Greek, the third to the Roman, the fourth to the Dark Ages, and the final paragraph to the Renaissance. Although each paragraph is a unit in itself, there is a steady progression in thought from the first to the last, and readers know where they are and where the authors are taking them. Throughout, the passage is marked by simplicity, clarity, and gracefulness.

45b Write unified paragraphs. Relate each sentence clearly to the central idea.

Every sentence in a good paragraph should bear on the main point. An irrelevant sentence which digresses from the main point puzzles the reader about its connection to other sentences and the purpose of the paragraph.

Notice in the following paragraph how the writer digresses and destroys the unity.

> Groups of people often seem to develop a definable and single personality. One group may differ markedly from another with a similar purpose but a different character. Classes in college, for example, often vary widely for no explainable reason. One section of a course may be lazy, passive, and dull. Another in the same subject may be energetic and bright, independent but respectful. The professor may hasten to one group with anticipation and drag his feet as he goes to meet the other. *Of course, professors differ as much as their classes do. One may be generous with his time and truly concerned about his students. Another may be selfish and indifferent.* The likenesses within one group of people and the differences from one group to another reflect many of the aspects of human personality.

This paragraph does not succeed. It establishes the central idea of the unique character of groups of people and then changes to the subject of professors. One interesting idea ran off the main track; the writer started another subject. The two together get nowhere. The last sentence makes a half-hearted effort to return to the main idea, but the discussion turns to what might easily become still a third subject. A paragraph that brings together two or three thoughts usually does not make even one good one.

▶ **Exercise 2**

By deleting extraneous material, improve the paragraphs below that are not unified (as many as three sentences may be extraneous). Put a check next to paragraphs that are acceptable. Underline all topic sentences (some paragraphs may have more than one).

1. The motion picture *All Quiet on the Western Front* was actually created as an antiwar protest. It deals with World War I from a German perspective. The hero has a professor he

first admires but comes to distrust. Even though it is about the Germans, it does not glorify the German cause. It depicts the plight of the sensitive human spirit caught in the terrible grip of war. World War I started when Archduke Ferdinand was assassinated. Probably no one would have guessed that this incident would grow quickly into the greatest war the world had ever known. The theme of the picture is expressed in the ending, where the hero is killed while reaching for a flower he sees on the battlefield.

2. Sensible business people who deal in realities every day will often go out of their way on the street to avoid walking under a ladder. Diners in restaurants throw salt over their shoulders to ward off bad luck when they spill a little. It is not at all unusual to see a perfectly sane adult knock on wood to insure continued good fortune. Many people moan over broken mirrors not because the accident will cost them the money to buy new mirrors but because they are worried that they may be in for seven years of bad luck. Superstitions, then, are many and various and still manifest themselves in the actions of a great many normal people.

3. As the basic social unit the family is as important today in America as it ever was, though perhaps in a different way. Family coherence was essential in the early days of the country to insure the survival of the individual members. They helped each other and protected each other. Today people need their families not so much to insure physical survival as to help them through the perils of modern times, especially through such psychological perils as loss of identity. America is not all bad, however. It offers the greatest freedom of all countries for individual development. America

is still the land of opportunity. The family gives one a sense of belonging, a sense of the past. When all else seems severed, the family can be the anchor to sanity.

4. A Saturday visit to the barber shop was once an exciting and meaningful experience for a boy. It offered an almost unique opportunity for a youngster to enter for a little while the adult masculine world. At school a boy had no opportunity to see this world. At home he was often with his father and perhaps his brothers, but that was not the same as sitting among men and listening to their jokes—often slightly off-color—and their strong opinions on people and politics and their stories, sometimes of violence and courage. If he were wise, the lad sat in the barber chair and listened carefully with silent respect, for he sensed that he was being given the rare opportunity of visiting a world he would someday enter.

45c Avoid short, skimpy paragraphs. Develop your paragraphs adequately.

In most expository writing, a series of short, skimpy paragraphs suggests that a writer does not know much to write about each point, has not grouped thoughts well, has not developed each thought fully, or has not been careful about paragraph divisions.

Do not omit the examples, the proof, the explanations, the exceptions—in short, the finer and the fuller details that make good paragraphs. Instead of merely mentioning points, you should develop and clarify them for the reader. Details flesh out your ideas.

The following three topic sentences alone lack the fullness of good writing. The basic principles are introduced, but nothing is developed.

Most of American history and much of American literature have been
conditioned or influenced by the existence of a changing frontier.

Until recently, a politician who had not been born in a log cabin was
handicapped in any election.

For Americans, the frontier has always been an ambivalent symbol.

In the paragraphs as they were originally written, the subject
—the frontier—comes alive:

> Most of American history and much of American literature
> have been conditioned or influenced by the existence of a changing
> frontier. In our homes and in our schools many of our greatest
> stories and legends are about men like Captain John Smith, Lewis
> and Clark, Daniel Boone, Davy Crockett, and Kit Carson. We
> celebrate not only Washington's achievements as our Revolu-
> tionary leader and first President, but also his exploits as an Indian
> fighter and surveyor of the wilderness. We remember Andrew
> Jackson as Old Hickory, a frontier figure. We honor Abraham
> Lincoln as a son of the prairie woodland, a rail-splitter who read
> the Bible by light from a fireplace.
>
> Until recently, a politician who had not been born in a log
> cabin was handicapped in any election. Theodore Roosevelt gained
> glamor from his career as a cattleman and his fame as the organ-
> izer of the Rough Riders. Even a New Englander like Calvin Cool-
> idge found it wise to visit the Black Hills of South Dakota and
> wear an Indian headdress for newspaper photographers. And in
> 1960 we elected as President another New Englander who prom-
> ised us a "New Frontier."
>
> For Americans, the frontier has always been an ambivalent
> symbol. It has been considered a source of freedom and a place of
> danger; an exciting challenge, but also a cause of hardship and
> exhaustion; a place for heroism, but also an excuse for racism,
> sadism, and brutality; an inexhaustible mine of humor, but humor
> too often tinged with cruelty or false sentimentality. It has been
> idealized as a source of health, vitality, and nobility; but it has
> been condemned as rude, ugly, and barbaric.
>
> PHILLIP DURHAM AND EVERETT L. JONES,
> *The Frontier in American Literature*

In the first two paragraphs, the topic sentences are developed by
references to typical and famous Americans related in some way
to the frontier. In the last paragraph, interpretation is more

significant, and the qualities in the men and the meaning of the frontier are the basis of development.

In some kinds of writing, short paragraphs are acceptable and expected. Newspapers, for example, generally use short paragraphs. They allow a reader to skim a story, to select the most interesting points and skip the others. It can be effective to use a short paragraph amid longer ones to put special stress on a point. To some extent the length of a writing assignment will influence the length of paragraphs. The theme of a thousand words may allow more room to develop full paragraphs than a short assignment.

▶ Exercise 3

In the following passage all the sentences are separated. Decide how many paragraphs the passage should contain. Indicate where the passage should be divided into paragraphs.

Perhaps we should beware of taking evidence of this sort too tragically, or of deducing from detective stories nothing but a pessimistic moral.

The condemnation of detective stories as drugs or cheap escapism may be pedantic.

For, if they are a symptom, they can also be a cure.

If we credit the Freudian view that socially dangerous impulses can be got rid of by removing them to the level of fantasy, then detectives stories could be described as a harmless safety valve, a wholesome therapy serving a desirable social purpose.

And yet one may wonder if this commonly accepted view is entirely correct, if fantasy and real life are actually so unrelated.

To some extent we may build our real life around our fantasy and, if this is so, sensation literature may not so much rid us of dangerous drives as reinforce and shape them.

In any case, if detective stories are not so sinister as they at first appear from analysis, neither are they as frivolous as some critics have judged them.

The drives they cater to are compelling and basic, and relate ultimately to the struggle for self-preservation.

It is the universal nature of their theme which explains the size and variety of their reading audience.

The intellectual, who scorns the cheap fantasies of the popular magazines, is not likely to be able to forgo the fantasies which give him hope for his survival in an alien world.

Detective stories deal, in their own way and on their own level, with the most essential and urgent problems in the human condition.

ADAPTED FROM WILLIAM O. AYDELOTTE,
"The Detective Story as a Historical Source"

45d Avoid excessively long paragraphs.

Very long paragraphs make it difficult for a reader to digest meaning easily. To reduce excessive length it may be necessary to reduce the scope of the controlling idea—to limit purpose. But sometimes a paragraph can be trimmed by simply discarding material. You may not need ten examples to prove or illustrate a point. Four or five may do it more effectively.

▶ Exercise 4

The authors divided the following passage into three paragraphs. Indicate the places where you believe they made the divisions, and underline the topic sentences.

Whereas most of us speak only to the relatively few people we meet face-to-face, reporters address an audience that ranges from a few hundred to several million. The average person can select subjects and wording to fit an individual listener, but the reporter ordinarily must write about actions and situations that interest large groups. And reporters must tell most of their stories in words that any reasonably literate person can understand. Professional reporters are the hired eyes, ears, legs, and brain of the reader, viewer, or listener. Everything they do is guided by the individual reader's interests. They are paid to survey a small fraction of the world's activities each day and tell the public what they find: what is happening, what is scheduled to happen, what people are saying about it, and (when they can be reasonably sure) what it means. If they do their job well, they supply much of the current information that each person needs to develop a workable picture of reality. If they do it poorly, they become responsible for part of the public's ignorance and prejudice. Continual awareness of this responsibility to the public marks the attitude of professional reporters. Reporters are individuals, but they also are vital elements in the social process of communication. By helping decide what constitutes news, how it should be written and to what length, they function as human valves and amplifiers in the vast machinery of mass communication. They select, reject, compile, interpret, explain, and highlight. But in so doing, they are geared more to the product than to the process. They do not serve simply as an open conduit between the reader and reality, as mechanical sifters of fact and opinion. If they are functioning properly, they are constantly attuned to the receiver. A reporter is a *thinking* agent of the reader.

JAMES M. NEAL AND SUZANNE S. BROWN,
Newswriting and Reporting

45e Develop a paragraph by the method most appropriate for the subject.

Topics for paragraphs may be developed in many ways. Good writers usually select a subject and then use their common sense to determine the way that it can be presented and then read and understood.

Definition

Whether you are using a new word or a new meaning for an old one, a definition explains a concept. It avoids the problems that arise when two persons use the same term for different things. Be as specific as possible; exemplify. Avoid definitions which are uniquely your own (unless you are willing to be challenged). Intellectual definitions, of course, may be much more elaborate than those given in dictionaries. Avoid the expression "According to Webster. . . ."

> Romantic love may be described as an emotion; it is translated into behavior. A person in love wants to do something to or with his loved one. The behavior a couple settles upon comprises their love. The better the translation of emotion into behavior, the less residual emotion will remain. Paradoxically, then, people who love each other do not feel love for each other.
>
> ADAPTED FROM GEORGE W. KELLING,
> *Blind Mazes: A Study of Love*

Comparison, contrast, and analogy

Two basic methods can be used in developing a paragraph by comparison and contrast: writing everything about one point and then everything about the other (XXXX YYYY) or writing about alternating points throughout the paragraph (XY XY XY XY). Either method can be effective, but in long and complex comparisons and contrasts the alternating method is generally better because it keeps both aspects in mind at the same time throughout.

Hot water is the most satisfactory form of heat for the small greenhouse. The heat is more evenly distributed than in the case of steam heat and there is less danger of a sudden drop in temperature. And it is an accepted fact that practically all plants thrive better under a system of hot water heat than under steam heat. It is a more natural kind of heat and is more nearly like the heat of the sun. Hot water heat has the added advantage of being more economical than steam, as it is possible to maintain a very low fire in mild weather.

JAMES BUSH-BROWN AND LOUISE BUSH-BROWN,
America's Garden Book

An analogy explains one thing in terms of another which is like it in some respects but not others. A comparison of a thing generally unknown to something much better known is a good and easy method of exposition or explanation. A common form of analogy is the comparison of life to a voyage or a journey.

Causes and effects

Generally a paragraph of this kind may state a condition or effect and then proceed by listing and explaining the causes. On the other hand, the first sentences may list a cause or causes and then conclude with the consequence, the effect. In either method of development, the writer usually begins with a phenomenon which is generally known and which moves on to the unknowns.

The following paragraph begins with an effect and proceeds to examine the causes.

This close-knit fabric [of the city] was blown apart by the automobile, and by the postwar middle-class exodus to suburbia which the mass-ownership of automobiles made possible. The automobile itself was not to blame for this development, nor was the desire for suburban living, which is obviously a genuine aspiration of many Americans. The fault lay in our failure, right up to the present time, to fashion new policies to minimize the disruptive effects of the automobile revolution. We have failed not only to tame the automobile itself, but to overhaul a property-tax system that tends to foster automotive-age sprawl, and to institute coordinated planning in the politically fragmented suburbs that have caught the brunt of the postwar building boom.

> EDMUND K. FALTERMAYER,
> *Redoing America*

Examples

Some topic sentences state generalizations which may not seem clear or true without evidence and illustration. Proof can be provided by an extended example or several short examples. They must be accepted as true in themselves and as representative of the generalization. Examples can add concrete interest as well as proof.

> It was during this period that some of our most notable examples of garden art were produced: the great villas of Italy, the palace gardens of Spain, the vast plaisances of the French châteaux, the careful parterres of the Dutch, and the beautiful manor house gardens of England.

> JAMES BUSH-BROWN AND LOUISE BUSH-BROWN,
> *America's Garden Book*

Classification

Paragraphs which classify explain by arranging a number of things into groups and categories. Seeing the distinctions should lead to clear understanding of the component parts and, then, an understanding of the larger group or concept. Analysis explains one thing by naming its parts. Synthesis lists several categories and then puts them into a single concept or classification.

> Modern pessimism and modern fragmentation have spread in three different ways to people of our own culture and to people across the world. *Geographically,* it spread from the European mainland to England, after a time jumping the Atlantic to the United States. *Culturally,* it spread in the various disciplines from philosophy to art, to music, to general culture (the novel, poetry, drama, films), and to theology. *Socially,* it spread from the intellectuals to the educated and then through the mass media to everyone.

> FRANCIS A. SCHAEFFER
> *How Should We Then Live?*

This list is by no means exhaustive. No one knows the number of possible ways of writing paragraphs. They can be developed by **details** (a method which in itself may mean many things), by **combinations of ways,** by **moving from the general to the particular** or **the particular to the general,** by **moving from the whole to the parts** and vice versa, by the **analysis of a process,** by **reasons** or **inferences,** by **alternatives,** and so on and so on. Paragraphs may be particularly adapted for use as **introductions** and **conclusions.**

45f Use transitional devices to show the relationships between the parts of your writing.

Transitional devices are connectors and direction givers. They connect content words to other words, sentences to sentences, paragraphs to paragraphs. Reading materials without transitions would be like traveling in a strange land with no signs. Practiced writers assume that they should keep their readers informed about where a paragraph and a paper are going.

CONNECTIVE WORDS AND EXPRESSIONS

but	indeed	likewise
and	in fact	consequently
however	meanwhile	first
moreover	afterward	next
furthermore	then	in brief
on the other hand	so	to summarize
nevertheless	still	to conclude
for example	after all	similarly

DEMONSTRATIVES

this   that   these   those

References to demonstratives must be clear.

OTHER PRONOUNS

many   each   some   others   such   either

Repeated key words, phrases, and synonyms

Repetitions and synonyms guide the reader from sentence to sentence and paragraph to paragraph.

Transitional words in topic sentences can contribute materially to clarity, coherence, and the movement of the discussion. Some writers meticulously guide readers with a connector at the beginning of almost every paragraph. H. J. Muller, for example, begins a sequence of paragraphs about science as follows:

In this summary, science . . .
Yet science does . . .
Similarly the basic interests of science . . .
In other words, they are not . . .
This demonstration that even the scientist . . .
This idea will concern us . . .
In other words, facts and figures . . .

Parallel structures

Repeating similar structural forms of a sentence can show how certain ideas within a paragraph are alike in content as well as structure. A sequence of sentences beginning with a noun subject or with the same kind of pronoun subject, a series of clauses beginning with *that* or *which,* a series of clauses beginning with a similar kind of subordinate conjunction (like *because*)— devices like these can achieve transition and show connection.

Excessive use of parallelism, however, is likely to be too oratorical, too dramatic. Used with restraint, parallel structures are excellent transitional devices.

General exercises

▶ Exercise 5
Write three paragraphs on any of the following subjects. Use at least two methods of development (see pages 227–230). Name the method you use in each paragraph.

1. Boredom
2. Politics and sincerity
3. The mercy of the white lie
4. The importance of being earnest
5. The loud-mouth

▶ Exercise 6
Find three good paragraphs from three different kinds of writing: from a book of nonfiction, an essay, a review, or a newspaper article. Discuss how effective paragraphs differ in different kinds of writing.

▶ Exercise 7
Find an ineffectual paragraph in a book or article. Analyze it in a paragraph.

46 Writing themes

A successful theme is the result of three important steps: careful planning, skillful composing, and intensive revision. These matters are covered in various aspects on the pages that follow. Before specifics, however, consider the following practical advice.

(1) System

Do not think that the actual writing of a paper will take care of itself when the inspiration moves you. Great writers—poets, novelists, essayists, and others—develop a well-defined system of working. Generally, they think hard, research diligently, plan well, set certain times aside during the day or night for writing, and continue to shape what they have written down. Set up your own method. Talent without system leads merely to unfulfilled promise; talent with system produces good writing. Even if you have just average insight, a system will help you realize your full potential.

(2) Motive

The word *serious* when applied to writers sets them apart in a favored category from shallow enthusiasts who wish merely to dabble or hacks who crank out inferior work mostly for material gain. Motive is one of the most important factors in writing. You should therefore determine to write for the best reasons. If you desire only to get through an assignment or to satisfy a require-ment, chances are your themes will lack thoughtfulness and conviction. Though you are not a professional author, cultivate the self-image of a serious writer. Set up the right motives along with a wise system of proceeding, and you will be able to pro-gress rapidly. In some way not entirely analyzable, earnestness of purpose and true interest creep into all types of writing, even college themes. Conversely, casualness and lack of interest also become evident.

(3) The nature of revision

If you were a sculptor attempting to create in marble a Greek discus thrower, what would the public say if you presented it as complete after you had merely hacked out the vague outline and no more? In assuming that you have finished, you might pos-sibly confuse what you had in mind to create with the actual result, but your viewers would rightly call your work a blob.

Writers can be just as subjective as a misguided sculptor, just as mistaken in the way they view their own work. Good writers develop a means of looking at their writing that corresponds with the way others will see it, while at the same time retaining the plan and purpose they started with. Revising requires a shift of gears, a disciplined change of mind from creator to critic, from participant to spectator, from writer to reader, and then a shift back. When revising, get in the habit of imagining that you are two people—the writer *and* the stranger who will be reading what you write. The process of revising ought to involve an active dialogue between these imaginary persons, a series of questions and answers from the perspectives of both. When you see your work both as you would like it to be and as others will see it, and when you determine that the two are as close as possible, then your revising will be completed. Full revision is thus a far more extensive process than simply a check to correct typographical mistakes, misspellings, and other quickly handled matters. Do not deceive yourself into believing that you have thoroughly revised just because you have looked over a draft for glaring errors.

(4) The Reviser's Eye

Athletes training hard for a contest would not ask friends to do their push-ups for them. Neither should you depend on a roommate or friend to go over your draft and revise it for you. That would be like asking another to train for you, for revising is training toward the development of the *Reviser's Eye*. You may miss some things that need changing by doing your own work, but the act of revising is an essential step in the educational process. You are becoming dependent when you ask others to tell you what to change; you are making yourself stronger and more self-reliant as a writer when you find your own problems and correct them. The *Reviser's Eye* is the ability to see in your rough draft what yet needs to be done, the talent for spotting what is out of place, illogical, vague, or unconvincing. Nothing is more valuable to a writer, but it is developed only through the repeated act of revising.

(5) Proofreading

Never fail to give your paper a final check for errors. The fundamental reason for proofreading is seldom understood, and many writers do great harm to themselves by neglecting it. The greatest value a clean and correct manuscript has is based on what it represents to the reader, what impression such a manuscript conveys. It shows the reader that here is a careful writer who pays attention to detail. A final draft marred with careless errors bespeaks a sloppy writer (and by implication, perhaps, a fuzzy thinker). If, for example, a writer submits to a magazine an essay about trends in college enrollments, an essay that is riddled with the kinds of mistakes proofreading would have caught, the editor tends to question whether anything in the essay can be trusted. How can one so careless as to let errors get by in the manuscript be trusted in other areas?

(6) Meeting deadlines

Whether or not your instructor applies a penalty for late papers, you should allow nothing short of a dire emergency to prevent you from completing and submitting your work on time. You may sometimes feel that deadlines are arbitrary and artificial, but remember that disciplining yourself to meet a deadline can be as important in self-improvement as the writing of the paper itself. By establishing sensible priorities, using what time you do have wisely, and then meeting your responsibilities, you are learning how a mature writer works under pressure. Further-more, experienced and consistently good writers know that having definite deadlines neither destroys nor dilutes the creative impulse. When they do not have externally imposed quotas or deadlines, they frequently set them for themselves—to complete a certain number of words a day or to have a chapter or an essay completed in a week or so. Such a routine of deadlines forms a creative *rhythm* for them and actually enhances their productivity. You can make time work for you, or you can make it your greatest enemy. Even though you have not quite shaped a theme to your liking, turn it in when it is due. Then on the next assignment get an earlier start, and never allow yourself to lose track of the deadline.

(7) Profiting from criticism

The process of revising and the act of learning do not come to an end when you submit your theme. Sadly, many students pay little attention to anything on a returned paper but the grade. Most teachers take care to mark weaknesses on papers (see pp. xv–xviii), and many write comments in the margins and at the end. Their purpose in doing so is not merely to justify a grade but to offer constructive advice about future writing. The student who ignores these marks and comments and who misunderstands the motive behind them fails to take advantage of a valuable tool in learning. Others fail to profit from suggestions because of various problems in attitude. Above all, cultivate a positive attitude toward criticism. Arrogance and defensiveness often stand in the way of improvement. It is painful when someone makes a low appraisal of writing you are proud to have composed; it may even be infuriating to think that the reader has failed to see what you intended. Your first thought is to defend your work and to charge the critic with stupidity, unfairness, or pickiness. Occasionally you may be right, but these attitudes are self-defeating. Instead of considering your writing sacrosanct just because *you* wrote it, instead of declaring impatiently that you *meant* to do what you are being criticized for, instead of defensively disagreeing and taking a superior attitude, instead of questioning the standards of your critic, try very hard to understand the other point of view. Ask yourself if there is not some validity in the objections.

To profit most from criticism, allow at least one full day to intervene between the time you get a theme back and a conference you have about it with your instructor. During this period study diligently all markings and comments and make a concerted effort to understand the point of view of your reader. One of the greatest mistakes you can make is to rush into a conference to discuss a paper as soon as it has been returned to you. You may be disappointed and sometimes angered by the grade and therefore not as objective as you need to be; you have not had time to digest comments and criticisms; you have not formulated definite and constructive questions.

So *use* your teachers to the maximum. Squeeze from their every comment the last drop of help it will yield. Forget your ego and learn more and more about writing.

46a Choose a significant and interesting subject.

Correct grammar and mechanics, precise diction, figures of speech—as important as they are—do not create attractive materials for a reader. The writer must have something worthwhile to say. Often the best papers come from the imaginative use of experience.

Draw on your experience, memory, imagination, knowledge, interests, and study. Good subjects can come to mind at unexpected moments. You may think of one while your thoughts are wandering in class or while you are taking your clothes to the laundry. Never let a possible subject escape you. Reserve a page or two in your notebook for all the topics and titles which occur to you. Even the less promising possibilities may evolve into good subjects. When a theme must be written, it is better to have an excess of ideas than a blank sheet of paper staring at you from your desk. You can avoid false starts and lost time by examining your list of possibilities and settling on one good topic at the outset. (For suggestions about subjects for themes, see pages 249–254.)

46b Limit your topic.

Tailor your subject to the length of the assignment. Do not skim the surface of a broad topic, but select a limited part of it and develop that part fully through discussion, analysis, illustration, and detail.

A 250-word paper calls for a more limited treatment than a 500-word or a 1000-word paper; it may demand a different subject altogether. Generalized treatments of large subjects can be successful if they are handled with intelligence, breadth of perspective, and insight; many good editorials are written on just such topics. But the best themes deal with topics limited enough to allow room for plenty of explanation and detail.

For an extended discussion of additional ways of limiting subjects, see **48a.**

Suppose a student starts with the idea of writing a 500-word theme on humor. The evolution of this subject in the student's mind can be shown as follows:

Humor: Too broad . . .

The Nature of Humor: Still too broad . . .

A Specific Kind of Humor: Might have something here . . . think of a kind . . .

Sick Humor: Sounds unpleasant . . . unattractive topic equals unattractive theme?

Jokes and Jokers: Getting close, but still too broad . . .

Practical Jokers: Almost have it, but what about practical jokers?
The Serious Intent of Practical Jokers: That's it. A subject I'm interested in and can say something about.

Through association of ideas, this student arrived at what looks
like a workable subject.

Even after the topic is thus limited, however, you cannot
know that it is the right size until you have (1) considered its
subdivisions and (2) sometimes actually written the theme. A
subject which at first seems limited may open up into greater
complexity and promise to yield a paper far beyond the assigned
length. If so, you must turn to another subject—perhaps a still
more limited aspect of the first.

Or if the paper is already written, you may reduce the
length of it, usually by cutting out whole sections. But a theme
shortened in this way is often confused, jerky, or badly propor-
tioned because of omissions and condensations. A fresh start
with a new topic may cost a high price in lost time. It is much
better to write a theme of the proper length in the first place.

46c   Formulate a thesis.

The central idea of a paper can usually be expressed in a single
sentence. Sometimes this statement can be phrased early in the
planning process, sometimes not until you are near the actual
writing. In any event, it should be expressed early in the written
paper, often in the opening paragraph.

A good **thesis statement** is specific and concise. It brings
the subject into focus for the reader, suggests the scope of the
paper, and shows coherently the idea or ideas that the theme
will develop.

VAGUE AND STEREOTYPED
It is the purpose of this theme to discuss the serious intent of practical
  jokers.

VAGUE

Practical jokers have similar motivations.

MORE PURPOSEFUL

Practical jokers have four basic motivations: to obtain applause, to feel
reassurance, to experience power, and to vent hostility.

46d   Select an appropriate tone and be consistent.

Tone is the quality which reveals the writer's attitude toward
the subject matter. It may be serious or humorous, ironical or
straightforward, zealous or casual, brisk or nostalgic. As a general rule, a moderately serious tone is a good choice for most
subjects. Unless you are extremely skilled, you should not run
the risk of alienating your readers by treating a serious subject
humorously. Whatever tone you choose, be consistent. Incon-
sistency confuses a reader about the purpose of a paper.

The tone, on the other hand, need not be held unvaryingly
in one key. It may, for example, move reasonably from the
serious to a touch of humor, but it should not run from one
extreme to another in the same piece of writing.

Avoid flippancy and sarcasm.

46e   Organize carefully.

You should never set out to write a paper without some kind
of outline, even if it is only in your mind. A **scratch outline** is
the simplest kind. It is a list of points you want to make in any
form you wish. It is a quick way to order your thoughts and
remind you of that order when you are writing the paper. For
brief themes or those written during the class hour, a scratch
outline will usually suffice. You might use the following points
to start a scratch outline for a paper on "The Serious Intent of
Practical Jokers":

practical jokes—variety of
serious motivations
to get attention
to be reassured
to experience power
to vent hostility

Add further points (some of which you may not use in the paper) as thoughts occur to you at different times.

A **topic outline** is a formal and detailed structure to help you organize your materials. In making a topic outline, observe the following rules:

1. Number the main topics with Roman numerals, the first subheadings with capital letters, the next with Arabic numerals. If further subheadings are necessary, use a, b, c, and (1), (2), (3).

I. . . . .
   A. . . . .
      1. . . . .
         a. . . . .
            (1) . . . .
            (2) . . . .
         b. . . . .
      2. . . . .
   B. . . . .
II. . . . .

2. Use parallel grammatical structures.
3. Use topics, not sentences. Do not place periods after the topics. Punctuate as in the example that follows.
4. Check to see that your outline covers the subject completely.
5. Use specific topics and subheadings arranged in a logical, meaningful order. Each indented level of the outline represents a division of the preceding level and has smaller scope.

Avoid single subheadings. Roman numeral I calls for II; subheading A calls for B, and so forth.

NOT
I. Nature of and reasons for practical jokes
   A. Variety   *B needed*
II. Applause

The following is an example of a topic outline with a title, a thesis statement, and a series of orderly and carefully developed topics.

The Serious Intent of Practical Jokers

Thesis Statement: Practical jokers share four basic motivations: to obtain applause, to feel reassurance, to experience power, and to vent hostility.

  I. Nature of and reasons for practical jokes
    A. Variety
    B. Motivations
 II. Applause
    A. For acting
    B. For cleverness
III. Reassurance
    A. Victim ridiculous
    B. Joker superior
IV. Power
    A. Over joke
    B. Over victim
 V. Hostility
    A. Harmless jokes, normal hostility
    B. Harmful jokes, abnormal hostility
VI. Practical jokes and human nature

The **sentence outline** represents a more extensive kind of preparation for writing a theme. More thinking goes into a sentence outline than into a scratch or topic outline, but the additional effort offers a tight control over your writing and makes it harder to wander from the subject. As a rule, the more time you spend on your outline, the less time you will need to do the actual writing. The sentence outline follows the same conventions as the topic outline except that the entries are expressed in complete sentences. Place periods after sentences in a sentence outline.

The Serious Intent of Practical Jokers

Thesis Statement: Practical jokers share four basic motivations: to obtain applause, to feel reassurance, to experience power, and to vent hostility.

I. The nature of practical jokes differs widely, but the motivations of practical jokers are common to all.
   A. Practical jokes vary from the humorous and harmless to the cruel.
   B. Practical jokers share four basic motivations: to obtain applause, to feel reassurance, to experience power, and to vent hostility.
II. Practical jokers, like most people, crave applause.
   A. They are actors expecting approval of an audience for playing a part well.
   B. They also expect approval for their cleverness.
III. Closely related to the desire for applause is the human need for reassurance.
   A. The practical joker always makes the victim look more or less ridiculous.
   B. By making the victim look silly, the practical joker feels superior.
IV. Practical jokes enable the performer to feel a sense of power.
   A. The joker controls the length and pace of the joke.
   B. The joker controls the victim like a puppeteer.
V. The practical joker is venting feelings of hostility toward others.
   A. Even harmless jokes reflect some degree of hostility in all of us.
   B. Cruel jokes show an abnormal degree of hostility in the performer.
VI. To understand the motivations of practical jokers is to see basic aspects of human nature.

46f   Use examples to illustrate generalizations.

Meaningful generalizations frequently rest on illustrations. An abstract truth may become evident only after concrete examples

Model theme

The Serious Intent of Practical Jokers

THESIS STATEMENT: Practical jokers share four basic motivations: to obtain applause, to feel reassurance, to experience power, and to vent hostility.

(Your assignment may not require that you place a thesis statement after the title.)

Practical jokes vary as much as the people who indulge in them. Everyone has probably witnessed numerous harmless and often funny pranks like those played on April Fool's Day. Other forms of practical joking, such as those that once characterized college hazing, are far from humorous. In fact, they can be sadistically cruel. Even though differences are evident in their tricks, practical jokers share four basic motivations: to obtain applause, to feel reassurance, to experience power, and to vent hostility. The intensity of these motivations determines whether the joke is pleasant to all (including the victim) or only to the practical joker.

In one way or another most people strive for applause. Practical jokers are in a sense actors. They desire approval for playing a part well. An executive who puts a big plastic spider in the chair of a typist and then with a straight face asks what that is beside her loses much of his fun if no one else is present in the office to see her reaction. If onlookers are present, they may laugh with him and thus show their mark of appreciation for his acting. He feels that they are also saying to him with their laughter that he is clever and intelligent for thinking up such a prank, pulling it off so well, and providing amusement and relief from routine.

Closely related to the desire for applause is the human need for reassurance. A practical joke is a reflection of this craving in all of us to make ourselves look better at someone else's expense. In varying degrees the victim of a practical joke is always made to look ridiculous. He may be tricked into talking into a mailbox where there is a hidden microphone, or he may slip on a banana peel planted in his path, or open a door with dirty grease on the knob. By making his victim look silly, the practical joker feels a momentary flash of superiority. He senses that he is better than his victim because he is rational and composed whereas the victim is off his guard.

Although one may not think of a practical joker as a person who wants power, he nevertheless performs his jokes partly because they enable him to experience the thrill of control. He feels power by controlling the length and pace of the joke itself. He can hurry it to its conclusion, or he can prolong it and add refinements as he chooses. In a small way, his is the power of creativity. He also experiences power over his victim because he is like a puppeteer pulling the strings. He is in command; the other person merely responds. He has the advantage because he knows what is going on; his victim is in the dark.

Psychologists say that we manifest hostility toward others in dozens of ways that we do not realize. The practical joke offers one of these ways to vent feelings of hostility and aggression in a fashion that is socially acceptable provided the joke is not destructive. The degree of hostility in the practical joker can often be measured by the nature of his prank. If he sends a novice mechanic out for a left-handed wrench, he is probably reflecting the mild hostility that most people feel toward the greenhorns of the world. If, on the other hand, he arranges for the novice to slip on a banana peel on the way and to be hit with a flower pot, his feelings of hostility are probably beyond those of normalcy.

To understand the motivations of practical jokers is to understand something fundamental about human nature. The reasons behind practical jokes may not appear attractive, but they are not in themselves abnormal. Whether we actually perform the jokes or not, we are all practical jokers because in varying degrees we all share the four basic motivations.

have been given. (See **45c**.) A string of unillustrated generalizations can make a theme dull and unconvincing. Examples give your paper clarity and color.

GENERALIZATION

In varying degrees the victim of a practical joke is always made to look ridiculous.

EXAMPLES

He may be tricked into talking into a mailbox where there is a hidden microphone, or he may slip on a banana peel planted in his path, or he may find himself trying to open a door with grease stuck to the knob.

In many ways, papers are developed with the same methods that paragraphs are except that the scale is much more extensive. For further suggestions, see pages 227–230.

46g Revise your themes. Use the following checklist of essentials.

Before submitting any paper, read over the final draft two or three times, at least once aloud for sound. (For methods of revising, see pages 233–235.) If possible, allow some time between readings. Watch especially for misspellings, typographical errors, faulty punctuation, and omissions made in revising or copying.

Revising papers after they have been read and marked by your instructor is always helpful and often required.

Checklist

Keep these points in mind as you begin your paper, and check them again when you finish.

Title

The title should accurately suggest the contents of the paper.

It should attract interest without being excessively novel or clever.

It should not be too long.

NOTE Do not underline the title of your own paper (to represent italics), and do not put quotation marks around it.

Introduction

The introduction should be independent of the title. No pronoun or noun in the opening sentence should depend for meaning on the title.

It should catch the reader's attention.

It should properly establish the tone of the paper as serious, humorous, ironic, or otherwise.

It should include a thesis statement which declares the subject and the purpose directly but at the same time avoids worn patterns like "It is the purpose of this paper to . . . ."

Body

The materials should develop the thesis statement.

The materials should be arranged in logical sequence.

Strong topic sentences (see **45a**) should clearly indicate the direction in which the paper is moving and the relevance of the paragraphs to the thesis statement.

Technical terms should be explained.

Paragraphs should not be choppy.

Enough space should be devoted to main ideas. Minor ideas should be subordinated.

Concrete details should be used appropriately. Insignificant details should be omitted.

Transitions

The connections between sentences and those between paragraphs should be shown by good linking words and repetition of parallel phrases and structures. (See **45f**.)

Conclusion

The conclusion should usually contain a final statement of the underlying idea, an overview of what the paper has demonstrated.

The conclusion may require a separate paragraph; but if the paper has reached significant conclusions all along, such a paragraph is not necessary for its own sake.

The conclusion should not merely restate the introduction.

Proofreading

Allow some time, if possible at least one day, between the last draft of the paper and the final finished copy. Then you can examine the paper objectively for wordiness, repetition, incorrect diction, misspellings, faulty punctuation, choppy sentences, vague sentences, lack of transitions, and careless errors.

Subjects for papers

Keep a notebook of items which you think may be useful to you as possible subjects and materials for papers. Some suggested subjects follow.

Fewer Years for College	The Center City
Old Photographs	Bad Teaching
Fair Journalism	Abortion
Return to the Country	Television Commercials
Political Cartoons	An Ice Storm
The New Music	Women's Equal Rights
Divorce	The Average Man
The New Freedoms	Working in a Political Campaign
Blackness	Good Fences and Good Friends
Patterns of Humor	Educating the Parent
City Folklore	Camping Out

Walking	Parks
A Deserted House	Censorship
Crime	The Subway at Night
Exploring	Credit
The Scientific Attitude	Welfare
The Emergency Ward	Acting in a Play
Trip Down River	A Description of a Painting

Axioms to suggest subjects for papers

Axioms are old ways of stating beliefs. Through the years they may have become trite. In themselves, they are not good subjects for papers. But they may lead you to good topics that are related to what they say. When appropriate for the assignment, look over the list and see if any one suggests a topic for a paper. Also, you may be given a chance to think of another axiom and to develop a theme subject from it.

1. All work and no play makes Jack a dull boy—or Jill a dull girl.
2. A bird in the hand is worth two in the bush.
3. A rolling stone gathers no moss.
4. A stitch in time saves nine.
5. Tomorrow never comes.
6. Eat, drink, and be merry, for tomorrow we die.
7. You cannot tell a book by its cover.
8. Old soldiers never die; they just fade away.
9. Cast bread on the waters, and it will surely return to you.
10. The early bird gets the worm.
11. The grass is always greener on the other side.
12. Life is not a bed of roses.
13. Rain falls on the just and the unjust alike.
14. A thing of beauty is a joy forever.
15. Beauty is but skin deep.
16. Laugh and the world laughs with you; weep, and you weep alone.

17. Birds of a feather flock together.
18. A dog is a person's best friend.
19. All people are created equal.
20. Pride goes before the fall.

Quotations to suggest subjects for themes

The following quotations may help you develop subjects for themes. Support, refute, exemplify, or use these quotations in any appropriate way. You may think of a subject only remotely related to what the author says.

> The older generation had certainly pretty well ruined this world before passing it on to us. They give us this Thing, knocked to pieces, leaky, red-hot, threatening to blow up; and then they are surprised that we don't accept it with the same attitude of pretty, decorous enthusiasm with which they received it. . . .
>
> JOHN F. CARTER, JR.,
> "The Overnight Realists"

> For the 15 per cent of adolescents who learn well in schools and are interested in subjects that are essentially academic . . . catch-all high schools are wasteful.
>
> PAUL GOODMAN,
> "Freedom and Learning:
> The Need for Choice"

> Never have the burdens of wealth been greater than they are today, and never have its rewards been slimmer.
>
> JEAN PAUL GETTY,
> "The World Is Mean to Millionaires"

> For generations we have tried to make the world a better place by providing more and more schooling, but so far the endeavor has failed.
>
> IVAN ILLICH,
> "The Alternative to Schooling"

The outstanding objection to the modern dance is that it is immodest and lacking in grace. It is not based on the natural and harmless instinct for rhythm, but on a craving for abnormal excitement.

THE HOBART COLLEGE *Herald*

For there is a cloud on my horizon. A small dark cloud no bigger than my hand. Its name is Progress.

EDWARD ABBEY,
Desert Solitaire

The humor in *Peanuts,* then, has a dimension apart from the obvious gag level. This is because the characters in *Peanuts* are reflections of ourselves, and we are funnier than any make-believe character could possibly be.

MARTIN JEZER,
"Quo Peanuts?"

Women's emancipation has in various ways made marriage more difficult.

BERTRAND RUSSELL,
Marriage and Morals

Problems are never solved by returning to a stage which one has already outgrown.

ERICH FROMM,
"Our Way of Life Makes Us Miserable"

We are not so weak and timorous as to need to be free of fear; we need only use our capacity to not be afraid of it and so relegate fear to its proper perspective.

WILLIAM FAULKNER,
"Faith or Fear"

Religion will not regain its old power until it can face change in the same spirit as does science.

ALFRED NORTH WHITEHEAD,
"Religion and Science"

No great and enduring volume can ever be written on the flea, though many there be who have tried it.

HERMAN MELVILLE,
Moby-Dick

Whoso would be a man, must be a nonconformist.

RALPH WALDO EMERSON,
"Self-Reliance"

Stay, stay at home, my heart and rest; / Homekeeping hearts are happiest.

HENRY WADSWORTH LONGFELLOW

A prophet is not without honor, save in his own country, and in his own house.

MATTHEW 13:57

Home life as we understand it is no more natural to us than a cage is natural to a cockatoo.

GEORGE BERNARD SHAW,
Getting Married

To some extent a citizen of any country will feel that the tourist's view of his homeland is a false one.

MARY MCCARTHY,
"America the Beautiful"

Labor disgraces no man; unfortunately you occasionally find men disgrace labor.

ULYSSES S. GRANT,
Speech at Birmingham, England

The mass of men lead lives of quiet desperation. What is called resignation is confirmed desperation.

HENRY DAVID THOREAU,
Walden

Our life is frittered away by detail.

THOREAU,
Walden

The preservation of the English language in its purity throughout the United States is an object deserving the attention of every American who is a friend to the literature and science of his country.

JOHN PICKERING,
A Vocabulary

The process of composition   253

Ah, one doesn't give up one's country any more than one gives up one's grandmother.

HENRY JAMES,
The Portrait of a Lady

The mobs of great cities add just so much to the support of pure government, as sores do to the strength of the human body.

THOMAS JEFFERSON,
Notes on Virginia

There is no "best" system of education, and the only really bad kind is one which is uniform and standardized.

LYNN WHITE, JR.,
Educating Our Daughters

47   Writing about literature

Poetry, fiction, and drama may be read for enjoyment, or they may be read and reread, studied, and then discussed. Casual readers frequently notice little more than what happens. Though nothing is wrong with this kind of quick and pleasurable reading, a deeper and more careful probing brings a different kind of satisfaction. In writing about literature, you should express your own reactions in a way that does justice to the richness and the complexity of the work. A good paper states the writer's opinions; it convinces others by solid evidence and proof cited or quoted from the work.

A poem, novel, short story, or play does not mean anything a reader wishes it to. Write about a topic which the story provides. Do not use the literary work as a diving board from which to plunge into subjects that are actually remote from it.

This short section is not intended to provide you with the basis for an entire course in literature or for a major in English. Instead, it is merely an introduction to the writing of essays on literary subjects.

47a   Choose a literary work which interests you. Write about the feature of the work which interests you most.

You can never hope to write about all you see in a work of litera-ture. Choose the best topic you can find. What is dull to you is almost certain to be dull also to your reader. If your teacher permits you to select your own topic, discard anything which does not have for you some degree of intellectual and perhaps even emotional excitement. Do not give up too soon in your search for a topic, however; for what seems uninteresting at first may later develop into a promising subject.

Literary works have parts: paragraphs, stanzas, divisions with Roman or Arabic numerals, chapters, and so forth. One good way to find a subject is to write down what each part does. Then see how the parts fit together. This process may provide you with a good subject.

Select a subject appropriate to the length of the assignment. A narrow topic can be important. A short paper on one crucial paragraph in fiction, the setting (or place of one scene), or one speech may provide perspective on an entire work.

Between the first reading of the work and the writing of your paper, study in detail every item which relates to your topic. Take notes. Do not read a work and then think that you can remember it well enough to write your paper from your memory and second looks at the printed page. As you read further into the work, it is natural to forget ideas that occurred to you at first; so it is important to write them down as you go along. Many first impressions will be proved wrong by what happens later in the work. Discard these and save the good ones.

Ideas for a paper should percolate before you write. It is dif-ficult to produce an instant topic that is good. Keep the literary work on your mind even while you are doing other things be-sides sitting at your desk to write. Think about it in idle mo-ments. The best idea you have for a paper may come while you are engaged in a trivial task, or when you are not much aware that you are thinking about your paper at all. The actual composing of the paper will be much simpler and the results much better if you think through a subject and plan well before you start your first draft. The more thinking ahead of time, the more thoughtful the essay.

47b Give the paper a precise title.

Do not search for a fancy title at the expense of meaning. Authors of literary works often use figurative titles like *Death in the Afternoon* and *The Grapes of Wrath,* but you would be wise to designate your subject more literally.

Vague and general titles of literary papers may be puzzling. As a title, "A Criticism of *Gravity's Rainbow*" provides no information about the subject except the name of the novel. "The Ending of *Gravity's Rainbow*" stands a better chance of revealing what the paper is about.

Stick to the topic named in the title. The topic sentence of every paragraph should point back to the introduction and to the title. Every paragraph should contribute to what you wish to say about the subject named at the beginning.

47c Give the subject an appropriate kind of development.

Announce the topic, and then explain what your methods will be. If you use secondary sources (depending perhaps on the assignment), show how your ideas are different from previous views (see **48c**). Describe the work or the situation in the work briefly and generally (see **47d, 48a**). Always make it clear to your reader what you are doing. The distinctions between the statement of your thesis, summary of what the author said, paraphrase, proof, analysis, and your critical conclusions should be self-evident. A good paper announces what it will prove, proves it, and then shows the significance of what has been proved.

Writings about literature fall into several categories. Explanations of a few of the more significant ones follow.

An interpretation

Most papers result from a close study of the work. An interpretative paper identifies literary methods and ideas. Through analyzing the techniques, the writer presents specific evidence to support the interpretation.

Distinguish carefully between the thinking of a character and that of the author. Unless an author speaks in his or her own person, you can only deduce from the work as a whole what the author thinks. Many works of literature depict a character whose whole way of life and thinking is the opposite of the author's views. To confuse the character with the author in this kind of work is to make a crucial mistake. Sometimes it is clear what authors think about their characters, but not always.

A review

A good review tells precisely what a work attempts to do and what methods it follows in carrying out its aim. If length permits, the review may include a brief outline of the contents. Such information should not be presented for its own sake, however, but as part of the attempt to give a fair and exact view of what the work accomplishes.

A character analysis

It is easy to seize on a character sketch as a kind of paper to write. Actually it is very difficult to compose a truly good character analysis. This kind of paper lends itself to superficiality. A paper accomplishes little by merely summarizing a character's traits and recounting actions without considering motivations, development, and interrelationships with other characters. Describe the method of characterization—*how* the author develops the character. Distinguish between *character* and *characterization.* Do not characterize; the author of the work is the one who characterizes.

Setting
Often the time and place in which a work is set suggest something significant about the way people interact with their environments. If you write about setting, show how it is more than just a backdrop for the action.

Technical analysis
The analysis of technical elements in literature—imagery, symbolism, point of view, structure, prosody, genre, and so on—requires special study of the technical term or concept as well as of the literary work itself. You might begin by consulting a good basic reference book like C. Hugh Holman's *A Handbook to Literature.*

Combined approaches
Many papers combine different kinds of approaches. A thoughtful paper on imagery, for example, does more than merely point out the images, or even the kinds of images, in the work under study. Rather, it uses the imagery to interpret, analyze, or clarify something else also—theme, structure, characterization, mood, relationship, recurrent patterns, and so on.

47d Do not summarize and paraphrase excessively.

Tell only as much of the story as is necessary to clarify your interpretations and prove your arguments. Summarizing a plot involves little or no thinking; your thoughts about literature are the crucial measure of your work. When you paraphrase, make it clear that it is the author's thinking which you are reporting, not your own.

47e Think for yourself.

The excellence of your paper will depend finally on the significance of your thinking. Do not merely report something you learned *from* the literature; write something you learned *about* it.

Spend little or no time telling your reader that it is your belief; it is understood that opinions expressed are your own. Your readers will determine for themselves the importance of your paper according to your accuracy, your evidence, your methods, and your thinking.

Wild and unsupported thoughts have a more negative effect on readers than pure summary or paraphrase.

47f Write about the literature, not about yourself or your reading process.

Your reader will not be interested in the difference between what you saw in a work on a first reading as opposed to your insight after a second reading. Omit such irrelevant information. Only your final and considered views should be presented in your paper.

Generally avoid the first person pronouns *I* and *we*. Excessive concern with your own methods and the development of your own thoughts detracts from what you say about literature and causes irrelevance and wordiness.

47g Provide sufficient evidence to support your ideas.

Strike a proper balance between generalizations and detailed support of your points. Do not write abstractly or too generally. Make a point; develop its particularities and ramifications;

quote the work; and show how your point is supported by the quotation. Do not use long quotations without comment and analysis. Show your readers the proof. Do not force them to find it for themselves.

Papers, or even paragraphs, usually should not begin with a quotation. Readers prefer to see what you have to say first. Then you can work in quotations to support your argument. As a rule, do not conclude paragraphs with quotations either. Do not assume that readers will recognize evidence unless you identify it.

47h Organize and develop the paper according to significant ideas.

Do not automatically organize your paper by following the sequence of the story or the poem. Often the result of this kind of order may be poor topic sentences, summary rather than thought, mechanical organization, and repetitive transitional phrases.

Usually it is better to break up your overall argument or thesis into several aspects and to move from the discussion of one of these topics on to the other.

Do not begin a sequence of paragraphs with such mechanical expressions as "In the first stanza . . ." and "In the second stanza. . . ."

47i Do not moralize.

Good criticism is not preachy. Do not use your paper as a platform from which to moralize on the rights and wrongs of the world. A literary paper that is otherwise excellent can be spoiled by an attempt to teach a moral lesson.

It is especially ineffective to begin with your own philosophical view of the world and then to discuss the work as an illustration of views you already had before you read it.

47j Acknowledge your sources.

If you study other critics' writings, you need to state your contribution, to define the difference between what they have written and what you think. Avoid beginning papers or paragraphs with the names of critics and their views before you present your own.

Develop your own thesis. Stress your views, not those of others. Use sources to show that other critics have interpreted correctly, to correct errors in some criticism that is otherwise excellent, to show that a critic is right but that something needs to be added, or to show that no one has previously written on your subject at all.

If no critic has written about the work or the point you are making, that is no problem (unless your instructor requires that you have a number of sources). On the other hand, it is a serious error to state that nothing has been done on your subject when it has. Be thorough in your investigation.

For bibliographies of writings about literature, see **48b.** For information about plagiarism and documentation, see **48f** and **48g.**

Some hints about reading a work and planning to write a paper

Let your subject grow out of your reading of the work and your questions about it. Do not begin with preconceived ideas about what you will write on. You may discover that the subject you had hoped to write about is not appropriate. If you plan to discuss setting, for example, a close reading of the work may show that setting is not important.

Preparing to write a paper—an example

Read the following poem.

My Papa's Waltz

The whiskey on your breath
Could make a small boy dizzy;
But I hung on like death:
Such waltzing was not easy.

We romped until the pans
Slid from the kitchen shelf;
My mother's countenance
Could not unfrown itself.

The hand that held my wrist
Was battered on one knuckle;
At every step you missed
My right ear scraped a buckle.

You beat time on my head
With a palm caked hard by dirt,
Then waltzed me off to bed
Still clinging to your shirt.

　　　　　　　THEODORE ROETHKE

　　Study the following questions. Write down the answers to the ones that seem most significant to you.

1. Who is the speaker of the poem? Is it the poet? A boy?
2. Why did the poet choose this speaker?
3. Considering the great number of words which may be used to name a father, what is the effect of calling him "Papa"?
4. Why does the poet refer to the movements around the room as a waltz?
5. That is, what kind of dance is a waltz, and how is it appropriate to the poem? Is it a happy dance? Graceful?
6. To whom is the poem addressed? Why?
7. What does "like death" mean in the poem?
8. Is the boy literally afraid, or is he exaggerating?
9. How long after the waltzing is the boy remembering the dance with his papa?
10. What does the falling of the pans show about the manner of dancing?
11. What is the reaction of the mother?
12. Later the boy or the man he becomes remembers that his father held him by the wrist. How does he probably hold him? Why? Is there a difference between his intentions in the holding and his manner of holding?
13. The speaker remembers that one of the father's knuckles was battered. What does that suggest? A fight? A fall?
14. Why does the father miss steps in the dance, and why does the boy remember his missing them?
15. What does *beat time* mean?
16. What is the significance of the father's dirty hands?
17. What is the point to the boy's right ear scraping a belt buckle?
18. What emotions are attached to the father's waltzing the boy off to bed?
19. What is the attitude of the speaker toward the drunken father?
20. What is the character or nature of the father, the boy, the situation, the emotions of the two, the memories of the boy when he is older? To sum up, what is the poem about?

Some final hints

Read the work once carefully.

Decide on a subject generally.

Narrow the subject as much as you can before a second reading.

Ask yourself questions as you read the work the second time, the third, and so on.

Write down the answers to your questions.

Arrange the answers by topics.

Decide on a final approach, topic, title, and thesis.

Discard the erroneous answers to your questions.

Discard the irrelevant points. Choose the one you wish to discuss.

Select the best topics.

Put them in logical order.

Rearrange them as you carry out the creative process of thinking through the subject and writing the paper.

Revise as many times as necessary.

Do not display or emphasize technical terms, which may sometimes be as distracting as they are helpful. Your reader will not be impressed by attempts to show off. That is no substitute for straight thinking and clear writing.

Be sure to name the work which you write about and the author. Do not misspell the author's name—as often happens. Ernest Hemingway, for example, spelled his last name with only one *m*.

In the body of your paper do not rely on your title for information. Do not assume that your reader knows anything about the work or the author except what you tell him or her.

▶ Exercise 8

From your answers to the questions above, write a paper about "My Papa's Waltz."

▶ Exercise 9

Find another poem or short story and compose twenty significant questions about it.

48 Writing the research paper

The research paper is based on a systematic investigation of materials found in a library. This section provides instructions about the way to assemble materials from sources and to document them with footnotes.

48a Choose a subject which interests you. Limit it to manageable size.

Your subject should allow you to use the library extensively, think for yourself, and come to a significant conclusion which will be of interest to your reader. Above all, it should engage your attention so that you enjoy reading and thinking about it and writing it up for others.

Begin by choosing a general subject area.

If you have long had a particular interest, it may be your starting point: photography, perhaps; or literature; or painting; or architecture. If nothing comes to mind, start with a list of broad areas, such as the following, decide on one you like, and then focus on a limited aspect of it.

art	government	industry
literature	sociology	science
philosophy	anthropology	archaeology
history	economics	medicine
religion	geography	ecology

At this stage you are trying to relate your investigation to an active interest.

Limit your subject adequately.

Suppose you have chosen photography as your general area. After a little thought and reading and a look at the card catalog of the library, you will see that this is too broad a topic for one paper. So you may begin by narrowing it to color photography, or aerial photography, or the history of photography. Any of these topics could be further restricted: for example, "The Effect of Color Photography on Advertising," or "Aerial Photography in World War II," or "Matthew Brady: Photographer of the Civil War." Still further limitation may be desirable, depending on the length of your paper and the resources of your library.

If you are starting with a broad area, such as anthropology, history, science, or literature, you may move gradually toward your final subject in a process like the following:

Anthropology—tribal societies—a tribal people still surviving—American Indians—the Navajo—the lore of the Navajo—Navajo songs.
Science—a study of science in some historical period—biology—evolution—evolution before Darwin—reactions to evolution in popular periodicals before Darwin.
Art—popular art—cartoons—American cartoonists—James Thurber's drawings.

In practice, narrowing down from a general to a specific subject is seldom smooth and orderly. Glean ideas for limiting a broad area by skimming an article in an encyclopedia or the subject headings in the card catalog. You may even be well into your preliminary research (see **48b**) before you arrive at the final topic.

As you read and work, consider whether you are trying to cover too much ground or whether, at the other extreme, you are too narrowly confined. If you are not satisfied with your subject after you get into your preliminary reading, try with your instructor's help to work out an acceptable modification of it instead of changing your topic completely.

Avoid inappropriate subjects.

Beware of subjects highly technical, learned, or specialized. Only a specialist can handle modern techniques in genetic research or experimental psychology. Avoid topics that do not lead to a wide range of source materials. If you find that you are using one or two sources exclusively, the fault may be with your method—or with your topic. For example, a process topic (how to do something) does not lend itself to library investigation. Instead of writing on "How to Ski," a student might harness an interest in skiing to a study of the effect of skiing on some industry or region in the United States.

48b Become acquainted with the reference tools of the library and use them to compile a working bibliography.

Certain guides to knowledge are indispensable to library investigation. From them you can compile a **working bibliography,** a list of publications which contain material on your subject and which you plan to read. The items on this list should have only the author's name, the title, and the information you need in order to find the source in the library.

The basic tool for finding books in the library is the **card catalog.** Books are listed alphabetically by author and title with helpful subject headings, subheadings, and cross-references which will lead you to new aspects of your topics. Reproduced on pages 268–269, 270 are four typical catalog cards—actually four copies of the same Library of Congress card filed for four different uses. Notice the typed title and subject headings.

The card catalog leads you to the books in your library. The

Subject Card
Subject (usually in red)

Library of Congress
call number ————→

Author ————————→
Title of book ————→

Pages and technical ——→
data

Subject headings under which ————→
this book is listed

Publication information

Dewey decimal
call number

PS3539   COMEDY
H94Z9

   Tobias, Richard Clark, 1925–
      The art of James Thurber [by] Richard C. Tobias.
   Athens, Ohio University Press [1970, ᶜ1969]

   196 p. 24 cm. 7.50

   Bibliography: p. 186–189.

        1. Thurber, James, 1894–1961. 2. Comedy. I. Title

   PS3539.H94Z9 1970   818′.5′209   68–20938
   SBN 8214–0058–4   MARO

   Library of Congress   (⁷)

Another Subject Card

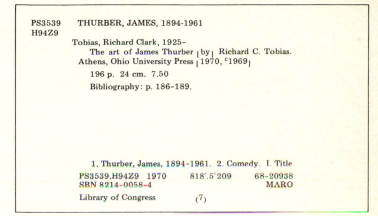

```
PS3539      THURBER, JAMES, 1894-1961
H94Z9
            Tobias, Richard Clark, 1925-
                The art of James Thurber ⌐by⌐ Richard C. Tobias.
            Athens, Ohio University Press ⌐1970, ᶜ1969⌐

                196 p.  24 cm.  7.50

                Bibliography: p. 186-189.




            1. Thurber, James, 1894-1961.  2. Comedy.  I. Title

            PS3539.H94Z9  1970        818'.5'209      68-20938
            SBN 8214-0058-4                            MARO

            Library of Congress            (⁷)
```

periodicals are indexed in special reference books, which list articles by author, title, and subject. The following periodical indexes are the most useful.

Periodical indexes

Readers' Guide to Periodical Literature, 1900– .
> An index to the most widely circulated American periodicals.

Nineteenth Century Readers' Guide to Periodical Literature, 1890–1899.
> Author and subject index to some fifty English language general periodicals of the last decade of the nineteenth century.

Poole's Index to Periodical Literature, 1802–1906.
> An index by subject to the leading British and American periodicals of the nineteenth century.

Humanities Index, 1974– .

Author Card

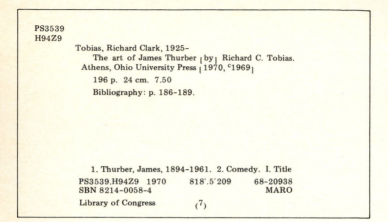

PS3539
H94Z9

    Tobias, Richard Clark, 1925–
        The art of James Thurber ₍by₎ Richard C. Tobias.
    Athens, Ohio University Press ₍1970, ᶜ1969₎

        196 p. 24 cm. 7.50

        Bibliography: p. 186–189.

        1. Thurber, James, 1894–1961. 2. Comedy. I. Title
        PS3539.H94Z9 1970   818′.5′209   68–20938
        SBN 8214-0058-4   MARO
        Library of Congress   (⁷)

Title Card

PS3539   The art of James Thurber
H94Z9

    Tobias, Richard Clark, 1925–
        The art of James Thurber ₍by₎ Richard C. Tobias.
    Athens, Ohio University Press ₍1970, ᶜ1969₎

        196 p. 24 cm. 7.50

        Bibliography: p. 186–189.

        1. Thurber, James, 1894–1961. 2. Comedy. I. Title
        PS3539.H94Z9 1970   818′.5′209   68–20938
        SBN 8214-0058-4   MARO
        Library of Congress   (⁷)

Social Sciences Index, 1974– . Preceded by *Social Sciences and Humanities Index.*

Social Sciences and Humanities Index, 1965–1974. Formerly *International Index,* 1907–1965.

Author and subject index to a selection of scholarly journals.

British Humanities Index, 1962– .

Supersedes in part *Subject Index to Periodicals,* 1915–1922, 1926–1961.

Subject index to British periodicals.

Applied Science and Technology Index, 1958– .

Cumulative subject index to a selection of English and American periodicals in such fields as aeronautics, automation, chemistry, electricity, engineering, physics.

Art Index, 1929– .

"Cumulative Author and Subject Index to a Selected List of Fine Arts Periodicals."

Biography Index, 1946– .

"Cumulative Index to Biographical Material in Books and Magazines."

Biological and Agricultural Index, 1964– .

Continues *Agricultural Index,* 1919–1964. "Cumulative Subject Index to Periodicals in the Fields of Biology, Agriculture, and Related Sciences."

Book Review Digest, 1905– .

Index to book reviews. Includes excerpts from the reviews.

Book Review Index, 1965– .

Business Periodicals Index, 1958– .

Cumulative subject index to periodicals in all fields of business and industry.

Current Index to Journals in Education, 1969– .

Covers "the core periodical literature in the field of education" and "peripheral literature relating to the field of education."

Education Index, 1929– .

"Cumulative Subject Index to a Selected List of Educational Periodicals, Proceedings, and Yearbooks."

General Science Index, 1978– .
   Science literature for the nonspecialist.
Industrial Arts Index, 1913–1957.
      In 1958 divided into the *Applied Science and Technology Index* and *Business Periodicals Index.* "Subject Index to a Selected List of Engineering, Trade and Business Periodicals."
Music Index, 1949– .
      Index by author and subject to a comprehensive list of music periodicals published throughout the world.
New York Times Index, 1851– .
      "Master-Key to the News since 1851."
Public Affairs Information Service. Bulletin, 1915– .
      Subject index to periodicals and government publications chiefly in the social sciences.

   Suppose you are writing on the drawings of James Thurber. Looking under *Thurber, James* in the *Humanities Index,* Volume Two, April 1975 to March 1976, you find the following entry:

THURBER, James
James Thurber: artist in humor. L.
Hasley. South Atlan Q 73:504–15 Aut '74

Subject heading
Title of article
Author of article
Abbreviation of the name of the
      periodical in which the article
      appears. Learn the complete
      name by checking inside the
      front cover of the periodical
      index.
Volume number
Pages
Date

With this information, you should be able to find the article if the periodical is in your library. Of course, you will be unable to read through all the articles written about a broad subject. But you will be able to exclude some merely by studying their titles in the periodical indexes.

Besides using the card catalog and the periodical indexes, you will need to know about several **general reference aids.** Many of these will give you bibliographical listings as well as surveys of your subject.

General reference aids

Articles on American Literature, 1900–1950; 1950–1967; 1968–1975.

Cambridge Histories: Ancient, 12 vols., rev. ed. in progress; Medieval, 8 vols.; Modern, 13 vols.; *New Cambridge Modern History,* 14 vols.

Cambridge Bibliography of English Literature, 1941–1957. 5 vols.; *New Cambridge Bibliography of English Literature,* 1969–1977. 5 vols.

Collier's Encyclopedia.

Columbia Lippincott Gazetteer of the World, 1962.

Contemporary Authors, 1962– .

Current Biography, 1940– . "Who's News and Why."

Dictionary of American Biography, 1928–1937. 20 vols. Supplements 1–6, 1944–1980.

Dictionary of American History, rev. ed., 1976–1978. 8 vols.

Dictionary of National Biography, 1885–1901. 22 vols. main work and 1st supplement; supplements 2–7, 1912–1971.

Encyclopedia Americana. Supplemented by the *Americana Annual,* 1923– .

Encyclopaedia Judaica, 1972. 16 vols.

Encyclopedia of Philosophy, 1967. 8 vols.

Encyclopaedia of Religion and Ethics, 1908–1927. 13 vols.

Encyclopedia of World Art, 1959–1968. 15 vols.

Encyclopedia of World History, 5th ed., 1972.

Essay and General Literature Index, 1900– . ."An Index to . . . Volumes of Collections of Essays and Miscellaneous Works."

Facts on File; a Weekly World News Digest . . . , 1940– .

Information Please Almanac, 1947– .

International Encyclopedia of the Social Sciences, 1968. 17 vols. *Biographical Supplement,* 1979.

Literary History of the United States: History, 1974. *Bibliography and Bibliography Supplement I,* 1963; *Bibliography Supplement II,* 1972.

MLA International Bibliography of Books and Articles on the Modern Languages and Literatures, 1919– .

McGraw-Hill Encyclopedia of Science and Technology, 3rd ed., 1971. 15 vols. Supplemented by *McGraw-Hill Yearbook of Science and Technology.*

McGraw-Hill Encyclopedia of World Drama, 1972. 4 vols.

The Mythology of All Races, 1916–1932. 13 vols.

New Catholic Encyclopedia, 1967–1979. 17 vols.

New Century Cyclopedia of Names, 1954. 3 vols.

New Encyclopaedia Britannica. Supplemented by *Britannica Book of the Year,* 1938– .

New Grove Dictionary of Music and Musicians, 1980. 20 vols.

Oxford Classical Dictionary, 2d ed., 1970.

Oxford History of English Literature, 1945– .

Princeton Encyclopedia of Poetry and Poetics, 1974.

Statesman's Yearbook: Statistical and Historical Annual of the States of the World, 1864– .

Statistical Abstract of the United States, 1878– .

Webster's Biographical Dictionary, 1980.

World Almanac and Book of Facts, 1868– .

Check your card catalog for special reference works in the area of your subject.

Your working bibliography should grow as you proceed. Be sure to include all the information that will help you find each item listed: along with the author and title, you will need the library call number for books and the date, volume, and page numbers for articles.

48c Distinguish between primary and secondary materials.

Primary materials are such things as a painting, a poem, a short story, a motor, a stock exchange, an animal, a fossil, a virus, or a public opinion poll. In a paper on gasolines, for example, the gasolines tested are primary materials; the writings of engineers about them are secondary. Primary materials for a study of tourists abroad would consist of published and unpublished diaries, journals, and letters by tourists; interviews of tourists; and anything that is part of the tourist's life. Select a topic which allows use of primary materials so that you can reach independent conclusions and not rely entirely on the thinking of others.

    Secondary materials are those written *about* your topic. In a study of tourists abroad, for example, the writings of journalists and historians about them are called secondary sources. The significance and accuracy of such materials should be evaluated (see page 207–208). It is important to consider when a work was written; what information was available to its author at that time; the general scholarly reputation of the author; the extent of the author's knowledge and reliability as indicated in the preface, footnotes, or bibliography; the logic the author has demonstrated in proving points; and even the medium of publication. A general article in a popular magazine, for example, is likely to be less reliable than a scholarly article in a learned journal.

48d Locate source materials, read, evaluate, and take notes.

Before you begin to take notes, it is a good idea to do some broad **preliminary reading** in an encyclopedia or in other general introductory works. Try to get a general view, a kind of map of the territory within which you will be working.

After you have compiled a working bibliography (**48b**), located some of the sources you wish to use, and done some preliminary reading, you are ready to begin collecting specific material for your paper. If you are writing a formally documented paper, make a **bibliography card** for each item as you examine it. This will be a full and exact record of bibliographical information, preferably on a 3 × 5 inch filing card. From these cards you will later compile a final bibliography for your paper. A sample card is shown on page 277. The essential information includes the name of the author, the title of the work, the place and date of publication, and the name of the publisher. If the work has an editor or a translator, is in more than one volume, or is part of a series, these facts should be included. For later checking, record the library call number.

For **note-taking,** your next step, use cards or slips of paper uniform in size. Cards are easier to use than slips because they withstand more handling. Develop the knack of skimming so that you can move quickly over irrelevant material and concentrate on pertinent information. Use the table of contents, the section headings, and the index to find chapters or pages of particular use to you. As you read and take notes, consider what subtopics you will use. The two processes work together: your reading will give you ideas for subtopics, and the subtopics will give direction to your note-taking. At this point you are already in the process of organizing and outlining the paper. Suppose you wish to make a study of the drawings of James Thurber. You might work up the following list of tentative topics:

Thurber's background
His beginnings as an artist
His stature as an artist
The nature and effects of his drawings
His most famous drawing
His world view as seen in the drawings

Bibliography Card

(reduced facsimile — actual size 3 × 5 inches)

A label which indicates that this is a bibliography card. Keep these cards separate from those on which you take notes. They will eventually be used in making up the bibliography for your paper.

Bibliography

Bernstein, Burton

Thurber: A Biography

New York: Dodd, Mead

1975

PS 3539
H94 Z57

Author's name

Title

Place of publication and name of publisher

Date of publication

Call number

These headings may not be final. You should always be ready to delete, add, and change headings as you read and take notes. At this stage, the final order of headings—the outline—may be neither possible nor necessary.

To illustrate the methods of note-taking, suppose you have found the following paragraph about James Thurber.

> Beyond question the foremost humorist of the twentieth century, James Thurber was a divided man. With minor exceptions he did not explore the century's large social and political problems. War, religion, crime, poverty, civil rights—these were not his subjects. Instead he struck at the immemorial stupidities, cruelties, and perversities of men that lie at the root of our ills. A disillusioned idealist, he satirized mean behavior to sound the clearest note of his discontent. Yet he considered himself an optimist or near kin to one. He insisted that the perceptive reader would detect in his work "a basic and indestructible thread of hope."
>
> LOUIS HASLEY,
> "James Thurber: Artist in Humor"

You may make a note on this passage by paraphrasing, by quoting, or by combining short quotations with paraphrasing.

To **paraphrase** is to express the sense of a passage entirely in your own words, selecting and summarizing only information and ideas that will be useful. The card on page 279 identifies the source, gives a subject heading, indicates the page number, and then records relevant information in the student's own words. It *extracts* items of information instead of merely recasting the entire passage and line of thought in different words. Notice the careful selection of details and the fact that the paraphrase is considerably shorter than the original.

If at the time of taking notes you cannot yet determine just what information you wish to extract, you may copy an entire passage. For later reference you must then be careful to show by quotation marks that it is copied verbatim.

A photoduplicating machine can guarantee accuracy and save you time. At an early stage in research it is not always possible to know exactly what information is needed. Photocopy

James Thurber's Optimism

Holey, "James Thurber: Artist in Humor."

504 Though he deals with the tragic ills
of mankind, Thurber thought of himself
not as a pessimist but as an optimist.

Subject heading

Identification of source.
Full bibliographical
information has been
taken down on the
bibliography card.

Page number

some of the longest passages, and then you can study them and digest them during the writing of the first draft of the paper. Do not copy so many passages that you leave too much of the thinking until the last moment, but make enough duplicates to prevent constant returns to the same books in the library.

When writing your paper, you may either quote directly, as in the note at the top of page 281, or paraphrase (see **28c**). Quoting and paraphrasing may be combined on a single note card, as in the card at the bottom of page 281. It is most important to use quotation marks accurately when writing the note, to use your own words when not quoting, and to transfer quotations and quotation marks from card to paper with scrupulous care.

Any single card should contain notes from only one source, and all the notes on any single card should be about one single topic, such as James Thurber's subjects on the cards above. This will give you maximum flexibility in organizing materials as the plan of the paper takes shape. Arrange the cards by topic before you write the paper.

The accuracy of your paper depends to a great extent on the accuracy of your notes. Indicate on each card the source, the page numbers, and an appropriate subject heading.

Note-taking is not a mere mechanical process; it involves interpretation and evaluation. Two persons writing on the same subject and using the same sources would not be likely to take quite the same notes, and their papers would differ accordingly in content and organization.

Study the following passage, which deals with the similarity of Thurber's cartoons to dreams.

Most of the drawings in *The Seal in the Bedroom* have a touch of that strange, dream-like quality which was always to be one of the hallmarks of Thurber's imagination. Neurosis, hallucination, the whole area of the irrational were subjects which held a particular fascination for him throughout his career. Many of his drawings haunt the imagination because they confront us directly with images which seem to have popped up from the unconscious or to have been recalled from dreams. His most famous cartoon,

Quotation

James Thurber's subjects

Hasley
504   "With minor exceptions he did not explore
the century's large social and political problems.
War, religion, crime, poverty, civil rights —
these were not his subjects. Instead he
struck at the immemorial stupidities,
cruelties, and perversities of men that lie
at the root of our ills."

Quotation and paraphrase

James Thurber's subjects

Hasley.
504   "With minor exceptions he did not
explore the century's large social and political
problems." Instead of addressing himself to
such things as war or crime, he chose to
point out the basic weaknesses of human
nature.

"All right, have it your way—you heard a seal bark," shows a man and a woman in bed, and looming up behind the headboard, a pleasant-looking seal. The woman is querulous and impatient at her husband's nonsense, and the man is silently exasperated because she won't believe him. The scene has that mixture of the familiar and the strange which is the essence of dreams, and like dream-images, it resists logical explanation.

CHARLES S. HOLMES,
The Clocks of Columbus:
The Literary Career of James Thurber

From a passage as full of information as this one, it is possible to take several kinds of notes under different subject headings. Most of this material might eventually be used in a paper, but to a certain extent the material is adapted to the purposes of the paper by the way it is selected and classified under the student's subject headings. By the very process of reading and note-taking, the student is thinking about the subject and organizing thoughts. This is the supreme importance of taking notes, of quoting and paraphrasing. Now study the notes on pages 283–284, all from the preceding paragraph by Holmes. Observe the variety in subject headings and treatment.

48e Construct an outline

No step in the writing of a research paper is more important than the working out of a good outline. The purpose of an outline is not to hold you rigidly to a preconceived form but to enable you to think through your topic and organize it logically and interestingly *before you begin to write*. Writing too soon is the most common of all flaws in composing a research paper. The outline may therefore be the most important single step in the process. After you have worked out a tentative outline, study it carefully to be sure that you have included all the major points you wish to make and that you have arranged them so that your discussion will flow rationally from one to the other.

Quotation

Thurber's drawings and dreams

Holmes, *Clocks*
134 "Most of the drawings in *The Seal in the Bedroom* have a touch of that strange, dream-like quality which was always to be one of the hallmarks of Thurber's imagination."

Quotation

Thurber's interest in the irrational

Holmes, *Clocks*
134 "Neurosis, hallucination, the whole area of the irrational were subjects which held a particular fascination for him throughout his career. Many of his drawings haunt the imagination because they confront us directly with images which seem to have popped up from the unconscious...."

Paraphrase

Thurber's Cartoon of the Seal

Holmes, *Clocks*
135 Thurber's cartoon of the seal in the
bedroom is difficult to analyze because
it blends the real world with a world
of fantasy and is therefore much like
a dream.

Quotation and Paraphrase

Thurber's Cartoon of the Seal

Holmes, *Clocks*
135 "His most famous cartoon," of
the seal in the bedroom, "has that
mixture of the familiar and the strange"
that makes it too much like a
dream to be easily analyzed.

If you have taken the time and effort to complete a full and effective outline, you will find that the writing of the paper itself will go much quicker and smoother and that the result will be a unified discussion. See the model outline on page 297.

48f Acknowledge your sources. Avoid plagiarism.

Acknowledge your indebtedness to others by giving full details of sources in footnotes and bibliography. Using others' words and ideas as if they were your own is a form of stealing called **plagiarism.**

Some of the principles of quoting and paraphrasing have already been discussed under the topic of taking notes (**48d**). They must be kept in mind during the writing and revision of the paper. Finally, quotations and paraphrases should be carefully checked for accuracy after the paper is written.

All direct quotations must be placed in quotation marks and acknowledged in your text.
If you are writing a documented paper, specific details of the citation must be completed in a footnote (see pages 287–291). Even when you take only a phrase or a single unusual word from a passage, you should enclose it in quotation marks. You may quote words, phrases, clauses, sentences, or even whole paragraphs. Generally you should quote a sentence or a paragraph only when a writer has phrased something especially well and when you need to supply all the information given. Do not quote excessively. A sequence of quotations strung together with a few words of your own is not satisfactory. Excessive quoting indicates that you have not properly digested your sources, thought about the ideas, and learned to express them in your own words and to relate them to your own ideas.

All paraphrases and citations must be acknowledged.

Credit a source when you cite ideas or information from it even when you do not quote directly. Altering the wording does not make the substance yours. An acknowledgment not only gives proper credit but also lends authority to your statement. Whenever you consult a source or a note card as you write, you are probably paraphrasing, and you probably need an acknowledgment.

In paraphrasing you are expressing the ideas of another writer in your own words. A good paraphrase preserves the sense of the original, but not the form. It does not retain the sentence patterns and merely substitute synonyms for the original words, nor does it retain the original words and merely alter the sentence patterns. It is a genuine restatement. Invariably it should be briefer than the source. In the example below, notice the difference between a satisfactory and an unsatisfactory paraphrase:

ORIGINAL

Hemingway's debt to journalism was a large one, and he always acknowledged it. Unlike many ex-newspapermen, however, he neither sentimentalized the profession nor misunderstood its essential threat to creative writing.

CHARLES A. FENTON,
The Apprenticeship of Ernest Hemingway

BADLY PARAPHRASED

Hemingway's indebtedness to journalism was very great, and he himself said so. Unlike so many writers who have been newspaper men, however, he did not sentimentalize journalism or misunderstand that it is a danger to creative talent.

BETTER

Hemingway admitted that he learned from newspaper work. But he also recognized that journalism can hurt writers as well as help them.

If the source has stated the idea more concisely than you can, you should quote, not paraphrase.

Do not make use of extended paraphrases. If a good many of your paragraphs are simply long paraphrases, your reader will assume that even your organization is taken from someone else, concluding that you have not assimilated your materials and thought independently about them — in short, that you have not done an acceptable piece of original work.

48g Follow accepted practices of documentation.

Although there is common agreement on the *principles* of documentation, the *forms* vary with fields, periodicals, publishers, and indeed even instructors. There are several good guides to documentation, but the most widely adopted style in language and literature is that recommended by the Modern Language Association of America in the *MLA Handbook for Writers of Research Papers, Theses, and Dissertations* (1977). With a few exceptions, the sample footnote and bibliographical entries listed below, as well as those in the model paper on pages 294-325, are based on the *MLA Handbook*. The entries below may serve you as models, though your instructor may require modifications.

Sample footnotes

Standard reference to a book
[1]Henry Nash Smith, *Mark Twain: The Development of a Writer* (Cambridge: Harvard Univ. Press, 1962), p. 83.

Subsequent reference to a book
[2]Smith, p. 81.

NOTE Some instructors prefer "Ibid., p. 81." in footnotes of this kind.

Standard reference to a book (same kind as footnote 1)
[3]Henry Nash Smith, *Virgin Land: The American West as Symbol and Myth* (Cambridge: Harvard Univ. Press, 1950), p. 143.
[4]Smith, *Mark Twain,* p. 79.

NOTE When two or more works by the same author, like Smith above, have been cited previously, a new footnote should give the title or an abbreviated version of it.

Standard reference to an article
[5]George Watson, "Quest for a Frenchman," *Sewanee Review,* 84 (1976), 474.

NOTE The abbreviation "p." is not used when the volume number is given. Inclusive page numbers for the article should be given in the bibliographical entry.

Standard reference to an article in a weekly or monthly magazine
[6]Alan Brien, "Take Me to Your Union Leader," *Punch,* 3 May 1972, p. 610.

NOTE Page numbers in most weeklies and monthlies begin anew with each issue.

Subsequent reference to an article
[7]Watson, p. 475.

NOTE See note for footnote 2 above.

Reference to a book by more than one author
[8]Walter R. Cuskey, Arnold William Klein, and William Krasner, *Drug-Trip Abroad: American Drug-Refugees in Amsterdam and London* (Philadelphia: Univ. of Pennsylvania Press, 1972), p. 90.

Reference to a book by more than three authors or editors
[9]Harvey A. Hornstein et al., eds., *Social Intervention: A Behavioral Science Approach* (New York: Free Press, 1971), p. 181.

NOTE The Latin abbreviation "et al." (from *et alii*) means "and others."

References to volumes in works of more than one volume
[10]George A. Simcox, *A History of Latin Literature from Ennius to Boethius* (New York: Harper, 1883), II, 438.

NOTE The abbreviation "p." is not used when the volume number is given. In works where separate volumes have different publication dates, the volume number cited is given immediately after the title.

[11]Herbert M. Schueller and Robert L. Peters, eds., *The Letters of John Addington Symonds,* III (Detroit: Wayne State Univ. Press, 1969), 667. [Bibliographical entry gives inclusive dates of all volumes.]

Reference to an essay in volume of essays

[12]Dorothy Emmet, "Coleridge and Philosophy," in *S. T. Coleridge,* ed. R. L. Brett (London: G. Bell, 1971), p. 210.

NOTE Use the following form to refer to essays and articles reprinted in casebooks and other collections of essays.

[13]Alain Renoir, "Point of View and Design for Terror in *Beowulf,*" *Neuphilologische Mitteilungen,* 63 (1962), 154–167; rpt. in *The Beowulf Poet: A Collection of Critical Essays,* ed. Donald K. Fry, Twentieth Century Views (Englewood Cliffs, N.J.: Prentice-Hall, 1968), p. 156.

Reference to a book that is part of a series

[14]Edward Hubler, *The Sense of Shakespeare's Sonnets,* Princeton Studies in English, No. 33 (Princeton: Princeton Univ. Press, 1952), p. 117.

Reference to second or later editions of a book

[15]Desmond King-Hele, *Shelley: His Thought and Work,* 2nd ed. (Teaneck, N.J.: Fairleigh Dickinson Univ. Press, 1971), p. 311.

NOTE A modern reprinting of an older edition of a book is listed as follows.

[16]Edwin E. Slosson, *Major Prophets of To-Day* (1914; rpt. Freeport, N.Y.: Books for Libraries Press, 1968), p. 91.

Reference to a book with an editor

[17]Ann Radcliffe, *The Mysteries of Udolpho,* ed. Bonamy Dobrée (London: Oxford Univ. Press, 1966), p. 363.

Reference to an introduction to a book

[18]Bonamy Dobrée, "Introd.," *The Mysteries of Udolpho,* by Ann Radcliffe (London: Oxford Univ. Press, 1966), pp. xv–xvi.

Reference to a book with a translator

[19]Erich Maria Remarque, *Shadows in Paradise,* trans. Ralph Manheim (New York: Harcourt, 1972), p. 123.

Reference to a signed article in an encyclopedia
    [20]Richard C. Tobias, "Thurber, James," *Encyclopedia Americana,* 1980 ed.

NOTE Authors with initials at the end of articles in encyclopedias are usually identified in a section (usually in the first volume) which lists contributors. Articles arranged alphabetically in reference books do not need to be identified by volume and page.

Reference to an unsigned article in an encyclopedia
    [21]"Midway Islands," *Encyclopedia Americana,* 1964 ed.

NOTE A subsequent reference to this anonymous article could be merely the title.

    [22]"Midway Islands."

Reference to a newspaper article
    [23]"Churchill's Account of His Early Wars Is Ridiculed in a Contemporary's Notes," *New York Times,* 23 July 1972, sec. 1, p. 12, cols. 1–6.

NOTE When an article is signed, the author's name should be given at the beginning of the footnote. When a newspaper issue has only one section, the section number, as given above, is not necessary.

Reference to a dissertation
    [24]Catherine McGehee Kenney, "The World of James Thurber: An Anatomy of Confusion," Diss. Loyola of Chicago, 1974, p. 16.

Reference to an article in *Dissertation Abstracts* (or its successor, *Dissertation Abstracts International*)
    [25]Catherine McGehee Kenney, "The World of James Thurber: An Anatomy of Confusion," *DAI,* 35 (1974), 2276A (Loyola of Chicago).

Biblical reference
    [26]I Kings iv.3. [Books of the Bible are not italicized.]

Reference to a play (with act, scene, and line)
    [27]*King Lear* v.iii.245.

Reference to one author quoted in a book by another author
    [28]Ian Watt, *The Rise of the Novel* (Berkeley: Univ. of California

Press, 1957), p. 125, quoted by Wayne C. Booth, *The Rhetoric of Fiction* (Chicago: Univ. of Chicago Press, 1961), p. 321.

Reference to an unsigned bulletin or pamphlet
[29]*Enforcement of the Selective Service Law,* Special Monograph No. 14, Selective Service System (Washington, D.C.: GPO, 1951), pp. 102–103.

Reference to a signed bulletin or pamphlet
[30]Charles E. Whieldon, Jr., and William E. Eckard, *West Virginia Oilfields Discovered before 1940,* Bulletin 607, Bureau of Mines, U.S. Dept. of the Interior (Washington, D.C.: GPO, 1963), p. 5.

Sample bibliography
Items are listed in alphabetical order. The most frequently used types of entries are found under *Smith* for a book and *Watson* for an article.

Article in weekly or monthly magazine
Brien, Alan. "Take Me to Your Union Leader." *Punch,* 3 May 1972, pp. 610, 612.

Newspaper article
"Churchill's Account of His Early Wars Is Ridiculed in a Contemporary's Notes." *New York Times,* 23 July 1972, sec. 1, p. 12, cols. 1–6.

Book by more than one author
Cuskey, Walter R., Arnold William Klein, and William Krasner. *Drug-Trip Abroad: American Drug-Refugees in Amsterdam and London.* Philadelphia: Univ. of Pennsylvania Press, 1972.

Introduction to a book
Dobrée, Bonamy, introd. *The Mysteries of Udolpho.* By Ann Radcliffe. London: Oxford Univ. Press, 1966.

Essay in a volume of essays
Emmet, Dorothy. "Coleridge and Philosophy." In *S. T. Coleridge.* Ed. R. L. Brett. London: G. Bell, 1971, pp. 195–220.

Unsigned bulletin or pamphlet
Enforcement of the Selective Service Law. Special Monograph No. 14,
   Selective Service System. Washington, D.C.: GPO, 1951.

Book by more than three authors or editors
Hornstein, Harvey A., et al., eds. *Social Intervention: A Behavioral
   Science Approach.* New York: Free Press, 1971.

Book that is part of a series
Hubler, Edward. *The Sense of Shakespeare's Sonnets.* Princeton Studies
   in English, No. 33. Princeton: Princeton Univ. Press, 1952.

A dissertation
Kenney, Catherine McGehee. "The World of James Thurber: An Anat-
   omy of Confusion." Diss. Loyola of Chicago 1974.

Article in *Dissertation Abstracts International*
Kenney, Catherine McGehee. "The World of James Thurber: An Anat-
   omy of Confusion." *DAI,* 35 (1974), 2276A (Loyola of Chicago).

Second or later edition of a book
King-Hele, Desmond. *Shelley: His Thought and Work.* 2nd ed. Teaneck,
   N.J.: Fairleigh Dickinson Univ. Press, 1971.

Unsigned article in an encyclopedia
"Midway Islands." *Encyclopedia Americana.* 1964 ed.

Book with a translator
Remarque, Erich Maria. *Shadows in Paradise.* Trans. Ralph Manheim.
   New York: Harcourt, 1972.

Essay reprinted in a casebook or other collection
Renoir, Alain. "Point of View and Design for Terror in *Beowulf.*" *Neuphilologische Mitteilungen,* 63 (1962), 154–167. Rpt. in *The Beowulf Poet: A Collection of Critical Essays.* Ed. Donald K. Fry.
   Twentieth Century Views. Englewood Cliffs, N.J.: Prentice-Hall,
   1968, pp. 154–166.

Volume in a work of more than one volume with different publication dates
Schueller, Herbert M., and Robert L. Peters, eds. *The Letters of John
   Addington Symonds.* 3 vols. Detroit: Wayne State Univ. Press,
   1967–1969.

Volume in a work of more than one volume with same publication date
Simcox, George A. *A History of Latin Literature from Ennius to Boethius*. 2 vols. New York: Harper, 1883.

Modern reprinting of an older edition
Slosson, Edwin E. *Major Prophets of To-Day*. 1914; rpt. Freeport, N.Y.: Books for Libraries Press, 1968.

Standard reference to a book
Smith, Henry Nash. *Mark Twain: The Development of a Writer*. Cambridge: Harvard Univ. Press, 1962.

Signed article in an encyclopedia
Tobias, Richard C. "Thurber, James." *Encyclopedia Americana,* 1980 ed.

Standard reference to an article
Watson, George. "Quest for a Frenchman." *Sewanee Review,* 84 (1976), 465–475.

Signed bulletin or pamphlet
Whieldon, Charles E., Jr., and William E. Eckard. *West Virginia Oilfields Discovered before 1940*. Bulletin 607, Bureau of Mines, U.S. Dept. of the Interior. Washington, D.C.: GPO, 1963.

Model research paper

A model research paper, with an outline and accompanying explanations, is given on the following pages for study. Generally this paper follows the form outlined in the *MLA Handbook for Writers of Research Papers, Theses, and Dissertations* (1977), with the following variations: blocked quotations in college papers are customarily single-spaced; footnotes and bibliographical entries are single-spaced with double-spacing between them. The *MLA Handbook* specifies that in research papers, blocked quotations, footnotes, and bibliography be double-spaced. In these, as in other matters of form, follow the preference of your instructor.

Allow ample and even margins.
Double-space the text.
Indent five spaces for paragraphs.
Leave two spaces after periods and other terminal punctuation.
Leave one space after other marks of punctuation.

The material on the title page should be spaced so that it appears balanced on the page. Center the title and place it about one-third from the top of the page. Include your name and the name and section number of the course as indicated on the opposite page, or follow the specific preferences of your instructor.

Hope Through Fantasy in James Thurber's Drawings

By

Debra Warwick

English 101

Section 1

If your instructor requests that you submit an outline with your paper, it should occupy a separate, unnumbered page following the title page and should follow the form for the outline illustrated on pages 242–243.

Hope Through Fantasy in James Thurber's Drawings

THESIS STATEMENT: Although the comic drawings of James Thurber seem
simple, they actually embody a complex world view with strong suggestions
of pessimism but with an even stronger sense of hope.

I.   Introduction--Thurber's career as a cartoonist

    A. His one-man exhibition at the Valentine Gallery

    B. Before the Valentine exhibit--his beginnings

        1. Collaboration with E. B. White

        2. Praise by British artist Paul Nash

        3. First collection of drawings: <u>The Seal in the Bedroom</u>

    C. After the Valentine exhibit--his later years

II. The nature of Thurber's drawings

    A. Subject matter

    B. Technique

    C. Captions

III. The effects of Thurber's drawings

    A. Before careful analysis

    B. After careful analysis

IV. An examination of "The Seal in the Bedroom"

    A. The woman

    B. The man

    C. The seal

V.   Thurber's world view

    A. Reputation for bitterness

    B. His complexity and affirmation

The writer has submitted a photocopy of the main cartoon to be discussed in order to provide a concrete example for the reader as well as to help establish a tone for the paper.

"All Right, Have It Your Way—
You Heard a Seal Bark!"

Center the title on the page. Triple-space between the title and the first line of the text.

Place footnote numbers slightly above the line of type and after marks of punctuation. Do not leave a space before the number; do not place a period after the number. Number footnotes consecutively throughout the paper. Never repeat a number in the text even if the references are exactly the same.

The source for the statement footnoted as 2 is given below. Notice how the quotation has been paraphrased in the paper.

> Gallery-goers, stepping sideways like crabs, passed from frame to frame in which were exposed the backs of old letterheads and odd sheets of scratch paper on which were scrawled the amiable bloodhounds, the horrid boneless women, the bald, browbeaten little men of Artist Thurber, associate editor and one of the two most successful members of the staff of *The New Yorker*.
>
> "MOROSE SCRAWLER,"
> *Time*

After capturing the reader's interest by recounting the story of Thurber's one-man art exhibition, the writer uses the final lines of the first paragraph to state the central idea of the paper.

The next paragraph then takes up the subject of Thurber's background as an artist.

The page number for the first page may be omitted or centered at the bottom.

Hope Through Fantasy in James Thurber's Drawings

In December of 1934 the highly respected Valentine Gallery in Manhattan held one of the most unusual exhibitions in all of its history. Less traditional than many of the art galleries in New York City, the Valentine "devoted itself to the more advanced of the socially acceptable left-wing artists."[1] Nevertheless, this was a particularly odd one-man show: as viewers shuffled from one frame to another, they witnessed childlike reproductions of gentle dogs, aggressive women, and emasculated men all casually drawn as doodles on various sorts and sizes of sheets, even scratch paper.[2] Much puzzlement and disbelief ran through these lovers of art; but the exhibition was widely reviewed, and the artist, James Thurber, was in the end compared with such giants as Picasso and Matisse.[3] Since then, Thurber's position as a serious artist as well as a serious writer has been solidly established, although his cartoons, known best from the pages of The New Yorker, are deceptively simple. His fame has been accompanied by a reputation for bitterness, which is in some measure justified; but if pessimism is reflected in Thurber's drawings, a sense of hope is even stronger.

Thurber never took his role as an artist as seriously as other people did. He was completely self-taught. In fact, his brother William was supposedly the Thurber with talent for drawing. James's early doodles were not drastically different from the ones that brought him acclaim, but his family dismissed them, and he was advised not to waste his time. An urge so deep that he did not himself understand it kept him at these spare, un-detailed, outline figures. He produced them so quickly and effortlessly that his respect for them was slight compared to his feelings for his writing,

Place the page number in the upper right-hand corner, two lines above the first line of text. Use Arabic numerals; do not put a period after the number.

The statement beginning with "Blending" illustrates the technique of combining in a sentence one's own words with quoted words.

In the quotation, brackets have been used to indicate that the word *Nash* is not in the original text (see **26**). Brackets are also used to enclose the scholarly term *sic* when a word in a quotation has been misspelled. This assures your reader that the misspelling is not yours and that you are quoting accurately.

which came slowly and painfully. Yet others saw depth in the drawings that seemed spontaneously dredged up from the unconscious mind of a genius. "Blending the worlds of reality and dream," as one critic has put it, the drawings, not the writings, "are the purest expression of his imagination."[4]

The person most responsible for getting Thurber's drawings into magazines and books was E. B. White. While sharing an office with him at The New Yorker, White noticed that Thurber produced dozens of drawings, which were promptly crumpled up and tossed into the trash. One of these turned out to be a seal resting on a large rock and looking dreamily off into the distant sea where there were two approaching specks. The caption read, "Hm, explorers." White was so amused and so convinced of a profound comic talent in Thurber that he tried to get the editor of The New Yorker to publish the cartoon.[5] This failed, but when they collaborated in 1929 on a satirical book, White insisted to the publishers that Thurber do the illustrations. Both for the writing and the drawings, Is Sex Necessary? was a hit, and Thurber was on his way. Seeing how well the book was selling, the editor of The New Yorker then asked Thurber if he could publish the seal drawing. Thurber had thrown it away, however, and when he tried to reproduce it, it came out differently and was destined to be the most famous of all his cartoons, the seal in the bedroom.[6]

The illustrations for Is Sex Necessary? and the cartoons that steadily appeared in The New Yorker magazine thereafter brought Thurber much attention as a funny and peculiar scrawler, but he was surprised to realize in 1931 that he was being taken seriously by artists and critics of high reputation. When the respected British artist Paul Nash came to America, he sought out Thurber. "In the paintings of his American contemporaries he [Nash] found

The writer now moves from Thurber's career as an artist to the nature of his drawings.

When an ellipsis is used to indicate omitted words at the end of a sentence, the three spaced periods are preceded by a fourth with no space before it.

Be extremely careful with all quotations. Do not change anything. For example, the word *Sex* with a capital "S" may look strange, but that is the way the author wrote it, the way it should be represented.

In quotations that are run in with the text (that is, not set off), use single quotation marks to designate a quotation within the quotation. Notice the word *psych*.

little to attract him, and he shocked them by his insistence on the importance of James Thurber's comic drawings."[7] Nash was only one of many serious artists and art critics to see in the witty Thurber a profundity and a complexity only half recognized by the man himself. In 1932 Thurber's first and perhaps most impressive collection of drawings was published as The Seal in the Bedroom and Other Predicaments. With the success of that volume and the one-man exhibition at the Valentine Gallery the next year, it was difficult even for Thurber not to recognize that he had achieved stature as an original artist. His reputation continued to grow until the 1950's, when he was forced to give up drawing because of blindness.[8]

Thurber's drawings present a world of men, women, and animals. The women tend to be large and angry. The men find themselves often intimidated by the female's size and manner. They appear constantly at odds with each other. The animals—frequently dogs but sometimes seals or penguins—are universally pleasant. In 1943, Newsweek called Thurber "America's most incredible artist," and described his typical woman figure as "a fiercely aggressive female with the figure of a potato sack, a face which is a cross between a weasel's and a swordfish's, and, the final indignity, perfectly straight and stringy hair.... She frowns grimly, smiles idiotically, and leers loomily. She stalks the male, rules him, bewilders him, and even, once, murders him."[9] The man of the drawings, writes another critic, is "bothered most of all by Sex, with its marital con-comitant, but also by all disciplines whose names begin with 'psych'; by mechanical devices; by the upper-middle-class ceremonials of suburbia; by the bureaucratic organization of modern society, and by the deterioration of communications between man and man and between man and woman."[10]

Prose quotations of about five lines or more generally should be set off as indicated here. Single-space within the quotation. Paragraphing within the passage should follow the source. Indent for paragraphs when you quote more than one. *Do not enclose blocked quotations in quotation marks.* When there is a quotation within the quotation, as here, use double quotation marks to indicate it.

The is usually capitalized and italicized as part of the title of *The New Yorker* magazine. Since it was not printed as part of the title in this particular article being quoted, it should not be here. Follow quotations exactly and recheck each one for accuracy when you have completed the draft of your paper.

The two words quoted, "been through," do not need to be footnoted because the reader can clearly see that they are taken from the long quotation above for which the source is given in footnote 12.

4

What the writer of one of Thurber's obituaries said about his dogs can also be said about most of the other animals: "His drawings of dogs, which he produced with abundance on the backs of envelopes, in telephone books and on tablecloths, had a quality that seemed to link them with no other beast on earth."[11]

If the general subject of Thurber's drawings is the war between men and women, with an animal of some sort frequently the innocent bystander, his technique is having no technique—that is, none that sophisticated training teaches. In answer to Alistair Cooke's question as to whether his cartoons had encouraged parents to submit their children's drawings, Thurber answered:

> It actually did—not only parents but very strange people. Some people thought my drawings were done under water; others that they were done by moonlight. But mothers thought that I was a little child or that my drawings were done by my grand-daughter. So they sent in their own children's drawings to the New Yorker, and I was told to write these ladies, and I would write them all the same letter: "Your son can certainly draw as well as I can. The only trouble is that he hasn't been through as much."[12]

With his usual tone of humility where his drawings were concerned, he was indulging in satire of others and himself, but he revealed nevertheless in his comment about how much he had "been through" an understanding of the relationship between his deepest inner self and his drawings. "No one understands," commented Dorothy Parker, "how he makes his boneless, loppy beings, with their shy kinship to the men and women of Picasso's later drawings," and likewise, no one knows "from what dark breeding-ground come the artist's ideas."[13] Like so many others, Dorothy Parker was intrigued, if not spellbound, by the drawing of the seal in the bedroom:

Notice the handling of single and double quotation marks at the end of the paragraph. Ordinarily the question mark would not separate the single and double quotation marks, but it does so here because the entire sentence is a question. No other end punctuation should be used with a question mark.

The parentheses used in the quotation of the second paragraph indicate that the words *the one-line cartoon* were in parentheses in the source as well. If these words were not in the source but were added by the writer of this paper, they would be in brackets, not parentheses.

After dealing with the nature of Thurber's drawings—their subject matter, their techniques, and their captions—the writer now moves to the next block of the discussion, the effects that the drawings produce on the viewers.

5

"How is one to shadow the mental process of a man who is impelled to depict a seal looking over the headboard of a bed occupied by a broken-spirited husband and a virago of a wife, and then to write below the scene the one line: 'All right, have it your way--you heard a seal bark'?"[14]

Thurber and his fellow artists who were drawing for The New Yorker created a "new kind of cartoon (the one-line cartoon), in which the words and drawing were inextricable and neither was witty without the other."[15] Many who have admired Thurber's art and compared it to such painters as Matisse have not realized the extent to which the drawing depends upon the caption for its effect. Dorothy Parker recalled that a friend of hers had overheard one woman say to another on a London bus: "Mad, I don't say. Queer, I grant you. Many's the time I've seen her nude at the piano." This was, she felt, precisely the kind of caption Thurber would write under a drawing of two women chatting, for Thurber, she argued, "deals solely in culminations. Beneath his pictures he sets only the final line.... It is yours to ponder how penguins get into drawing-rooms and seals into bedchambers.... He gives you a glimpse of the startling present and lets you construct the astounding past."[16]

The effect of a Thurber drawing is both immediate and long lasting. As his general popularity suggests, his cartoons create laughter spontaneously in the viewer, who in most cases is not interested in questioning why. If the question is raised and if viewers contemplate the drawings over a period of time, they discover that the cartoons lose none of their humor with time but that other emotions are evoked. After the initial amusement comes the awareness of the characters' state of mind or situation, which is usually that of confusion or unhappiness or both. "Thurber is

Quoting an important critic of art here is especially effective, for it indicates that Thurber is more than a cartoonist drawing for the funny papers, that he is taken seriously in the art world for his ability to project the depths of his imagination. The length of the quotation is such that it could be either set off or run in with the text. It is set off to give it emphasis.

The writer is now ready to illustrate much of what has previously been said in the paper with a close analysis of the drawing which has been submitted with the paper.

Dorothy Parker has been cited in footnotes three times previously, but it is clear that the writer of this paper is not relying too heavily on one source, for she has selected a subject for which there are abundant resources, and she is using a great variety of them. Be careful not to pick a subject on which you cannot find adequate secondary research materials.

The drawing of the seal in the bedroom is primary material, the writings about Thurber and his art, secondary materials. The discussion of the specific cartoon is much enhanced by the fact that the writer included as an illustration a photocopy of the drawing itself.

almost alone in using, as a comedian, material which in other hands is tragic."[17] On the heels of this unpleasant recognition of predicament, however, follows that sense of wonder and mystery that attracted Dorothy Parker. In his ability to evoke this world of dreams, he has been called a "fantast" and compared favorably with such artists as Goya, William Blake, and Pieter Bruegel, the Elder. Speaking of these as well as Thurber, one art critic writes:

> Perhaps it is the fantast who, after all, gets closer to the
> truth than anyone else, for instead of giving us an idealized
> transmutation of reality or a photographically accurate record,
> he gives us only its most salient and telling features after
> they have been distilled in the alembic of his fantasy.[18]

The fantasy, of which innocence is frequently a component, works to offset the pessimism of the overt subject matter, and one is brought full circle back to humor. Before and after contemplation and analysis, a Thurber drawing is comic--in the best and deepest sense of the word.[19]

A detailed examination of one cartoon, the one picturing a seal in the bedroom, will illustrate more specifically the complexity of Thurber's art. The only active figure in the scene is a woman in bed with her husband. As is often the case in a Thurber cartoon, she is large, almost formless. Dorothy Parker wrote that Thurber's characters "have the outer semblance of unbaked cookies" and that "the women are of a dowdiness so overwhelming that it becomes tremendous style."[20] Thurber himself claimed that he could not draw a beautiful woman.[21] Her hair is represented by a few almost straight lines that add to the overall impression of a person who has ceased to be concerned about her appearance, one who could care less whether she is appealing to the opposite sex. The action of the drawing comes from her mouth, opened angrily and snarling out the words

It is evident that the writer has studied many of Thurber's drawings, not merely the one being analyzed, for she makes comparisons and contrasts. A good paper may center upon a single work or a single aspect of a subject, but the writer is wise to become familiar with other works of the same author or artist or other aspects of the general subject. Otherwise, the analysis will tend to be without that richness of reference that comes only after the writer has devoted enough hours to research to become steeped in the subject.

of the caption, "All right, have it your way--you heard a seal bark!"
Her hands, like those of most Thurber figures, "do not look much like
hands," as one of his collaborators observed.[22] They are more like
the feet of a goat in this drawing. Her impatience, her lack of tenderness
and warmth pervade the scene. She is what every man dreads, a dominating,
overbearing, loud-mouthed, insensitive female.

The man is larger than many of Thurber's men, who tend to be smaller
than the women. As usual, he is without hair, and that feature seems to
increase the implied distance between the man and the woman. Thurber's
figures are so much alike that the slightest difference in detail points
up vast differences in the characters. They may be in the same bed, but
they are worlds apart. One imagines that they have had such exchanges
before, the man escaping her shrewish domination for a world of fancy.
He does not understand this other world--nothing is so evident on his
face as a sense of bewilderment--but at least he can experience it. The
woman in the drawing does not represent women in general but a literal and
unimaginative world, the real world.

The seal is the center of the drawing. It looms over the headboard
of the bed, but it is not looking down at the man and woman. It stares
out dreamily into space, with an expression of innocence. It is difficult
to imagine how anyone could view it without smiling the kind of smile that
comes from seeing a baby, the result of a feeling of comic tenderness.
Something more is in that seal, however. It should not be there in the
bedroom; it is out of place. A sense of mystery surrounds it. It is like
a benign ghost that one person sees but another cannot. Perhaps it is
something in the man that causes the seal to be there for him.

The process of composition   313

Underlining should be used sparingly, but since the writer has not used it previously and since both an original and, for this argument, crucial point is being made, it is effective to underline the words.

No footnote is used in this entire paragraph because the writer found none of these ideas in a source but is making an original contribution. If the ideas had been derived from secondary sources, however, a footnote would have been necessary. Indeed, not footnoting in such an instance would constitute the serious act of plagiarism.

With the paragraph beginning with "Because," the writer moves into the concluding section of the paper where the charge of pessimism is examined and rejected and the note of hope and affirmation stressed.

The writer wished to use this anecdote about Churchill. It was first found in the Bernstein biography of Thurber, then in Holmes' book, and also in Morsberger's book. It can, therefore, be safely assumed that this is common knowledge, and thus there is no need to footnote a single source for it.

8

Probably the most striking discovery that one makes after viewing the cartoon for a while is that the seal looks very much like the man. In fact, the man's hands look more like flippers than hands. From that point one notices that neither the man nor the seal has any hair and that the shape of their heads is the same. The arc of their eyebrows is practically identical, making their eyes appear the same. They both look off in the distance as if expecting to hear something. Their mouths are both closed whereas the woman's is open. In fact, if the man's nose were made larger and given whiskers, he would be the seal.

The seal, then, is a projection of something in the man himself, that sense of wonder, that remarkable imagination that enables him to dwell for a while in the realm of fantasy, a world of innocence and tenderness that is in stark opposition to the actual world. This drawing, as a critic has said of Thurber's works as a whole, "affirms the power of imagination."[23]

Because Thurber so often depicted the need to escape the real world and perhaps because he was known as an eccentric given to moments of sourness, he acquired a reputation among some critics as a pessimist. Time magazine referred to him as a "morose scrawler," and commented that his drawings are "enormously funny" but "are the products of an unhappy mind."[24] An acquaintance once told Thurber that when Winston Churchill heard Thurber's name called, he thought briefly and then said, "Oh, that depraved and insane American artist." Sometimes a pessimistic or abnormal outlook is attributed to Thurber for other reasons. For example, W. H. Auden severely criticized Thurber because his drawings are so bare, because they leave out details, "even sexual differences almost disappear." To Auden, Thurber is a sample of the "inward-looking artist" who draws as

The source for the paraphrasing and quoting of W. H. Auden is given below to indicate how the writer used these valuable tools of research and writing.

> Is it not, then, a little disconcerting to find how little of life has today any iconographic significance, that is, seems both universal and capable of inspiring reference and love? Not only landscape but the human figure itself has to be reduced to the barest outline —even sexual differences almost disappear. All detail, all portraiture belong to the world of the enemy, those unpleasant and powerful forces which Lear called "They" and Thurber calls the Liberators, the world whose art is the realistic bosh of society portraits and statues representing the workers of tomorrow. The realm of modern freedom is indeed limited. . . . Just as we have still to discover the proper relations of the private and public life, so the inward-looking artist has to unlearn his puritanical distrust of matter. . . . Logos and Eros have yet to be reconciled in a new Agape.
>
> W. H. AUDEN,
> "The Icon and the Portrait"

Merely because a statement is in print is no reason to accept it as true. The writer of this paper reveals both self-confidence and thoughtfulness in taking issue with W. H. Auden. Such disagreements should always be tactful and should never reflect bad manners. Sources can be used for purposes of disagreement as well as for agreement and support.

The passage beginning with "It is true" and running to footnote number 26 is a paraphrase with no actual quoting. The source is given below for comparison. Notice that the ideas have been followed but not the words of the source.

> Beyond question the foremost humorist of the twentieth century, James Thurber was a divided man. With minor exceptions he did not explore the century's large social and political problems. War, religion, crime, poverty, civil rights—these were not his subjects. Instead he struck at the immemorial stupidities, cruelties, and perversities of men that lie at the root of our ills. A disillusioned idealist, he satirized mean behavior to sound the clearest note of his discontent. Yet he considered himself an optimist or near kin to one. He insisted that the perceptive reader would detect in his work "a basic and indestructible thread of hope."
>
> LOUIS HASLEY,
> "James Thurber: Artist in Humor"

Although it is tempting to end a paper with an appropriate and eloquent quotation, it is generally more effective to end with your own words, carefully chosen to give the effect of your own thoughtfulness and a sense of finality.

he does because of a lack of "Agape" and because of a deep distrust of the world. If an artist distrusts the world, Auden suggests, he will reproduce as little of its details as possible in his art.[25] If this were true, then it would seem to follow that all those artists who do reproduce fully the details of the external world are necessarily optimistic lovers of matter.

Thurber was not in love with the world of ordinary activity, but Auden and many like him who see bitterness behind Thurber's comedy have missed something fundamental in his drawings. It is true that the subjects of Thurber's work generally were not political or social issues but the even larger and more basic problems, the weaknesses of human nature. He was something of an idealist who had become disappointed. In spite of his discontent, however, he thought of himself as an optimist rather than as a pessimist, and he believed that a sensitive audience would detect this positive note in his works.[26] Admittedly he, like many great writers and artists before him, despised certain aspects of a modern mechanized existence, but the very fact that he saw in mankind the ability to transcend that realm into a world of fantasy and innocence represents a strong and definite note of hope. There is both danger and promise in human existence. He "insisted that the menace to the individual lurks in the world of man-made systems, whether mechanical or mental, and that the promise waits in the uncircumscribed realms of the instinct and the imagination."[27] To the man in the drawing of the bedroom scene, the woman is but a representation of a threatening world of cold and harsh realities. But in the drawing, and in mankind's existence, the seal is just as real and is there to represent that other world we can--whether we be man or woman--experience if our ears are tuned aright.

The process of composition   317

Footnotes may be grouped together at the end of the paper as shown here, or they may be placed at the bottom of the pages on which they occur as illustrated on p. 325.

The word *Footnotes* (or *Notes*) is centered on the page. Triple-space between this title and the first footnote; double-space between footnotes.

Indent the first line of every footnote five spaces; do not indent succeeding lines.

In footnotes (but not in the bibliography) the author's name is written in normal order, first name first.

Footnote 1 shows the proper form for a reference to a weekly magazine.

Since full information was given in footnote 1, this reference in footnote 2 to the same article can be shortened as indicated.

Footnote 3 illustrates an important function of footnotes, to supplement what is said in the body of the paper with additional commentary. Also shown here is the standard way to refer to a book with a single author and a commercial publisher.

Footnote 4 shows how to refer to an article in an edited book of essays written by different authors. In this instance the author and the editor are the same person. Notice also that this is a book in a series.

Footnote 5 illustrates the proper way to refer to a monthly magazine in which the pagination begins anew with each issue.

Two separate works by Holmes have been cited, the first in footnote 3 and the second in footnote 4. A reference like "Holmes, p. 136" in footnote 6 would thus be confusing. Consequently, an abbreviated form of the title of the work referred to is necessary as shown.

Since the information given in footnote 8 is to be found in all accounts of Thurber's life, it is not necessary to cite a source.

Footnote 11 illustrates the proper form for referring to a daily newspaper and to a quarterly journal with continuous pagination throughout a yearly volume. Notice that the abbreviation *p.* or *pp.* is not used with the volume number.

10

Footnotes

1 "Morose Scrawler," _Time_, 31 Dec. 1934, p. 38.

2 "Morose Scrawler," p. 38.

3 In the previous year Smith College exhibited Thurber's drawings and those of George Grosz. Then after the one-man show at the Valentine Gallery, "it was clear that he had arrived as a comic artist," Charles S. Holmes, _The Clocks of Columbus: The Literary Career of James Thurber_ (New York: Atheneum, 1972), p. 163.

4 Charles S. Holmes, Introd., _Thurber: A Collection of Critical Essays_, ed. Charles S. Holmes. Twentieth Century Views (Englewood Cliffs, N. J.: Prentice-Hall, 1974), p. 7.

5 Thurber recounted this incident in an interview with Alistair Cooke. "James Thurber in Conversation with Alistair Cooke," _The Atlantic_, Aug. 1956, p. 38.

6 Burton Bernstein calls it "one of the most celebrated and often-reprinted cartoons of the twentieth century." _Thurber: A Biography_ (New York: Dodd, Mead, 1975), p. 190. The eminent humorist Robert Benchley was so taken with it that he sent Thurber a telegram that read as follows: "Thank you for the funniest drawing caption ever to appear in any magazine." See Holmes, _Clocks_, p. 136.

7 Margot Eates, _Paul Nash: The Master of the Image_, 1889-1946 (London: John Murray, 1973), p. 48.

8 His older brother accidently shot him in the eye with an arrow when they were children, causing the immediate loss of that eye. Thurber gradually lost the sight of the other eye because of complications from the accident and a cataract.

9 "That Thurber Woman," _Newsweek_, 22 Nov. 1943, p. 84.

10 Norris W. Yates, _The American Humorist: Conscience of the Twentieth Century_ (Ames: Iowa Univ. Press, 1964), p. 278.

11 "James Thurber Is Dead at 66; Writer Was Also Comic Artist," _New York Times_, 3 Nov. 1961, p. 1, col. 3. An art critic remarked that Thurber's dog figure is "a fantasy dog, which arouses sympathy and laughter in many people and faintly depresses others." Alan Priest, "Mr. Thurber's Chinese Dog," _The Metropolitan Museum of Art Bulletin_, 4 (1946), 261.

Footnote 13 indicates the way to refer to an introduction to a book by another author.

When only one work is involved, it is necessary in a subsequent reference to give only the author's last name and the page number as in footnote 14. Some writers would prefer the word *Ibid.* (not underlined) here.

Footnote 15 shows the way to refer to a book with an introduction by another author when the reference is to something in the book proper rather than in the introduction (as was the case in footnote 13).

Footnote 17 refers to a book in a series.

Although the information in footnote 19 is important and interesting, it does not belong in the text of the paper because it does not fit in with the progress of the argument. This footnote therefore illustrates a primary function of footnotes.

Since the writer did not have access to *The Nation,* it was satisfactory to refer to a reprinting of Auden's essay in footnote 25. The collection of essays gives the original place of publication, and it is helpful to pass this information on to readers. If the original source is available, always use that instead of a reprinting. Notice the difference between "pp. 60, 61" as given in footnote 25 and "pp. 60–61." Written the first way, the reference is to materials found on both pages but not in a consecutive passage. Written the second way, the reference means that the source is a single passage that runs from p. 60 into p. 61.

11

12 "James Thurber in Conversation with Alistair Cooke," p. 39. In another place, Thurber wrote that a rumor was abroad that he wrote the captions while his nephew made the drawings. James Thurber, "The Lady on the Bookcase," in The Beast in Me and Other Animals (New York: Harcourt, Brace, 1948), p. 67.

13 Dorothy Parker, Introd., The Seal in the Bedroom and Other Predicaments by James Thurber (New York: Harper, 1932), p. ix.

14 Parker, p. ix.

15 Stephen Becker, Comic Art in America, introd. Rube Goldberg (New York: Simon and Schuster, 1959), p. 128.

16 Parker, pp. vii-viii.

17 Stephen A. Black, James Thurber: His Masquerades. Studies in American Literature, 23 (The Hague: Mouton, 1970), p. 16.

18 E. M. Benson, "Phases of Fantasy," The American Magazine of Art, 28 (1935), 299.

19 It is natural to question whether Thurber's failing eyesight, and not some deeper reason, was responsible for his sparse, unrealistic drawings. Robert E. Morsberger points out, however, the following: "Thurber's visual problems had no relation to the technique of his art. His drawings were most devoid of detail when his sight was strongest; and his later illustrations, even after the operations, have considerably more detail than the earlier ones." James Thurber, Twayne's United States Authors Series, 62 (New York: Twayne, 1964), p. 170.

20 Parker, p. viii.

21 "That Thurber Woman," p. 84.

22 Elliott Nugent, "Notes on James Thurber the Man, or Men." The New York Times, 22 Feb. 1940, Sec. 10, p. 3, col. 4.

23 Richard C. Tobias, The Art of James Thurber (Athens: Ohio Univ. Press, 1969), p. 172.

24 "Morose Scrawler," p. 38.

25 W. H. Auden, "The Icon and the Portrait," in Thurber: A Collection of Critical Essays, pp. 60, 61. This essay originally appeared in The Nation, 13 Jan. 1940, p. 48.

26 Louis Hasley, "James Thurber: Artist in Humor," The South Atlantic Quarterly, 73 (1974), 504.

27 Robert H. Elias, "James Thurber: The Primitive, the Innocent, and the Individual," The American Scholar, 27 (1958), 356.

Start the bibliography on a new page as the last section of your paper. Head the page Works Cited, centered. Triple-space below the heading.

Do not indent the first line of an entry; indent succeeding lines five spaces.

Double-space between entries, single-space within an entry.

List only those sources actually used in your paper and referred to in footnotes.

Authors are listed with surnames first. If a book has more than one author, however, the names of authors after the first one are put in normal order.

List entries alphabetically. When more than one book by the same author is listed, use a line (about one inch) in place of the author's name in entries after the first. An entry without an author (for example, an unsigned magazine article) is listed alphabetically by the first word.

List the inclusive pages of articles.

Notice that the important divisions of entries are separated by periods.

A bibliographical entry should include all the information that will enable readers to find the source readily if they wish to do so.

12

Works Cited

Auden, W. H. "The Icon and the Portrait." The Nation, 13 Jan. 1940, p. 48;
    rpt. in Thurber: A Collection of Critical Essays. Ed. Charles S.
    Holmes. Twentieth Century Views. Englewood Cliffs, N. J.: Prentice-
    Hall, 1974, pp. 59–61.

Becker, Stephen. Comic Art in America. Introd. Rube Goldberg. New York:
    Simon and Schuster, 1959.

Benson, E. M. "Phases of Fantasy." The American Magazine of Art, 28 (1935),
    290–299.

Bernstein, Burton. Thurber: A Biography. New York: Dodd, Mead, 1975.

Black, Stephen A. James Thurber: His Masquerades. Studies in American
    Literature, 23. The Hague: Mouton, 1970.

Eates, Margot. Paul Nash: The Master of the Image, 1889–1946. London: John
    Murray, 1973.

Elias, Robert H. "James Thurber: The Primitive, the Innocent, and the
    Individual." The American Scholar, 27 (1958), 355–63.

Hasley, Louis. "James Thurber: Artist in Humor." The South Atlantic Quarterly,
    73 (1975), 504–15.

Holmes, Charles S. The Clocks of Columbus: The Literary Career of James
    Thurber. New York: Atheneum, 1972.

_____, introd. Thurber: A Collection of Critical Essays. Ed.
    Charles S. Holmes. Twentieth Century Views. Englewood Cliffs, N. J.:
    Prentice-Hall, 1974.

"James Thurber in Conversation with Alistair Cooke." The Atlantic, Aug.
    1956, pp. 36–40.

"James Thurber Is Dead at 66; Writer Was Also Comic Artist." New York Times,
    3 Nov. 1961, p. 1, cols. 3–4, p. 35, cols. 2–4.

"Morose Scrawler." Time, 31 Dec. 1934, p. 38.

Morsberger, Robert E. James Thurber. Twayne's United States Authors Series,
    62. New York: Twayne, 1964.

Nugent, Elliott. "Notes on James Thurber the Man, or Men." New York Times,
    22 Feb. 1940, Sec. 10, p. 3, cols. 1–4.

Parker, Dorothy, introd. James Thurber, The Seal in the Bedroom and Other
    Predicaments. New York: Harper & Row, 1932.

Priest, Alan. "Mr. Thurber's Chinese Dog." The Metropolitan Museum of Art
    Bulletin, 4 (1946), 260–61.

"That Thurber Woman." Newsweek, 22 Nov. 1943, pp. 84–86.

Thurber, James. "The Lady on the Bookcase." In The Beast in Me and Other
    Animals. New York: Harcourt, Brace, 1948, pp. 66–75.

Tobias, Richard C. The Art of James Thurber. Athens: Ohio Univ. Press, 1969.

Yates, Norris W. The American Humorist: Conscience of the Twentieth Century.
    Ames: Iowa Univ. Press, 1964.

The process of composition   323

This sample shows how footnotes can be placed at the bottom of pages on which they occur. Follow your instructor's preference as to where you place the footnotes.

Separate footnotes from the text by a short ruled or typed line starting at the left-hand margin and placed far enough below the last line of the text so that it will not be mistaken for underlining to indicate italics.

Hope Through Fantasy in James Thurber's Drawings

In December of 1934 the highly respected Valentine Gallery in Manhattan held one of the most unusual exhibitions in all of its history.
Less traditional than many of the art galleries in New York City, the
Valentine "devoted itself to the more advanced of the socially acceptable
left-wing artists."[1] Nevertheless, this was a particularly odd one-man
show: as viewers shuffled from one frame to another, they witnessed childlike reproductions of gentle dogs, aggressive women, and emasculated men
all casually drawn as doodles on various sorts and sizes of sheets, even
scratch paper.[2] Much puzzlement and disbelief ran through these lovers of
art; but the exhibition was widely reviewed, and the artist, James Thurber,
was in the end compared with such giants as Picasso and Matisse.[3] Since
then, Thurber's position as a serious artist as well as a serious writer has
been solidly established, although his cartoons, known best from the pages
of The New Yorker, are deceptively simple. His fame has been accompanied by
a reputation for bitterness, which is in some measure justified; but if
pessimism is reflected in Thurber's drawings, a sense of hope is even stronger.

---

[1] "Morose Scrawler," Time, 31 Dec. 1934, p. 38.

[2] "Morose Scrawler," p. 38.

[3] In the previous year Smith College exhibited Thurber's drawings and
those of George Grosz. Then after the one-man show at the Valentine Gallery, "it was clear that he had arrived as a comic artist." Charles S.
Holmes, The Clocks of Columbus: The Literary Career of James Thurber (New
York: Atheneum, 1972), p. 163.

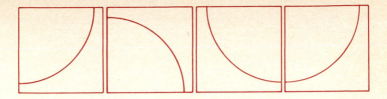

Glossaries of Usage
and Grammatical Terms

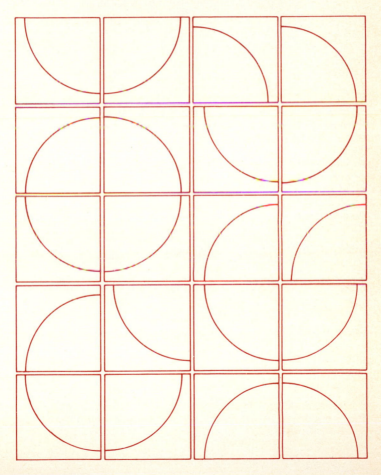

49   **Glossary of usage**   *gl / us*

Many items not listed here are covered in other sections of this book and may be located through the index. For words found neither in this glossary nor in the index, consult a good dictionary. The usage labels (*informal, dialectal,* and so on) affixed to words in this glossary reflect the opinions of two or more of the dictionaries listed on page 176.

A, an   Use *a* as an article before consonant sounds; use *an* before vowel sounds.

a nickname	*an* office
a house	*an* hour
(the *h* is sounded)	(the *h* is not sounded)
a historical novel	
(though the British say *an*)	
a union	*an* uncle
(long *u* has the consonant	
sound of *y*)	

Accept, except   As a verb, *accept* means "to receive"; *except* means "to exclude." *Except* as a preposition also means "but."

Every legislator *except* Mr. Whelling refused to *accept* the bribe.
We will *except* (exclude) this novel from the list of those to be read.

Accidently   A misspelling usually caused by mispronunciation. Use *accidentally*.
Advice, advise   Use *advice* as a noun, *advise* as a verb.
Affect, effect   *Affect* is a verb meaning "to act upon" or "to influence." *Effect* may be a verb or a noun. *Effect* as a verb means "to cause" or "to bring about"; *effect* as a noun means "a result," "a consequence."

The patent medicine did not *affect* (influence) the disease.
The operation did not *effect* (bring about) an improvement in the patient's health.

The drug had a drastic *effect* (consequence) on the speed of the patient's reactions.

Aggravate Informal in the sense of "annoy," "irritate," or "pester." Formally, it means "to make worse or more severe."

Agree to, agree with *Agree to* a thing (plan, proposal); *agree with* a person.

He *agreed to* the insertion of the plank in the platform of the party.
He *agreed with* the senator that the plank would not gain many votes.

Ain't Nonstandard or illiterate.

All ready, already *All ready* means "prepared, in a state of readiness"; *already* means "before some specified time" or "previously" and describes an action that is completed.

The riders were *all ready* to mount. (fully prepared)
Mr. Bowman had *already* bagged his limit of quail. (action completed at time of statement)

All together, altogether *All together* describes a group as acting or existing collectively; *altogether* means "wholly, entirely."

The sprinters managed to start *all together*.
I do not *altogether* approve the decision.

Allusion, illusion An *allusion* is a casual reference. An *illusion* is a false or misleading sight or impression.

Alot Nonstandard for *a lot*. See **Lot of, lots of.**

Alright Not standard spelling for *all right*.

A.M., P.M, or a.m., p.m. Used only with figures, as in "6:00 P.M." Not to be used for *morning* or *afternoon* as in "The parade began this P.M."

Among, between *Among* is used with three or more persons or things; *between* is used with only two.

It will be hard to choose *between* the two candidates.
It will be hard to choose *among* so many candidates.

Amount, number *Amount* refers to mass or quantity; *number* refers to things which may be counted.

That is a large *number* of turtles for a pond which has such a small *amount* of water.

An See **A.**
And etc. See **Etc.**
Anticlimax See **Climactic order.**
Anyplace Prefer *anywhere*.
Anyways Prefer *anyway*.
Anywheres Prefer *anywhere*.
As Weak or confusing in the sense of *because*.

The client collected the full amount of insurance *as* her car ran off the cliff and was totally demolished.

Awful A trite and feeble substitute for such words as *bad, shocking, ludicrous, ugly*.
Awhile, a while *Awhile* is an adverb; *a while* is an article and a noun.

Stay *awhile*.
Wait here for *a while*. (object of preposition)

Bad, badly See page 73.
Because See **Reason is because.**
Being as, being that Use *because* or *since*.
Beside, besides *Beside* means "by the side of," "next to"; *besides* means "in addition to."

Mr. Potts was sitting *beside* the stove.
No one was in the room *besides* Mr. Potts.

Between See **Among.**
Between you and I Wrong case. Use *between you and me*.

Bust, busted Slang as forms of *burst*. *Bursted* is also unacceptable.

Can, may In formal English, *can* is still used to denote ability; *may*, to denote permission. Informally the two are interchangeable.

FORMAL
May (not *can*) I go?

Capital, capitol *Capitol* designates "a building which is a seat of government"; *capital* is used for all other meanings.

Center around Illogical: use center *in* (or *on*) or cluster around.

Climactic, climatic *climactic* pertains to a climax; *climatic* pertains to climate.

Climactic order and anticlimax In climactic order, the elements of a series are arranged according to increasing importance. Ordering by decreasing importance may result in anticlimax and loss of emphasis.

UNEMPHATIC
The hurricane left thousands of people homeless, ruined the crops, and interrupted transportation.
CLIMACTIC
The hurricane interrupted transportation, ruined the crops, and left thousands of people homeless.

Colloquial See page 176.

Compare to, compare with After *compare* in similes, use *to*; in analyses of similarities and differences, use *with*.

He *compared* the wrecked train *to* strewn and broken matches.
He *compared* this train wreck *with* the one that occurred a month ago.

Complement, compliment *To complement* means "to complete"; *to compliment* means "to praise."

Considerable Basically an adjective, though used informally as a noun.

He had a *considerable* influence on his students.
He earned *considerable* each week.

Contemptible, contemptuous *Contemptible* means "deserving of scorn"; *contemptuous* means "feeling scorn."

The sophomore who was *contemptuous* toward freshmen was *contemptible*.

Continual, continuous *Continual* refers to a prolonged and rapid succession; *continuous* refers to an uninterrupted succession.

Contractions Avoid contractions *(don't, he's, they're)* in formal writing.

Criteria Plural. Use *criterion* for the singular.

Cute Overused, many think, for such expressions as *pretty, dainty, attractive.*

Data *Data* is considered singular or plural; the singular form, *datum,* is rare.

Deal Informal and overused for *bargain, transaction,* or *business arrangement.*

Done Past participle of *to do:* not to be used in place of *did,* as the past tense of *to do* (He *did* it *not* He *done* it).

Don't Contraction of *do not;* not to be used for *doesn't,* the contraction of *does not.*

Double negative Avoid such uneducated phrases as *can't help but, didn't have scarcely,* and so on.

Effect See **Affect.**

Enthused Use *enthusiastic* in formal writing.

Etc. Do not use *and etc. Etc.* means "and so forth."

Ever, every Use *every* in *every day, every other, everybody, every now and then;* use *ever* in *ever and anon, ever so humble.*

Every day, everyday *Every day* is used as an adverb; *everyday,* as an adjective.

He comes to look at the same picture in the gallery *every day.*
His trip to the gallery is an *everyday* occurrence.

Exam Informal: use *examination* in formal writing.

Except See **Accept.**

Expect Informal for *believe, suspect, think, suppose,* and so forth.

Fabulous Informal for *extremely pleasing.*

Fantastic Informal for *extraordinarily good.*

Farther, further Generally interchangeable, though many persons prefer *farther* in expressions of physical distance and *further* in expressions of time, quantity, and degree.

My car used less gasoline and went *farther* than his.
The second speaker went *further* into the issues than the first.

Fewer, less Use *fewer* to denote number; *less,* to denote amount or degree.

With *fewer* advertisers, there will also be *less* income from advertising.

Finalize Bureaucratic. Avoid.

Fine Often a poor substitute for a more exact word of approval or commendation.

Fix Informal for the noun *predicament.*

Flunk Informal: prefer *fail* or *failure* in formal usage.

Folks Informal for *family* or *relatives.*

Funny Informal for *strange, remarkable,* or *peculiar.*

Further See **Farther.**

Good Incorrect as an adverb. See page 72.

Grand Often vaguely used in place of more exact words like *majestic, magnificent, imposing.*

Great Informal for *first-rate.*

Hang, hanged, hung See page 37.

Hardly See **Not hardly.**

Has got, have got Use simply *has* or *have.*

Himself See **Myself.**

Illusion See **Allusion.**

Imply, infer *Imply* means "to hint" or "suggest"; *infer* means "to draw a conclusion."

The speaker *implied* that Mr. Dixon was guilty.
The audience *inferred* that Mr. Dixon was guilty.

In, into *Into* denotes motion from the outside to the inside; *in* denotes position (enclosure).

The lion was *in* the cage when the trainer walked *into* the tent.

Infer See **Imply.**
In regards to Unidiomatic: use *in regard to* or *with regard to.*
Into See **In.**
Irregardless Nonstandard for *regardless.*
Is when, is where Ungrammatical use of adverbial clause after a linking verb. Often misused in definitions and explanations.

NONSTANDARD
Combustion *is when* (or *is where*) oxygen unites with other elements.
STANDARD
Combustion occurs when oxygen unites with other elements.
Combustion is a union of oxygen with other elements.

Its, it's *Its* is the possessive case of the pronoun *it; it's* is a contraction of *it is.*

It's exciting to parents when their baby cuts *its* first tooth.

Kind of, sort of Informal as adverbs: use *rather, somewhat,* and so forth.

INFORMAL
Mr. Josephson was *sort of* disgusted.
FORMAL
Mr. Josephson was *rather* disgusted.

FORMAL (not an adverb)
What *sort of* book is that?

Kind of a, sort of a Delete the *a;* use *kind of* and *sort of.*

What *kind of* (not *kind of a*) pipe do you smoke?

Lay, lie See page 37.

Lead, led *Lead* is an incorrect form for the past tense *led*.

Learn, teach *Learn* means "to acquire knowledge." *Teach* means "to impart knowledge."

She could not *learn* how to work the problem until Mrs. Smithers *taught* her the formula.

Less See **Fewer.**

Liable See **Likely.**

Lie See page 37.

Like Instead of *like* as a conjunction, prefer *as*, *as if*, or *as though*.

CONJUNCTION
She acted *as if* she had never been on the stage before.

PREPOSITION
She acted *like* a novice.

CONJUNCTION
She acted *like* she had never had a date before. (informal)

Such popular expressions as "tell it like it is" derive part of their appeal from their lighthearted defiance of convention.

Do not use *like* for *that* as in *feel like*.

Do not use *like* (the verb) for *lack*.

Likely, liable Use *likely* to express probability; use *liable,* which may have legal connotations, to express responsibility or obligation.

You are *likely* to have an accident if you drive recklessly.
Since your father owns the car, he will be *liable* for damages.

Loose A frequent misspelling of *lose*. *Loose* is an adjective; *lose* is a verb.

She wore a *loose* and trailing gown.
Speculators often *lose* their money.

Lot See **A lot.**
Lot of, lots of Informal in the sense of *much, many, a great deal.*
May See **Can.**
Most Informal for *almost* in such expressions as the following:

He is late for class *almost* (not *most*) every day.

Myself, yourself, himself, herself, itself These words are reflexives or intensives, not strict equivalents of *I, me, you, he, she, him, her, it.*

INTENSIVE
I *myself* helped Father cut the wheat.
I helped Father cut the wheat *myself.*

REFLEXIVE
I cut *myself.*

NOT
The elopement was known only to Sherry and *myself.*
BUT
The elopement was known only to Sherry and *me.*

NOT
Only Kay and *myself* had access to the safe.
BUT
Only Kay and *I* had access to the safe.

Neat Slang for *appealing.*
Nice A weak substitute for more exact words like *attractive, modest, pleasant, kind,* and so forth.
Not hardly Double negative. Avoid.
Nowheres Dialectal. Use *nowhere.*
Number See **Amount.**
Off of *Off* is sufficient.

He fell *off* (not *off of*) the water tower.

O. K., OK, okay Informal.
Percent (or per cent) Use after figures, as "50 percent." Do not use for *percentage:*

Only a small *percentage* (not *percent*) of the people had degrees.

Phenomena Plural. The singular is *phenomenon.*
Photo Informal.
P.M. See **A.M.**
Principal, principle Use *principal* to mean "the chief" or "most important." Use *principle* to mean "a rule" or "a truth."

The *principal* reason for her delinquency was never discussed.
The *principal* of Brookwood High School applauded.
To act without *principle* leads to delinquency.

Quote A verb: prefer *quotation* as a noun.
Raise, rise See page 38.
Real Informal or dialectal as an adverb meaning *really* or *very.*
Reason is (was) because Use *the reason is (was) that.* Formally, *because* should introduce an adverbial clause, not a noun clause used as a predicate nominative.

NOT
The *reason* Abernathy enlisted *was because* he failed in college.
BUT
The *reason* Abernathy enlisted *was that* he failed in college.
OR
Abernathy enlisted *because* he failed in college.

Respectfully, respectively *Respectfully* means "with respect"; *respectively* means "each in the order given."

He *respectfully* thanked the president for his diploma.
Crossing the platform, he passed *respectively* by the speaker, the dean, and the registrar.

Revelant A misspelling and mispronunciation of **relevant.**

Sensual, sensuous *Sensual* connotes the gratification of bodily pleasures; *sensuous* refers favorably to what is experienced through the senses.

Set, sit See page 38.

Shall, will In strictly formal English, to indicate simple futurity, *shall* is conventional in the first person (I *shall,* we *shall*); *will,* in the second and third persons (you *will,* he *will,* they *will*). To indicate determination, duty, or necessity, *will* is formal in the first person (I *will,* we *will*); *shall,* in the second and third persons (you *shall,* he *shall,* they *shall*). These distinctions are weaker than they used to be, and *will* is increasingly used in all persons.

So For the use of *so* in incomplete constructions, see page 84. The use of *so* for *so that* sometimes causes confusion.

Sometime, some time *Sometime* is used adverbially to designate an indefinite point of time. *Some time* refers to a period or duration of time.

I will see you *sometime* next week.
I have not seen him for *some time*.

Sort of See **Kind of.**
Sort of   See **Kind of a.**
Super Informal for *excellent*.
Sure Informal as an adverb for *surely, certainly*.

INFORMAL
The speaker *sure* criticized his opponent.
FORMAL
The speaker *certainly* criticized his opponent.

Sure and, try and Use *sure to, try to*.

Be *sure to* (not *sure and*) notice the costumes of the Hungarian folk dancers.

Suspicion Avoid as a verb; use *suspect*.

Swell Slang or informal for *good;* often vaguely used for more exact words of approval.

Teach See **Learn.**

Terrible Often a poor substitute for a more exact word.

Than, then Do not use one of these words for the other.

Their, there Not interchangeable: *their* is the possessive of *they; there* is either an adverb meaning "in that place" or an expletive.

Their dachshund is sick.
There it is on the corner. (adverb of place)
There is a veterinarian's office in this block. (expletive)

These (those) kinds, these (those) sorts *These (those)* is plural; *kind (sort)* is singular. Therefore use *this (that) kind, this (that) sort; these (those) kinds, these (those) sorts.*

Thusly Prefer *thus*.

Transitive verb See **Voice** (Glossary of Grammatical Terms).

Try and See **Sure and.**

Unique Means "one of a kind"; hence it may not logically be compared. *Unique* should not be loosely used for *unusual* or *strange*.

Use Sometimes carelessly written for the past tense, *used*.

Thomas Jefferson *used* (not *use*) to bathe in cold water almost every
    morning.

Wait on Unidiomatic for *wait for*. *Wait on* correctly means "to serve."

Ways Prefer *way* when designating a distance.

a long *way*
NOT
a long *ways*

When, where See **Is when, is where.**

Where Do not misuse for *that*.

I read in the newspaper *that* (not *where*) you saved a child's life.

Where at The *at* is unnecessary.

NOT
Where is he *at?*
BUT
Where is he?

Whose, who's *Whose* is the possessive of *who; who's* is a contraction of *who is*.

-wise A suffix overused in combinations with nouns, such as *budget-wise, progress-wise,* and *business-wise*.

Without Dialectal for *unless,* as in "I cannot come *without* you pay for the ticket."

50 Glossary of grammatical terms gl/gr

This is by no means a complete list of terms used in discussing grammar. See other sections of this book and consult dictionaries.

Absolute phrase See **20L.**
Active voice See **Voice.**
Adjective A word which modifies a noun or a pronoun. (See pages 8, 72–74.)

Her young horse jumped over *that high* barrier for *the first* time.

Adjective clause See **Dependent clause.**
Adverb A word which modifies a verb, an adjective, or another adverb. See pages 9, 72–74.
Adverbial clause See **Dependent clause.**
Antecedent A word to which a pronoun refers.

antecedent   *pronoun*

When the ballet *dancers* appeared, *they* were dressed in pink.

Appositive A word, phrase, or clause used as a noun and placed beside another word to explain it.

appositive

The *poet John Milton* wrote *Paradise Lost* while he was blind.

Article *A* and *an* are indefinite articles; *the* is the definite article.
Auxiliary verb A verb used to help another verb indicate tense, mood, or voice. Principal auxiliaries are forms of the verbs *to be* and *to do*. (See pages 6–7.)

I *am* studying.
I *do* study.
I *shall* go there next week.
He *may* lose his job.

Case English has remnants of three cases: subjective, possessive, and objective. Nouns are inflected for case only in the possessive *(father, father's)*. An alternative way to show possession is with the "of phrase" *(of the house)*. Some pronouns, notably the personal pronouns and the relative pronoun *who,* are still fully inflected for three cases:

SUBJECTIVE (acting)
I, he, she, we, they, who

POSSESSIVE (possessing)
my (mine), your (yours), his, her (hers), its, our (ours), their (theirs),
    whose

OBJECTIVE (acted upon)
me, him, her, us, them, whom

Clause A group of words containing a subject and a predicate. See **Independent clause; Dependent clause.** See page 23.

Collective noun A word identifying a class or a group of persons or things. See page 3.

Comparative and Superlative degrees See **10a** and **10b.**

Complement A word or group of words used to complete a predicate. Predicate adjectives, predicate nominatives, direct objects, and indirect objects are complements. See pages 17–19.

Complex, compound, compound-complex sentences A *complex sentence* has one independent clause and at least one dependent clause. A *compound sentence* has at least two independent clauses. A *compound-complex sentence* has two or more independent clauses and one dependent clause or more. See page 24.

Compound structures See page 15.

Conjunction A word used to connect sentences or sentence parts.

See also **Coordinating conjunctions, Correlative conjunctions, Subordinating conjunctions,** and pages 10–11.

Conjunctive adverb An adverb used to relate two independent clauses which are separated by a semicolon: *however, therefore, moreover, then, consequently, besides,* and so on (see **22a**).

Coordinate clause See **Independent clause.** When there are two independent clauses in a compound or a compound-complex sentence, they may be called coordinate clauses.

Coordinating conjunction A simple conjunction which joins sentences or parts of sentences of equal rank *(and, but, or, nor, for, yet, so)*. See page 10.

Correlative conjunctions Conjunctions used in pairs to join coordinate sentence elements. The most common are *either — or, neither — nor, not only — but also, both — and.*

Degrees (of modifiers) See **10a** and **10b.**

Demonstrative adjective or pronoun A word used to point out *(this, that, these, those)*.

Dependent (subordinate) clause A group of words which contains both a subject and a predicate but which does not stand alone as a sentence. A dependent clause is frequently signaled by a subordinator *(who, which, what, that, since, because,* and so on) and always functions as an adjective, adverb, or noun.

ADJECTIVE
The tenor *who sang the aria* had just arrived from Italy.

NOUN
The critics agreed *that the young tenor had a magnificent voice.*

ADVERB
When he sang, even the sophisticated audience was enraptured.

Diagramming Diagramming uses systems of lines and positioning of words to show the parts of a sentence and the relationships between them. Its purpose is to make understandable the way writing is put together. (See example on following page.)

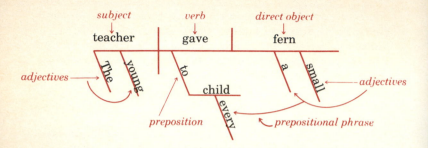

Direct object A noun, pronoun, or other substantive receiving the action of the verb. (See page 18.)

The angler finally caught the old *trout*.

Elliptical clause A clause in which one or more words are omitted but understood.

understood

The director admired no one else as much as *(he admired* or *he did)* her.

Expletive See **7h.**
Gerund See **Verbal.**
Indefinite pronoun A pronoun not pointing out a particular person or thing. Some of the most common are *some, any, each, everyone, everybody, anyone, anybody, one,* and *neither.*
Independent (main) clause A group of words which contains a subject and a predicate and which grammatically can stand alone as a sentence.
Indirect object A word which indirectly receives the action of the verb. (See pages 18–19.)

The actress wrote the *soldier* a letter.

Infinitive See **Verbal.**
Inflection A change in the form of a word to indicate its gram-

matical function. Nouns, adjectives, and pronouns are declined; verbs are conjugated. Some inflections occur when *-s* or *-es* is added to nouns or verbs or when *'s* is added to nouns.

Intensive pronoun A pronoun ending in *-self* and used for emphasis.

The director *himself* will act the part of Hamlet.

Interjection A word used to exclaim or to express an (usually strong) emotion. It has no grammatical connections within its sentence. Some common interjections are *oh, ah,* and *ouch.* See page 13.

Interrogative pronoun See **9i.**

Intransitive verb See **Voice.**

Inversion A change in normal word order, such as placing an adjective after the noun it modifies or placing the object of a verb at the beginning of a sentence.

Linking verb A verb which does not express action but links the subject to another word which names or describes it. See page 7 and **10c.** Common linking verbs are *be, become,* and *seem.*

Modifier A word (or word group) which limits or describes another word. See pages 92–94.

Mood The mood (or mode) of a verb indicates whether an action is to be thought of as fact, command, wish, or condition contrary to fact. Modern English has three moods: the indicative, for ordinary statements and questions; the imperative, for commands and entreaty; and the subjunctive, for certain idiomatic expressions of wish, command, or condition contrary to fact.

INDICATIVE
Does she *play* the guitar?
She *does.*

IMPERATIVE
Stay with me.
Let him stay.

The imperative is formed like the plural present indicative, without -*s*.

If I *were* you, I would go.
I wish he *were* going with you.
I move that the meeting *be* adjourned.
It is necessary that he *stay* absolutely quiet.
If this *be* true, no man ever loved.

The most common subjunctive forms are *were* and *be*. All others are formed like the present-tense plural form without -*s*.

Nominative case See **Case.**

Noun A word which names and which has gender, number, and case. There are proper nouns, which name particular people, places, or things *(Thomas Jefferson, Paris,* the *Colosseum);* common nouns, which name one or more of a group *(alligator, high school, politician);* collective nouns (see **7d** and **8c**); abstract nouns, which name ideas, feelings, beliefs, and so on *(religion, justice, dislike, enthusiasm);* concrete nouns, which name things perceived through the senses *(lemon, hatchet, worm).*

Noun clause See **Dependent clause.**

Number A term to describe forms which indicate whether a word is singular or plural.

Object of preposition See **Preposition** and **9b** and page 12.

Objective case See **Case.**

Obsolete words Not used in modern English, for example, *jump* for "exactly" and *shrewd* in the sense of "bad" or "evil."

Participle See **Verbal.**

Parts of speech See pages 2–13.

Passive voice See **Voice.**

Personal pronoun A pronoun like *I, you, he, she, it, we, they, mine, yours, his, hers, its, ours, theirs.*

Phrase A group of closely related words without both a subject and a predicate. There are subject phrases (*the new drill sergeant*), verb phrases (*should have been*), verbal phrases (*climbing high mountains*), prepositional phrases (*of the novel*), appositive phrases (my brother, *the black sheep of the family*), and so forth. See pages 20–22.

Predicate The verb in a clause (simple predicate) or the verb and its modifiers, complements, and objects (complete predicate). See pages 14, 16–17.

Predicate adjective An adjective following a linking verb and describing the subject (see page 18 and **10c**).

The rose is *artificial.*

Predicate nominative A noun following a linking verb and naming the subject.

Preposition A connective which joins a noun or a pronoun to the rest of a sentence. A prepositional phrase may be used as either an adjective or an adverb. See page 12.

Pronominal adjective An adjective which has the same form as a possessive pronoun (*my* book, *their* enthusiasm).

Pronoun A word which stands for a noun. See **Personal pronoun; Demonstrative adjective or pronoun; Reflexive pronoun; Intensive pronoun; Interrogative pronoun; Indefinite pronoun; Relative pronoun.**

Reflexive pronoun A pronoun ending in -*self* and indicating that the subject acts upon itself. See **Myself** (Glossary of Usage).

Relative pronoun See **9i.**

Simple sentence A sentence consisting of only one independent clause and no dependent clauses. See page 24.

Subject A word or group of words about which the sentence or clause makes a statement. (See pages 14–15.)

Subjective case See **Case.**

Subordinate clause See **Dependent clause.**

Subordinating conjunction A conjunction which joins sentence parts of unequal rank. Most frequently these conjunctions begin dependent clauses. Some common subordinating conjunctions are *because, since, though, although, if, when, while, before, after, as, until, so that, as long as, as if, where, unless, as soon as, whereas, in order that.* See pages 10–11.

Substantive A noun or a sentence element which serves the function of a noun.

Superlative degree See **10a** and **10b.**

Transitive verb See **Voice.**

Verb A word or group of words expressing action, being, or state of being. (See pages 6–7).

Automobiles *burn* gas.
What *is* life?

Verb phrase See **Phrase.**

Verbal A word derived from a verb and used as a noun, an adjective, or an adverb. A verbal may be a gerund, a participle, or an infinitive. See pages 20–22.

Voice Transitive verbs have two forms to show whether their subjects act on an object (active voice) or are acted upon (passive voice). See page 44.

Index

A, an, 328
Abbreviations
  for agencies and organizations,
    170
  for personal titles, 170
  improper use of, 170
  in bibliographies, 170
  in footnotes, 170
  periods with, 140–141
  with dates and times, 170
Absolute adjectives and adverbs,
  73
Absolute phrases, 121
Abstract nouns, 3
Abstract words, 197–198
Accept, except, 328
Accidently, 328
Accurate data, 207
Active voice, 44, 191
A.D., B.C., capitalized, 169
Addresses, commas with, 119–
  120
Adjectives
  absolute, 73

after linking verbs, 73–74
after verbs and objects, 74
articles as, 8
comparative, 72–73
coordinate, 111–112
cumulative, 111–112
defined, 8, 341
demonstrative, 8, 343
distinguished from adverbs,
  72–74
indefinite, 8
possessive, 8
predicate, 8, 17–18, 73–74,
  342, 347
pronominal, 347
superlative, 72–73
Adverbs
  absolute, 73
  comparative, 72–73
  conjunctive, 30, 118–119, 343
  defined, 9, 341
  distinguished from adjectives,
    72–74
  -ly ending of, 72

Adverbs *(cont.)*
   not after verbs and objects, 74
   not with linking verbs, 73–74
   superlative, 72–73
Advice, advise, 328
Affect, effect, 328–329
Agencies and organizations,
      abbreviations for, 170
Aggravate, 329
Agreement, pronouns and
      antecedents
   ambiguous reference,60
   antecedents such as *each,
      either,* 57–58
   collective noun antecedents, 57
   compound antecedents with
      and, 56–57
   compound antecedents with *or,
      nor,* etc., 57
   definite antecedents, 56, 60
   he or she, his or her, 58
   intensive pronouns, 60–61
   vague references, 59–60
   which, who, that, whose, 58–59
Agreement, subjects and verbs
   collective noun subjects, 49
   compound subjects with *and,*
      47–48
   compound subjects with *or, nor,*
      etc., 48
   indefinite pronoun subjects
      (*each, either,* etc.), 50
   intervening phrases or clauses,
      48–49
   none, some, such, etc., 50
   not with subjective
      complement, 52
   noun subjects plural in form,
      singular in meaning, 49–50
   number as subject, 51
   person and number, 47–53
   relative pronouns as subjects, 52
   titles as subjects, 52–53
   with *here, there,* 51–52
Agree to, agree with, 329

Ain't, 329
All, 50
All ready, already, 329
All together, altogether, 329
Allusion, illusion, 329
Alot, 329
Already, all ready, 329
Alright, 329
Alternatives (in reasoning), 212
Altogether, all together, 329
A.M., P.M. or *a.m., p.m.,* 329
Among, between, 329
Amount, number, 330
An, a, 328
Analogy, 227–228
And which, 99–100
And who, 99–100
Antecedents
   agreement with pronouns,
      56–60
   ambiguous (one not two), 60
   collective noun, 57
   compound with *and,* 56–57
   defined, 341
   definite, 56, 60
   for pronouns ending in *-self* or
      -selves, 60–61
   of relative pronouns, 52, 69–70
Anticlimax, 331
Anybody, 50, 57–58
Anyone, 50, 57–58
Anyplace, 330
Anyways, 330
Anywheres, 330
Apostrophes
   for joint possession, 166
   for plurals of numerals, letters,
      words, 166
   for possessive of indefinite
      pronouns, 166
   for possessive of nouns, 165
   not with possessive of personal
      pronouns, 67–68, 166
   to form contractions, 166
   to show omissions, 166

Apostrophes *(cont.)*
   with possessive forms of
     indefinite pronouns, 67–68
Appeal to emotions, 210–211
Appositives
   case of, 65–66
   colons before, 134
   defined, 341
   nonrestrictive and restrictive,
     114–115
Archaic words, 178
Argument, *see* Clear and logical
   thinking
Argumentum ad hominem, see
   Name-calling
Articles (*a, an, the*)
   as adjectives, 8
   defined, 341
   repeated, 98
Articles (literary), quotations
   with titles of, 138
As, case after, 66
As . . . as, no comma between,
   127
Authorities, reliable, 207–208
Auxiliary verbs, 6–7, 20, 341–342
Awful, 330
Awhile, a while, 330
Axioms, to suggest theme
   subjects, 250–251

Bad, badly, 73
Balanced sentences, 102–103
B.C., A.D., capitalized, 169
Begging the question, 209–210
Being as, being that, 330
Beside, besides, 330
Between, among, 329
Between he and I, 65
Between you and I, 330
Bible
   books of not underlined, 154
   referred to in footnotes, 290
Bibliography
   abbreviations in, 170

   cards for preparing, 276
   colons in, 135
   sample, 291–293, 322–323
   working, 267–275
Blocked quotations, 137
Books
   quotation marks with chapter
     titles of, 138
   underlining titles of, 154
Brackets
   for interpolations, 136, 302
   for parentheses, 136
Business letters
   envelopes for, 152
   folding, 153–154
   paragraphing in, 150
   proper stationery for, 154
   salutations of, 120–121, 135,
     150
Bust, busted, 331

Can, may, 331
Capital, capitol, 331
Capitalization, *see* Capital letters
Capital letters
   for B.C. and A.D., 169
   for days of the week, 169
   for first words of sentences,
     167
   for holidays, 169
   for interjection *O,* 167
   for months of the year, 169
   for names of specific courses,
     169–170
   for pronoun *I,* 167
   for proper nouns, 169
   for sacred books, 169
   for words of family relationship,
     168
   in direct quotations, 167
   in literary titles, 167, 306
   in personal titles, 167–168
   not for *a, an, the* in titles, 167
   not for conjunctions in titles,
     167

Capital letters *(cont.)*
  not for prepositions in titles,
    167
  not for seasons of the year, 169
  not with parenthetical sentence
    within another sentence, 136
  to designate religious
    denominations, 169
  to designate the Deity, 169
  with degrees, 168
Card catalog, 266, 267–270
Case
  after *as,* 66
  after *than,* 66
  defined, 342
  objective, 65–67, 68–70, 342
  of appositives, 65–66
  of interrogative pronouns,
    68–69
  of personal pronouns, 67–68
  of phrase for possession, 67
  of pronouns, 64–70
  of relative pronouns, 68–70
  possessive, 64, 66–67, 165, 342
  subjective, 64, 65–66, 68–70,
    342
Cause and effect, 211, 228–229
Center around, 333
Character analysis, in literary
    paper, 258–259
Characterization, 258–259
Checklist for revising themes,
    247–249
Choosing a subject
  literary paper, 255–256
  research paper, 265–266
  theme, 237–238, 249–254
Choppy sentences, 78, 101
Circular reasoning, 209–210
Classification, type of
    paragraph, 229
Clauses
  coordinate, 343
  defined, 23, 342
  dependent, 23, 343

  elliptical, 66, 93, 344
  independent, 23, 29–30, 78,
    80–81, 108, 109, 130–131,
    134
  intervening, 48–49
  introductory, 113–114
  nonrestrictive, 114–115
  overlapping, 81
  subordinate, 23, 30, 80–81, 343
Clear and logical thinking
  allowing for adequate
    alternatives, 212
  appeals to emotions, 210–211
  cause and effect, 211
  deductive reasoning, 206–207
  dogmatism, 212
  factual errors, 207
  false conclusions, 210
  flattery, 211
  inductive reasoning, 206–207,
    217–218
  labeling, 211
  loaded words, 211
  mass appeal, 211
  moderation, 211–212
  name-calling, 210–211
  omissions of steps in
    arguments, 210
  overstatements, 212
  prejudice, 210–211
  reasoning in a circle, 209–210
  recognizing conflicting facts, 209
  sampling, 209
  slanted words, 208
  snob appeal, 211
  sticking to the point, 209
  sweeping generalizations, 208
  unwarranted conclusions, 210
  using accurate data, 207
  using evidence, 209
  using reliable authorities,
    207–208
Clichés, 183–184
Climactic, climatic, 331
Climactic order, 331

Collective nouns, 3, 49, 57, 342
Colloquial English, 176
Colons
    after salutations of business
        letters, 135
    before appositives, 134
    before elements introduced, 134
    between hours and minutes,
        135
    between independent clauses,
        134
    improper use of, 135
    in bibliographical entries, 135
    with quotation marks, 139
Comma faults, 29–30
Comma splices, 29–30
Commas
    after abbreviations, 141
    after introductory phrases and
        clauses, 113–114
    between adjectives, 111–112
    for contrast and emphasis, 120
    in series, 108–109
    to avoid misreading, 109, 121
    to indicate omission, 121
    unnecessary, 126–128
    with absolute phrases, 121
    with conjunctive adverbs, 118–
        119
    with degrees, titles, dates,
        places, addresses, 119–120
    with direct address and
        salutation, 120–121
    with elements out of normal
        word order, 118–119
    with he said, etc., 121
    with however, 119
    with independent clauses, 29–
        30, 108
    with mild exclamations, 143
    with mild interjections, 120
    with nonrestrictive modifiers,
        114–115
    with other punctuation, 127
    with parentheses, 128

    with quotation marks, 139
    with quotations, 121
    with sentence modifiers, 118–
        119
    with short interrogative
        elements, 120
    with yes and no, etc., 120
Common nouns, 3
Comparative degree, 72–73
Compare to, compare with, 331
Comparison and contrast, 227–
    228
Comparisons
    awkward and incomplete,
        86–87
    of similar terms, 85–86
    other in, 86
Complement, compliment, 331
Complements
    defined, 17–19, 342
    direct objects, 342, 344
    indirect objects, 342, 344
    predicate adjectives, 342
    predicate nominatives, 342, 347
    subjective, 17–18, 64
    verbs with, 52
Complete predicates, 16
Completeness
    not omitting that, 85
    not omitting verbs or
        prepositions, 84
    with so, such, and too, 84
Complete subject, 14–15
Complex sentences, 24, 342
Compositions, see Themes
Compound antecedents, 56–57
Compound-complex sentences, 24,
    342
Compound numbers, 163
Compound objects, 65
Compound predicates, 16–17
Compound sentences, 24, 342
Compound subjects, 14–15, 47–48
Compound words, 163
Conciseness, 191–192

Conclusions, in themes, 249
Conclusions, unwarranted, 210
Concreteness, 192, 198
Concrete nouns, 3
Conditional verbs, 89
Conflicting evidence, 209
Conjunctions
  consistency in use of, 90
  coordinating, 10, 29–30, 48,
    78, 97–98, 108, 343
  correlative, 11, 98–99, 343
  defined, 342–343
  subordinating, 10–11, 78, 347–
    348
Conjunctive adverbs, 30, 118–
  119, 343
Connotation, 199–200
Considerable, 331–332
Consistency
  in mood, 89
  in number, 89
  in person, 89
  in relative pronouns, 90
  in use of conjunctions, 90
  in verb tenses and forms, 89
  in voice, 90
  with statements and questions,
    90
Contemptible, contemptuous, 332
Continual, continuous, 332
Contractions, 68, 166, 332
Coordinate adjectives, 111–112
Coordinating conjunctions
  commas with, 108
  defined, 10, 343
  excessive use of, 78
  prepositions mistaken for,
    48–49
  with independent clauses,
    29–30
  with parallel constructions,
    97–98
Coordinate clauses, 343
Coordination, excessive, 78

Correlative conjunctions
  defined, 11, 343
  parallelism with, 98–99
Course names, capitalization,
  169–170
Criteria, 332
Criticism of literature, *see*
    Literature, writing about
Criticism, profiting from,
  236–237
Cumulative adjectives, 111–112
Cute, 332

Dangling modifiers
  elliptical clauses, 93
  gerunds, 92
  infinitives, 93
  participles, 92
  prepositional phrases, 93
Dashes
  excessive, 156
  for emphasis, 135–136
  for parenthetical remarks, 135
  to indicate interruptions, 135
  to introduce summaries, 135
Data, 332
Dates
  commas with, 119–120
  question marks with, 142
Days of the week, capitalized,
  169
Deadlines, 235–236
Deal, 332
Deductive reasoning, 206–207
Definition, 227
Degrees, commas with, 119–120
Degrees of adjectives and adverbs,
  72–73
Deity, capitalization of words for,
  169
Demonstrative adjectives, 8, 343
Demonstrative pronouns, 4, 343
Denotation, 199–200
Dependent clauses, 23, 343

Diagramming, 344
Dialect, 176, 177–178
Dialogue
  fragments in, 29
  paragraphing in, 137
  quotation marks with, 137
  tenses in, 40
Diction
  archaic words, 178
  building a vocabulary, 186
  clichés, 183–184
  colloquial English, 176
  dialect, 176, 177–178
  dictionaries, 176
  exactness, 184–185
  gobbledygook, 183
  idioms, 180–181
  illiteracies, 177–178
  improprieties, 179–180
  informal English, 176
  labels, 176
  nonstandard English, 176
  precision, 184–185
  slang, 177
  specialized vocabulary, 182–183
  Standard English, 176
  technical words, 182–183
  triteness, 183–184
  vocabulary tests, 186–191
  see also Style
Dictionaries, 176
Different, 87
Direct address, comma with, 120
Direct and indirect discourse, 90
Direct objects, 18, 342, 344
Direct quotations, 167
Dissertations, quotation marks with titles of, 138
Documentation, 287–293
Dogmatism, 212
Done, 332
Don't, 332
Double negative, 332

Each, 50, 57–58
Effect, affect, 328–329
Either, 50, 57–58
Either . . . or, 48, 57
Ellipses
  periods with, 141
  to show omission, 141
  with quotations, 304
Elliptical clauses, 66, 93, 344
Emotions, appeal to, 210–211
End punctuation, 140–143
Enthused, 332
Envelopes, addressing, 152
Essays, quotation marks with titles of, 138
Et al., 288
Etc., 332
Ever, every, 332
Everybody, 50, 57–58
Every day, everyday, 332
Everyone, 50, 57–58
Evidence, 209, 259–260
Exactness, 184–185, 200
Exam, 333
Except, accept, 328
Excessive coordination, 78
Exclamation points
  excessive, 156
  for strong feeling, 142
  not for humor or sarcasm, 142
  sparing use of, 143
  with quotation marks, 139, 140
Expect, 333
Expletives, 51–52

Fabulous, 333
Fact and opinion, 208
False conclusions, 210
False dilemma, 212
Fantastic, 333
Farther, further, 333
Faults, comma, 29–30
Feel like, 335
Fewer, less, 333

Figurative language, 201–202
Figures
  colon with, 135
  for numbers, 171
  question mark with, 142
Figures of speech, 201–202
Finalize, 333
Fine, 333
Fine writing, *see* Flowery
  language
First person, avoiding, 259
Fix, 333
Flattery, 211
Flowery language, 203
Flunk, 333
Folks, 333
Footnotes
  abbreviations in, 170
  numbering of, 300
  positioning of, 318–321, 324,
    325
  samples, 287–291
  to acknowledge sources, 285
  unnecessary, 314
Foreign words, underlining, 155
Forms of verbs, 38–41
Fragments, sentence, 28–29
Funny, 333
Further, farther, 333
Fused sentences, 29–30
Future tenses, 38–41

Gender, *he or she,* 58
Generalizations, 208, 243, 247
General reference aids, 273–275
Genitive, *see* Possessive case
Gerunds
  case before, 66–67
  commas with, 114
  dangling, 92
  defined, 21
Glossary of grammatical terms,
  341–348
Glossary of usage, 328–340

Gobbledygook, 183
Good, 333
Grammar, 2–24
Grammatical terms, glossary of,
  341–348
Grand, 333
Great, 333

Half, 50–51
Has got, 333
He or she, instead of *he,* 58
Here, with singular or plural
  verbs, 51–52
Herself, 336
Himself, 336
His or her, instead of *his,* 58
Historical present tense, 39, 89
Holidays, capitalized, 169
Hours and minutes, colon with,
  135
However, comma with, 119
Humor, no question mark or
  exclamation point for, 142
Hyphenation and syllabication,
  162–164
Hyphens
  at ends of lines, 163–164
  improper use of, 163–164
  with capital letters, 167
  with compound numbers, 163
  with compound words, 163
  with two words used as single
    modifier, 163

I, capitalized, 167
Ibid., 287, 320
Idioms, 180–181
Illiteracies, 177–178
Illusion, allusion, 329
Imperative mood, 345–346
Imply, infer, 333–334
Improprieties, 179–180
In, into, 334
In regards to, 334

Incomplete comparisons, 85–87
Incomplete constructions, 84–85
Incomplete sentences, 28–29
Indefinite adjectives, 8
Indefinite pronouns, 4, 50, 67–68, 166, 344
Independent clauses
 colons with, 134
 commas with, 108, 109
 coordinating conjunctions with, 29–30
 defined, 23, 344
 for excessive coordination, 78
 main ideas in, 80–81
 punctuation with, 29–30
 semicolons with, 130–131
Indexes, periodical, 269, 271–273
Indicative mood, 345–346
Indirect and direct discourse, 90
Indirect objects, 18–19, 342, 344
Indirect questions, 140
Indirect quotations, 137
Inductive reasoning, 206–207, 217–218
Infer, imply, 333–334
Infinitives
 commas with, 114
 dangling, 93
 defined, 21–22
 present, 36–37
 subjects of, 65
 split, 97
 tenses of, 40–41
Inflection, 344–345
Informal English, 176
Intensive pronouns, 4, 60–61, 336
Interjections, 13, 120, 345
Interpolations, brackets for, 136
Interpretation of literature, 257
Interrogative elements, commas with, 120
Interrogative pronouns, 4, 68–69
Interrogative sentences, 142

Intervening phrases or clauses, 48–49
Into, in, 334
Intransitive verbs, 44
Introductory phrases or clauses, punctuation of, 113–114
Introductions for themes, 248
Inverted word order, 103–104, 345
Irregardless, 334
Irregular verbs, 36–39
Is when, is where, 334
It
 as subject, 52
 as vague reference, 59–60
Italics, 154–156
It is, avoiding, 192
Its, it's, 334
Itself, 336
It's, it is, 68
It's me, it's us, 64

Joint possession, 166

Kind of, sort of, 334
Kind of a, sort of a, 334–335

Labels
 in dictionaries, 176
 reflecting prejudice, 211
Learn, teach, 335
Lead, led, 335
Less, fewer, 333
Letters, *see* Business letters
Letters, words, and figures, italicized, 155
Liable, likely, 335
Library
 card catalog in, 267–270
 general reference aids in, 273–275
 periodical indexes in, 269, 271–273

Library *(cont.)*
  reference tools in, 267–275
  using, 265
Library paper, *see* Research
      paper
Lie, lay, 37
Like, 335
Likely, liable, 335
Linking verbs, 7, 64, 73–74, 345
Literary paper, *see* Literature,
      writing about
Literature, writing about
  acknowledging sources, 261
  analyzing characters, 257–258
  analyzing technical aspects,
      258
  avoiding first person pronoun,
      259
  choosing a subject, 255–256
  closing with quotations, 260
  combining approaches, 258
  developing subjects
      appropriately, 256–258
  discussing setting, 258
  distinguishing character from
      characterization, 257–258
  expressing originality, 259
  interpreting, 257
  moralizing, 260–261
  opening with quotations, 260
  organizing, 260
  paraphrasing excessively, 258
  planning, 255–256, 261–264
  proving points, 259–260
  reviewing, 257
  selecting appropriate titles, 256
  summarizing excessively, 258
  taking notes, 255
  using evidence, 259–260
  using proper verb tenses, 39
Loaded words, 211
Local expressions, 178
Logic, *see* Clear and logical
      thinking

Loose for *lose,* 335–336
Loose sentences, 101–102
Lot of, lots of, 336

Magazine indexes, *see* Periodical
      indexes
Main clauses, *see* Independent
      clauses
Main verbs, 6–7
Manuscript form, 150–154, 235
Margins, 150
Mass appeal, 211
May, can, 331
Mechanics
  abbreviations, 170
  apostrophes, 165–167
  capital letters, 167–170
  hyphenation and syllabication,
      162–164
  manuscript and letter form,
      150–154
  numbers, 171
  spelling, 157–162
  underlining (italics), 154–156
Metaphors, 202
Misplaced modifiers, 92–94
Misreading, commas to prevent,
      109, 121
Mixed figures of speech, 201
*MLA Handbook for Writers of
      Research Papers, Theses, and
      Dissertations,* 287, 293
Mode, *see* Mood
Model papers
  Research, 265–327
  Theme, 244–246
Moderation, 211–212
Modifiers
  dangling, 92–94
  defined, 345
  hyphenated, 163
  misplaced, 92–94
  nonrestrictive, 114–115
  position of, 92–94

Modifiers *(cont.)*
　restrictive, 115
　sentence, 94, 118–119
　squinting, 94
Monosyllables, not hyphenated,
　　164
Months, capitalized, 169
Mood
　consistency in, 89
　defined, 345–346
　imperative, 345–346
　indicative, 345–346
　subjunctive, 46, 345–346
Moralizing, 260–261
Most, 336
Motion pictures, underlining
　　titles of, 154
Ms., 150
Musical compositions, titles of,
　　138, 154–155
Myself, 336

Name-calling, 210–211
Namely, colon before, 134
Narrowing theme subjects,
　　238–239
Natural or scientific law, tense
　　with, 39
Neat, 336
Neither, 50, 57–58
Neither . . . nor, 48, 57
Newspapers, underlining titles of,
　　154
Nice, 336
No, comma with, 120
Nobody, 50, 57–58
Nominative case, *see* Subjective
　　case
Nominatives, predicate, 17–18
None, 50–51
Nonrestrictive modifiers,
　　114–115

Non sequitur, see False
　　conclusions
Nonstandard English, 176
No one, 50, 57–58
Nor, 48, 57
Not . . . but, 48, 57
Note-taking, 255, 276–282
Not hardly, 336
Nouns
　abstract, 3
　case of before gerunds, 66–67
　collective, 3, 49, 57, 342
　common, 3
　concrete, 3
　defined, 2–3, 346
　possessive, 64, 67, 165
　proper, 3, 160
　singular in meaning, plural in
　　form, 49–50
Nowheres, 336
Number
　consistency in, 89
　defined, 346
　of subjects and verbs, 47–53
Number, amount, 330
Numbers
　beginning sentences with, 171
　figures for, 171
　for pages, 150, 300, 302
　hyphens with, 163
　plurals of, 166
　spelled out, 171

O, capitalized, 167
Objective case, 65–67, 68–70,
　　342
Objects
　direct, 18, 342, 344
　indirect, 18–19, 342, 344
　of prepositions, 12, 19, 64, 65
Obsolete words, 346
Off of, 336–337
Of phrase, for possessive, 67
O.K., OK, Okay, 337

One, 50, 57–58
Opinion and fact, 208
Or, 48, 57
Order of words in sentences, 103–104, 345
Order, climactic, 331
Originality, 259
Other, in comparisons, 86
Outlines
  constructing, 282–285
  scratch, 240–241
  sentence, 242–243
  topic, 241–242, 297
Overlapping subordination, 81
Overstatement, 212

Padding, 191–192
Page numbers, 150, 300–302
Paintings, underlining titles of, 154
Papers, *see* Themes
Paragraphs
  analogy as type of, 227–228
  cause and effect as type of, 228–229
  classification as type of, 229
  comparison and contrast as type of, 227–228
  definition as type of, 227
  details in, 222–224
  development, 222–224
  excessively long, 225
  extended example as type of, 229
  in business letters, 150
  in dialogue, 137
  in quotations, 306
  main idea, 216–217
  methods of developing, 227–230
  skimpy, 222–224
  too short, 222–224
  topic sentences, 216–219
  transitional devices for, 230–231

  types of, 227–230
  unity, 219–220
Parallelism
  excessive, 231
  in balanced sentences, 102–103
  repetition for, 98
  with *and who* and *and which,* 99–100
  with coordinating conjunctions, 97–98
  with correlatives, 98–99
Paraphrasing, 258, 278–282, 286–287, 316
Parentheses
  commas with, 128
  for loosely related material, 136
  to enclose figures, 136
Parenthetical sentences, punctuation with, 136
Part, 50
Participles
  comma with, 114
  dangling, 92
  defined, 21
  past, 36–38
  perfect, 41
  present, 36
Parts of speech
  adjectives, 8
  adverbs, 9
  conjunctions, 10–11
  interjections, 13
  nouns, 2–3
  prepositions, 12
  pronouns, 3–5, 8
  verbs, 6–7
Passive voice, 44
Past participle, 36–38
Past tense, 36–41
Percent, per cent, 337
Perfect participles, 41
Perfect tenses, 38–41

Period fault, *see* Sentence fragment

Periodic sentences, 102

Periodical indexes, 269, 271–273

Periodicals, underlining titles of, 154

Periods
after abbreviations, 140–141
at end of sentence, 140
commas with, 141
no commas with, 141
not after titles, 141–142
not with parenthetical sentence within another sentence, 136
with ellipses, 141
with quotation marks, 139

Person
consistency in, 89
of subject and verb, 48, 52

Personal pronouns, 5, 67–68, 166, 346

Personifications, 202

Phenomena, 337

Photo, 337

Photoduplication, 278–279

Phrases
absolute, 121
defined, 346–347
gerund, 21
infinitive, 21–22
intervening, 48–49
introductory, commas after, 113–114
nonrestrictive, 114–115
participial, 21
prepositional, 12, 20, 93
verb, 20
verbal, 20–22, 92–93, 114

Place names, commas with, 119–120

Plagiarism, 261, 285–287

Plays, underlining titles of, 154–155

Plurals, of numerals, letters, words, 166

P.M., A.M., 329

Poetry, quoted, 137–138

Position of modifiers, 92–94

Possession, joint, 166

Possessive adjectives, 8

Possessive case
defined, 342
of nouns, 64, 67, 165
of personal pronouns, 67–68
of phrase, when needed, 67
preceding gerund, 66–67

Predicate adjectives, 8, 17–18, 73–74, 342, 347

Predicate nominatives, 17–18, 342, 347

Predicates
complete, 16
compound, 16–17
defined, 14–15, 16–17, 347
simple, 16

Prejudice, appeals to, 211

Prepositional phrases, 12, 20, 93

Prepositions
defined, 12, 347
idioms with verbs, 180–181
not omitting, 84–85
object of, 12, 19, 65
with singular subjects, 48

Present infinitive, 36–37

Present participles, 36

Present tense, 38–41

Primary and secondary sources, 275

Principal parts of verbs, 36–38

Principal, principle, 337

Progressive tenses, 38–39

Pronominal adjectives, 347

Pronouns
agreement and reference of, 56–61
before gerunds, 66–67

Pronouns *(cont.)*
  capitalizing pronouns referring
    to the Deity, 169
  case of, 64–70
  defined, 3, 347
  demonstrative, 4, 343
  ending in *-self* or *-selves,*
    60–61
  indefinite, 4, 8, 50, 67–68,
    166, 344
  intensive, 4, 60–61
  interrogative, 4, 68–69
  personal, 5, 67–68, 166, 346
  reference of, 56–60
  reflexive, 5, 347
  relative, 5, 52
  relative (case), 68–70
  relative (consistency in use of),
    90
  to avoid repetition, 194
  vague reference of, 59–60
Proofreading, 235, 249
Proper nouns, 3, 160
Punctuation
  brackets, 136
  colons, 133–135
  commas, 108–121
  dashes, 135–136
  ellipses, 141
  end, 140–143
  exclamation points, 142–143
  parentheses, 136
  periods, 140–142
  question marks, 142
  quotation marks, 137–140
  semicolons, 130–132
  single quotation marks, 138
  unnecessary commas, 126–128

Questions, indirect, 140
Question marks
  after doubtful dates or figures,
    142
  after interrogative sentence,
    142
  at ends of sentences, 142
  not for humor or sarcasm, 142
  with quotation marks, 139–140
Quotation marks
  improper use of, 137, 138–139
  not for blocked quotations, 306
  other punctuation with,
    139–140, 308
  single, 138, 304
  to enclose quotation within
    quotation, 138
  with dialogue, 137
  with direct quotations, 137–138
  with titles, 138
Quotations
  avoiding at beginning of paper,
    260
  avoiding plagiarism, 285–287
  blocked, 137, 306
  brackets in, 136, 302
  causing separation of elements,
    97
  colon before, 134
  commas with, 121
  direct, 167
  ellipses in, 141
  ending with, 260
  excessive, 285
  for titles of themes, 251–254
  indirect, 137
  not at end of paper, 316
  paragraphing in, 306
  poetry, 137–138
  prose, 137
  quotation marks with, 137–138
  within quotations, 138
Quote, 337

Raise, rise, 38
Real, 337
Reading, 254

Reasoning in a circle, 209–210
Reason is because, 337
Redundancy, 194–195
Reference aids, general, 273–275
Reference of pronouns, 56–60; *see also* Agreement, pronouns and antecedents
Reference tools, 267–275
Reflexive pronouns, 5, 336, 347
Regular verbs, 36–39
Relative clauses, 69
Relative pronouns
  case of, 68–70
  consistency with, 90
  definition of, 5
  verbs with, 52
Reliability of sources, 207–208, 275
Repetition, 98, 194–195
Research paper
  acknowledging sources, 285–287
  avoiding plagiarism, 285–287
  bibliography, 276, 291–293, 322–323
  blocked quotations in, 306
  brackets in, 302
  card catalog, 266, 267–270
  choosing a subject, 265–267
  documentation, 287–293
  ellipsis in, 304
  excessive quoting in, 285
  extended paraphrases, 287
  footnotes, 285, 287–291, 300, 318–321, 324–325
  general reference aids, 273–275
  inappropriate subjects for, 267
  limiting the subject, 265–267
  model paper, 293–327
  note-taking, 276–282
  outline, 282, 285, 296–297

page numbers, 300, 302
paraphrasing, 278–282, 286–287, 316
periodical indexes, 269, 271–273
photoduplicating, 278–279
preliminary reading for, 276
primary materials, 275
quotations, 280–282, 283–284, 285–287
reference tools for, 267–275
secondary materials, 275
underlining in, 314
unnecessary footnoting, 314
working bibliography, 267–275
Respectfully, respectively, 337
Restrictive modifiers, 115
Revelant, 338
Reviews, 257
Revision, xv–xvii, 233–235, 236–237, 247–249
Rise, raise, 38
Run-on sentences, 29–30

Salutations
  colon after, 135
  comma after in personal letters, 120–121
  in business letters, 150
Sarcasm, no question mark or exclamation point for, 142
Scientific law, tense with, 39
Scratch outline, 240–241
Sculptures, underlining titles of, 154
Seasons, not capitalized, 169
Secondary materials, 275
-self or *-selves,* pronouns ending in, 60–61
Semicolons
  between independent clauses, 130–131

Semicolons *(cont.)*
  improper use of, 131–132
  in a series, 131
  with independent clauses,
    29–30
  with quotation marks, 139
Sensual, sensuous, 338
Sentence fragments, 28–29
Sentence modifiers, 94, 118–119
Sentence outlines, 242–243
Sentences
  balanced, 102–103
  choppy, 78, 101
  complete, 28
  complex, 24, 342
  compound, 24, 342
  compound-complex, 24, 342
  fused, 29–30
  interrogative, 142
  kinds of, 24
  loose, 101–102
  order in, 103–104
  order of for variety, 101,
    103–104
  parenthetical, 136
  periodic, 102
  run-on, 29–30
  simple, 24, 347
  stringy, 78–81
  structure, 101–103
  subject of, 347
  topic, 216–219
  word order in, 118–119
Separation of elements, 96–97
Sequence of tenses, 38–41
Series
  colon before, 134
  commas with, 108–109
  semicolons in, 131
Set, sit, 38
Setting, treatment of in literary
    work, 258
Sexism and pronouns, 58
Shall, will, 338

Shifts
  in conjunctions, 90
  in mood, 89
  in number, 89
  in person, 89
  in tense, 89
  in voice, 90
  with direct and indirect
    discourse, 90
Ships, underlining names of, 155
Short paragraphs, 222–224
Short stories, quotation marks
    with titles of, 138
Sic, 302
Similes, 202
Simple predicates, 16
Simple sentences, 24, 347
Simple subjects, 14–15
Single quotation marks, 306
Sit, set, 38
Skimpy paragraphs, 222–224
Slang, 177
Slanted words, 208
Snob appeal, 211
So, 84, 338
So . . . as, no comma between,
    127
Some, 50
Somebody, 50, 57–58
Someone, 50, 57–58
Sometime, some time, 338
Sort of, kind of, 334
Sort of a, kind of a, 334–335
So . . . that, no comma between,
    127
Sources
  acknowledging, 261, 285–287
  primary and secondary, 275–
    282
Speech, parts of, 2–14
Specialized vocabulary, 182–183,
    267
Spelling
  adding *s* or *es,* 159

Spelling *(cont.)*
  adding syllables, 157
  changing syllables, 157
  changing *y* to *i,* 158
  doubling final consonant, 158
  dropping final *e,* 158
  frequently misspelled words,
    160–162
  ie or *ei,* 157–158
  mispronunciation and
    misspelling, 157
  omission of syllables, 157
  plurals of proper names, 160
Splice, comma, 29–30
Split infinitives, 97
Squinting modifiers, 94
Standard English, 176
Stringy sentences, 78–81
Structure, sentence, 101–103
Style
  abstract words, 197–198
  active voice, 191
  avoiding *it is* and *there are,* 192
  conciseness, 191–192
  concreteness, 192, 198
  connotation, 199–200
  denotation, 199–200
  figurative language, 201–202
  flowery language, 203
  padding, 191–192
  redundancy, 194–195
  repetition, 194–195
  tautology, 192
  vagueness, 197–198
  wordiness, 191–192
  see also Diction
Subject and verb, agreement,
    see Agreement, subject and
    verb
Subjective case, 64, 65–66,
    68–70, 342
Subjective complements, 17–18,
    52, 64
Subject of infinitive, 65

Subjects
  case of, 64
  complete, 14–15
  compound, 14–15, 47–48
  of infinitive, 65
  of sentence, 14–15
  simple, 14–15
  understood, 15
Subjunctive mood, 46, 345–346
Subordinate clauses, 23, 80–81
Subordinating conjunctions,
    10–11, 78, 347–348
Subordination
  faulty, 80–81
  of clauses, 30
  overlapping, 81
  placing main idea, 80–81
  placing subordinate idea,
    80–81
  upside-down, 81
  with subordinating
    conjunctions, 78
Substantive, 348
Such, completeness with, 84
Summary, excessive, 258
Superlative degree, 72–73
Super, 338
Sure, 338
Sure and, 338
Suspicion, 339
Sweeping generalizations, 208
Swell, 339
Syllabication and hyphenation,
    162–164
Synonyms, 194

Tautology, 192
Teach, learn, 335
Technical analysis of literature,
    258
Technical words, 182–183, 267
Television programs, quotation
    marks with titles of, 138

Tenses
  consistency in, 89
  future, 38–41
  historical present, 39, 89
  in dialogue, 40
  in writing about literature, 39
  natural truth or scientific law,
    39
  of verbs, 38–41
  perfect participle, 41
  past, 36–38, 38–41
  perfect, 38–41
  present, 38–41
  progressive, 38–39
  sequence of, 38–41
  shifts in, 89
Term paper, *see* Research paper
Terrible, 339
Than
  case after, 66
  no comma before in
    comparisons, 127
Than, then, 339
That
  for animals, things, or persons,
    58–59
  not omitting, 85
  not with nonrestrictive clauses,
    115
  verbs with, 52
That is, colon before, 134
Their, there, 339
Them, as vague reference, 59–60
Themes
  appropriate subject for, 150
  body of, 248
  checklist, 247–249
  choosing a subject, 237–238
  conclusions, 249
  consistency, 240
  formulating a thesis, 239–240
  illustrating generalizations,
    243, 247
  introductions, 248
  limiting the topic, 238–239

  margins in, 150
  meeting deadlines, 235–236
  motivation, 233
  organizing, 240–243
  page numbers, 150
  positioning of title, 150
  profiting from criticism,
    236–237
  proofreading, 235, 249
  revising, xv–xvii, 233–235,
    236–237, 247–249
  scratch outline, 240–241
  sentence outline, 242–243
  spacing in, 150
  suggested subjects for, 249–254
  system for, 232–233
  thesis statement, 239–240
  titles of, 156, 248
  tone, 240
  topic outline, 241–242
  transitions in, 248–249
Then, than, 339
There, their, 339
There, with singular or plural
    verbs, 51–52
There are, avoiding, 192
These kinds, 339
These sorts, 339
Thesis, of theme, 239–240
Thesis statement, 239–240
They, vague, 59–60
This, vague, 59
Thusly, 339
Titles, literary
  capital letters in, 167, 306
  of papers about literature, 256
  quotation marks with, 138
  underlining, 154–155, 156
  verbs with, 52–53
Titles, personal
  abbreviations of, 170
  commas with, 119–120
Titles, theme, 150, 248
Tone, 240
Too, completeness with, 84

Topic outlines, 241–242
Topic sentences, 216–219
Trains, underlining names of, 155
Transitional devices, 230–231
Transitions, 248–249
Transitive verbs, 37–38, 44
Triteness, 183–184
Troublesome verbs, 36–37
Try and, 338
Typescript
  example of, 151
  model research paper, 295–325

Underlining
  for emphasis, 155, 156
  foreign words, 155
  for names of ships and trains,
    155
  not for title of theme, 156
  sparing use of, 314
  titles, 154–155
  words, letters, and figures
    being named, 155
Unique, 339
Unity in paragraphs, 219–220
Unnecessary commas, 126–128
Unwarranted conclusions, 210
Upside-down subordination, 81
Usage
  glossary of, 328–340
  labels in dictionary, 176
  see also Diction
Use, 339

Vagueness, 59–60, 197–198
Variety
  in order of sentences, 101,
    103–104
  in sentence structure, 101–103
  subordination for, 80–81
Verbals
  defined, 20–21, 348
  gerunds, 21, 66–67, 92, 114

  infinitives, 21–22, 40–41
  participles, 21, 40–41
  phrases loosely attached, 93
Verbs
  agreement with subjects,
    47–53
  auxiliary, 6–7, 20, 341–342
  conditional, 89
  consistency, 40
  consistency in tenses, 89
  defined, 348
  emphatic forms, 38
  forms, 35–38
  future tense, 38–41
  historical present tense, 39
  intransitive, 37–38, 44
  irregular, 36–39
  linking, 7, 64, 73–74, 345
  main, 6–7
  natural truth and scientific
    law, 39
  not omitting, 84–85
  number with subjective
    complements, 52
  past participle, 36–38
  past tense, 36–38, 38–41
  perfect tenses, 38–41
  present infinitive, 36–37
  present tense, 38–41
  principal parts, 36–38
  progressive tense, 38–39
  regular, 36–39
  sequence of tenses, 38–41
  tense with infinitives, 40–41
  tenses, 38–41
  transitive, 37–38, 44
  with literary titles, 52–53
  troublesome, 36–37
Vocabulary
  building, 186
  specialized, 182–183
  tests, 186–191
Voice
  active, 34, 191
  consistency in, 90

Voice *(cont.)*
    defined, 348
    passive, 44

Wait on, 339
Ways, 339
Where, 340
Where at, 340
Which
    for animals and things, 58–59
    verbs with, 52
Who
    for persons, 58–59
    verbs with, 52

Who, whom, 68–70
Whose, 59
Whose, who's, 340
Will, shall, 338
-wise, 340
Without, 340
Wordiness, 191–192
Working bibliographies, 267–275

Yes, comma with, 120
You, as vague reference, 59–60
You and I, you and me, 64
Yourself, 336

Abbreviations Often Used in Marking Student Papers

numerals refer to page numbers

ab — abbreviations, 170

adj/adv — adjectives and adverbs, 72

agr — agreement: pronouns, 56; subject and verb, 47

archaic — archaic, 178

c — case, 64

cap/no cap — capital letters, 167

co — coordination, 78

coh — coherence, 92

comp — comparison, 85

con — connotation, 199

cons — consistency, 89

cs — comma splice, 29

d — diction, 176

dial — dialect, 178

dg — dangling, 92

exact — exactness, 184

fig — figurative language, 201

fl — flowery language, 203

frag — sentence fragment, 28

fus — fused sentence, 29

gl/gr — see Glossary of Grammatical Terms, 341

gl/us — see Glossary of Usage, 328

id — idiom, 180

imp — impropriety, 180

inc — incomplete, 84

ital/no ital — use of italics, 154

k — awkward, 80, 96, 194

log — logic, 206

mo — mood, 46

ms — manuscript form, 150

num — use of numerals, 171

o — omission

obs — obsolete word, 178

pct — punctuation, 108

po — position of modifiers, 92

pv — point of view, 89

ref — vague or faulty reference, 60

rep — repetition, 194

sep — separation, 96

seq — sequence of tenses, 38

sl — slang, 176

sp — spelling, 157

sub — subordination, 80

t — tense, 38

tech — technical diction, 182

tr — transition, 230

trite — triteness, 183

ts — topic sentence, 216

vag — vague, 197

var — sentence variety, 101

vb — verb form, 35

vo — voice, 44

vocab — vocabulary, 182

w — wordy, 191

x — obvious error

∧ — insert

¶/no ¶ — paragraphing, 216

‖ — parallelism, 97

⌐⌐ — transpose